Ton

THE WAR AGAINST MEN

Tom Kirkpatrick

THE WAR

AGAINST

MEN

PERPETRATORS, WEAPONS, FALLOUT,
AND
COUNTER-ATTACK STRATEGIES

RICHARD T. HISE

Red Anvil Press

Copyright © 2004 Richard T. Hise

All rights reserved.

No part of this publication, except for brief excerpts for purpose of review, may be reproduced, stored in a retrieval system, or transmitted in any form or by any means, electronic, mechanical, photocopying, recording, or otherwise without the prior written permission of the publisher.

RED ANVIL PRESS

1393 Old Homestead Drive, Second floor
Oakland, Oregon 97462—9506.
TEL/FAX: 541.459.6043
www.elderberrypress.com

RED ANVIL books are available from your favorite bookstore, amazon.com, or from our 24 hour order line: 1.800.431.1579

Library of Congress Control Number: 2003103181
Publisher's Catalog-in-Publication Data
The War Against Men/Richard T. Hise
ISBN 1-930859-61-9
1. Men.
2. Feminism.
3. Father's Rights.
4. Equality.
5. Divorce Law
I. Title

This book was written, printed and bound in the United States of America.

This book is dedicated to all of the God-fearing,
family-loving, hard-working men of America

Contents

PREFACE

I had become aware of and concerned in recent years about the number of friends and acquaintances who were being savagely victimized by the women in their lives. Premature deaths, extra-marital affairs (with tragic consequences for husbands and children), false allegations that destroyed lives, physical and mental abuse, excessive and uncontrolled spending that jeopardized families' finances, and humiliating and embarrassing incidents in public are just some of what I saw or was told about. In virtually all of these cases, the victims were God-fearing, family-loving and hard-working men—the individuals to whom this book is dedicated.

My concern led me to reflect on the plight of these men and men in general as America moved into the 21st century. These reflections became more defined and focused as I perused hundreds of articles, a dozen books, and volumes of statistical data provided mainly by the United States government. My conclusion: War is being waged against men, its savagery has increased over the last 30 years, it is occurring over an increasing number of fronts, and women are in the vanguard of this battle, especially their attack-dog National Organization for Women (NOW) and other groups of that ilk, along with liberal politicians and judges, federal departments and agencies, media, corporations, colleges and universities, and organized religion—in short, a wide spectrum of major institutions in the United States arrayed against American men.

The War Against Men: Perpetrators, Weapons, Fallout, and Counter-Attack Strategies describes this war. As the sub-title suggests, this book will more fully discuss the perpetrators and will identify the weapons they use, the results of this war thus far, and what we need to do to stem the tide and claim victory.

The first chapter in *The War Against Men* provides the reader with a number of vignettes that describe how various men in my relatively narrow circle of friends and acquaintances have been mistreated by women. It describes the careful, objective research methods I used that resulted in the conclusion that war is being waged against men. In stark contrast to the process I used to research and write *The War Against Men*, the lies women and women's groups used to gain their nefarious objectives—such as the legal right to abort over 41 million babies since 1970 and gain passage of discriminatory, anti-male legislation—are presented in this inaugural chapter.

Chapter Two discusses a little-known phenomenon: why it is especially difficult to be a man in the 21st century. The vast number of constituencies with which men must contend are identified, including wives, children, siblings, parents, in-laws, bosses, fellow workers, creditors, and governments. Home-front problems and economic/financial difficulties are highlighted.

Chapter Three discusses female efforts to homogenize the female and male genders through their efforts to look and act like men or, treacherously, their attempts to get us and our sons to be more like them. This chapter tells why the differences between men and women are desirable, even necessary, and pinpoints why female efforts to homogenize the sexes need to be thwarted.

Chapter Four employs copious data to reveal the ever-increasing levels of power that women have achieved in the United States over the last 30 years— in the home, work place, politics, education, entrepreneurship, military, and religion. The impact of demographics (population and life spans) are identified.

Chapter Five exposes the rank discrimination in favor of woman and against men that has fueled this female rise to power. Such discrimination occurs in virtually every aspect of American life— education, the work place, health care, legal system, colleges and universities, military, government, and abortions—all of which are discussed in this chapter.

Chapter Six uses objective data to ascertain what has occurred in the United States as women have gained greater levels of power. The unmistakable conclusion is that our nation has been in a precipitous decline since 1970, as evidenced by what has occurred in the "killing fields" (abortion) and in the areas of health, mental health, education, crime, military and, most importantly, in our homes

How women have contributed to this decline is covered in Chapter Seven. Some of the reasons presented are female hatred for men; the liberal, pro-female, anti-male media which is controlled by women; women working outside the home; their liberal ideology which culminates in their voting for liberal politicians; female control of our public school systems; and their resistance to what the Bible mandates about what should be the relationship between men and women and husbands and wives.

Chapter Eight offers a series of recommendations men should implement now on the political front to turn the tide in the war being waged against us. Specific areas addressed are the legal system, voting, education, abortion, gun control, taxes, drugs, and health care.

Chapter Nine indicates what we must do on the personal front to win the war. These recommendations—more emotional and more people-oriented than those in the political arena— focus on the pre-marital and marital stages of men's lives. What to look for in a potential mate and how the engagement period should evolve are emphasized in the premarital discussion; father-son and husband-wife relationships are examined in the marital aspect of men's lives, with heavy emphasis on financial and economic issues. What we need to do to take care of ourselves physically is also stressed.

In writing *The War Against Men*, I relied heavily on the thinking of highly-regarded experts as reflected in their writings in respected outlets. I also took advantage of the abundance of objective data available from the U.S. Government. Some of the experts (both historical and current) include George Will, Christina Hoff Sommers, Abigail Adams, Cathy Young, Elaine Donnelly, St. Thomas Aquinas, James Dobson, Ann Coulter, Abigail Kohn, John Leo, Thomas Sowell, Walter Williams, Norman Podhoretz, David Hume, the apostle Paul, Tom Clancy, Alfred Lord Tennyson, Diane Ravitch, and Phyllis Schlafly. (Note the large number of women cited). A partial list of sources used are *The Economist, U.S. News & World Report, National Review, Newsweek, Reason, Commonweal, Human Events, Washington Times*, and the *Bible*. Various *Statistical Abstracts of the United States* are the major U.S. government sources used.

I wrote this book as a husband, father, son, brother, and uncle—in short, as a man. It is written, thus, from a male perspective. While the book's major purpose is to alert us to the war being waged against us and what to do about it, I do seize the opportunity to recognize and extol the contributions men have made to our nation. In all honesty, you will not find the same sentiment expressed about women in *The War Against Men*. If you want books lauding the female gender and, as is often the case, also demeaning males, please read one or more of these; there are so many of them around.

I am deeply indebted to my good friend and colleague of 25 years, Dr. James U. McNeal, former professor of marketing at Texas A&M University, who was the only person aware that this book was a work in progress. I thank him for his advice, encouragement, discretion, and sources of information provided. I am highly appreciative of the enthusiasm and help provided by David W. St. John, editor, Red Anvil Press.

    Richard T, Hise
    College Station, Texas
    January 2004

ONE

What in the World is Going On?

"The long-run consequences of the war on males are potentially more injurious than those posed by terrorists."

Joan mistreated and bullied her seriously ill husband, Will, into continuing to work because she would lose a large insurance settlement if he had to quit working. He died after a strenuous day of work, rehab and having to take his wife out to eat because she "was tired." After his burial, she spent lavishly on herself and began to "come on" to other men.... Ruth spread lies about her husband, undermining him with his children, at work and church. Clandestinely removing over $100,000 from their joint bank account and hiding it in Canada, she sued John for divorce. The court allowed her to keep their $150,000 home, the purloined funds, valuable paintings, half of his retirement and also granted her $800 a month in child support. After the divorce, he received anonymous telephone calls at night, his house was broken into on several occasions, and a threatening letter with his forged signature was received by a public official, causing John to be questioned

at length by the police and the FBI.... Diane badgered her octoge-
narian brother to move in with her. She demanded and was granted
power of attorney for health and financial matters. His children
discovered four years later that he had been abused and over
$100,000 was missing from his bank accounts.... A retired Army
officer is constantly berated, embarrassed and humiliated by his
wife in front of friends, relatives and neighbors.... Tom was falsely
accused by his estranged wife of having sexually molested their
five year-old son. He avoids prison, but his reputation is sullied
and he is ruined financially.... The administration of a university
finds out that a male professor, whom they wanted rid of, had had
a consensual affair with a female graduate student—which he had
broken off. Although the student had flunked out, she was rein-
stated in "good standing" after testifying to their relationship,
effecting the teacher's ouster.... Veronica marries a widower who is
25 years older than she. She is provided with expensive cars, a
wonderful house and a sumptuous, in-the-ground swimming pool.
In appreciation of his goodness, she engages in a number of open,
adulterous relationships. After George died, his children by his
first wife were appalled to discover that he had left them nothing;
everything went to Veronica

    One day in 1999, I began to ponder these and similar inci-
dents. It certainly seemed to me that good men were getting shafted,
even brutalized, and that, in each instance, the perpetrators were
the women in their lives. I had no idea as to how widespread this
phenomenon was for, after all, I had a job to do, children to raise,
and had drastically cut back on the amount of reading and reflection on societal issues that I had previously done. In any event, I
became convinced that this was something that deserved some of
my attention, indeed, a lot of my attention, as I got more information as to how men in the United States have been faring over the
last thirty years and, more importantly, what effect this has had on
the United States.

    As a trained researcher in business (marketing), I am well aware
of the value of the inductive method of analysis and the use of the

scientific method. Starting with the premise that men in my narrow circle of friends and acquaintances were potentially representative of males as a whole in the United States, I diligently set out to see if this were the case by pouring over close to 300 articles, a dozen books, and reams of statistics contained in various reference sources, mainly those provided by the United States government. The temporal focus was 1970-2000, the time period when, among other trends, the "women's movement" in our country picked up steam. The culmination of over three years of research, reflection and writing is this book.

What I found—and what is presented in subsequent chapters—is, to say the least, disturbing. Over the last 30 years, women have achieved decidedly greater levels of leadership and the subsequent increase in power across all major facets of our society that that entails. Unfortunately, these have been obtained at the expense of males; as female levels of leadership and power have increased, those of males, quite naturally, have gone down or, as they say in business and economics circles, it is a zero-sum game: One side's gain is the other side's loss. Undergirding these phenomena has been the blatant anti-male, pro-female discrimination which exists in most facets of our society and, unfortunately, is given legal sanction through legislation, the rules, regulations and edicts of female-dominated federal departments and agencies which have the force of law, and the biased decisions rendered by liberal judges. Also contributing have been the vitriolic, anti-male rhetoric employed by the radical feminists, the all-pervasive, relentless pro-female propaganda machine they employ, the gullibility of vast numbers of women, and the apparent hatred that many women have toward men (remember Joan, Ruth, Diane, and the others from earlier in the chapter?).

I became more concerned (and upset) as I examined and, thus, became aware of what has occurred in our nation as leadership roles and the accompanying power have increased for women from 1970-2000 and those of men waned. On a wide variety of fronts—families, education, health, crime, military, drug addiction, government, the economy, religion, male-female relationships and, of course, the 41 million abortions since 1970—the United States has been, alarmingly, in a state of precipitous decline.

The next logical step in my research program was to ask why this had happened. Were there a large number of factors, or did they tend to coalesce toward one or two? While more than one factor did emerge, one unshakable conclusion was that women were much more responsible than men and that there was one major difference between the transgressions of the two genders: While men tended to commit sins of omission—not noticing what was happening culturally in the United States because of over-involvement with families and careers—women's decidedly much more egregious sins were of the commission type, fueled in large part by dubious values, immorality and rebellion against God's prescriptions regarding women's roles in society—particularly in marriage—self indulgence, and greed.

Once I had grasped how much trouble our country is in and the reasons why this has occurred, it was possible to develop a plan for action—a blueprint that, I believe, will stem our nation's downhill slide and will result in a restoration of the proper roles for males and females in our society which, itself, will be a potent force for getting our nation back on track.

The recommendations are divided into two categories: political and personal. In the political arena, we need to keep informed, vet political candidates primarily on issues important to men, and vote. Education, the military, abortion, gun control, taxes and the war on drugs are the principal areas covered. Personal prescriptions deal with how men need to manage their relationships with women (before and during marriage), their daughters and especially their sons, as well as, what we need to do in the work place, the courts, churches, and in the health care arena. These recommendations are specific, practical and achievable if the men in America wake up to the dangers that exist and are willing to make the sacrifices of time and resources required.

Undergirding our efforts to get our political and personal agendas accepted must be our willingness to play the "minority card," that is, to realize that we are indeed a minority in the United States and, as such, we need to consistently and aggressively invoke the equal protection clause of the U.S. Constitution (the 14th Amendment) to regain our lost rights and stop the slide into second-class citizen status. We also need to have an aggressive propaganda effort that can effectively rebut the lies and the unfair and prejudiced comments made about men in America and that will extol our virtues and the indisputable contributions we have made and are currently making to our nation.

During the 20th century, the United States engaged in a number of wars; World War I (the "war to end all wars"), World War II, the Korean War, and the Vietnam War are the most notable. Then, during September of 2001, we began the war on terrorism as a result of the heinous, despicable terrorist attacks on New York and the Pentagon. However, there is another war that has been waged in the United States, but is so unlike the others mentioned. This war has been going on much longer than any of the others. The longer it goes on, the more intense it seems to be getting. Yet, despite its duration and intensity, almost all Americans are unaware that it is occurring. Even the victims are seemingly oblivious to their plight and its implications and, thus, are not defending themselves. Astonishingly, most of the perpetrators are blind as well. Yes, this war can he termed a class war, but does not involve the usual combatants: proletariat vs. bourgeoisie, royalty vs. commoners, black vs. white, Christians vs. Moslems, rich vs. poor, and so on.

What I am referring to is women vs. men. I suspect that this battle has been raging in our country for at least a century, but its fervor has accelerated over the last 30 years. The vast majority of men do not realize that they are under attack, besieged, if you will, on a daily basis by the radical feminists and their unwitting dupes, the vast majority of American women. To be sure, married men may be annoyed by some of the things their wives do but brush them off because they are too involved with careers and family or feel that this is what a "real man" has to endure, thus, remaining oblivious to the dire consequences for them, their children (especially their sons), and our nation. Because of the martial nature to the threat we are facing, I will make liberal use in subsequent chapters of such terms as "war," "battles," and "fronts."

The war on terrorism will occupy our minds and soak up vast amounts of resources—and rightly so. However, let us be aware of the downsides: The war against men—the assault on our manhood, our accomplishments and contributions, the ways we operate and function because we were created by God as men—and, in particular, what must be done about it, will, in all likelihood, not receive the attention it deserves. This is indeed, unfortunate for, in my opinion, the long-run consequences emanating from the war on males are potentially more injurious than those posed by terrorists. The support for this assertion is found in the history books: Civilizations die out because of internal rot and decay, not from those forces external to them.

Am I the only one aware of the war against men? Thank God, no. Howard S. Schwartz's book, *The Revolt of the Primitive : An Inquiry into the Roots of Political Correctness* (Praeger Publishers, 2001) was reviewed in the *Washington Times* (October 22-23, 2001) by nationally syndicated columnist, Paul Craig Roberts. In discussing Mr. Schwartz's book, Mr. Roberts says that Schwartz shows that feminism has metamorphosed from demands for greater equality into *gender warfare* against masculinity. "The feminists holy war against 'toxic man' is as ferocious in its ways as the Muslim holy war against the West." In concluding his review, Roberts says "!t is ironic that American males, *demonized and second-class citizens in their own society*, are at work liberating Afghan women from Osama bin Laden and the Taliban. Perhaps the American male should reconquer his home before he shows his prowess abroad" (emphasis added).

I had in mind (and adhered to) several rules-of-thumb as I conducted the research for this book and wrote the various chapters. As far as possible, I wanted to uncover and report facts and figures. To be sure, there is plenty of opinion reported in this work—including mine—but I did make a conscientious effort to support opinion with appropriate data. I wanted this book to exude honesty. This should be almost a shibboleth of any academic researcher—as my training, experience and previous writing have been—but apparently is the direct antithesis of the "facts and figures" used by the women's movement in America to gain their nefarious ends. To put it bluntly, there are a number of examples where the data were created out of whole cloth; in other words, they lied. Dr. Bernard Nathanson was one of the founders in 1969 of the National Abortion Rights Action League (NARAL) and was a leading advocate of legalizing abortion. (He also performed thousands of abortions himself). Dr. Nathanson—now pro-life and a Christian—admitted that false data were used by the feminists to get Roe vs. Wade passed. 'We fabricated data. We put out statistics saying there were one million illegal abortions a year. That wasn't true. There were 150,000 to 200,000. We said four to five thousand women died each year from illegal abortions. The real figure was 200 to 300.' Norma McCorvey was the "Roe" in Roe vs. Wade. Ms. McCorvey, like Dr. Nathanson now pro-life and a Christian, admitted she lied when she said her pregnancy was caused by rape. 'I lived in a park. I was a hippie. I was a street person. I would sell flowers on a street corner. I was not stable. I was not politically minded. I just wanted an abortion' (Joseph A. D'Agostino, "Shake The Nation Back To Life Is Back," *Human Events,* January 21, 2002).

Women's groups and politicians charged that medical research in the U.S. had short changed women. Pat Schroeder (D-Colo.) said that 'male researchers were more worried about prostate cancer than breast cancer.' Donna Shalala (Health and Human Services Secretary) stated that health care had been addressed from the male point of view, and President Clinton vowed that women would never again be "second-class citizens" in medical research and care.

Nothing could have been further from the truth. Since 1979, four-fifths of National Institutes of Health studies have included both men and women and 75% of the single-sex studies were female-only. Between 1975 and 1995, single-sex trials were evenly split and, in cancer research between 1966 and 1985, all-female studies outpaced all-male studies by a 2-1 ratio.[1] Katherine Hanson, Director, Women's Educational Equity Act Publishing Center, alleged that every year, *four million* women are beaten to death, violence is the leading cause of death among women, the leading cause of injury among women is being beaten by a man at home, and between 1990 and 1991, there was a 59% increase in rapes. Lies, lies and more lies! Ms. Hanson's allegations are patently false and are clearly rebutted by the true facts as reported by Christina Hoff Sommers, W. H. Brady Fellow at the American Enterprise Institute (Washington D.C.) and former professor of philosophy at Clark University:

•The leading cause of death for women is heart disease *(370,000* deaths annually).

•About *3,600* women a year die from homicide.

•*One percent* of women's injuries are caused by men.

•Between 1990-1991, rapes increased by only *four percent* and the number of rapes has dropped since then.[2]

Ms. Sommers charges that Hanson and other 'gender-fair' activists "regularly whip themselves into an anti-male frenzy with their false statistics."[3]

The National Organization for Women (NOW) claimed on its web site that 1.2 million women are raped each year by their current or past male partners, some more than once. The site even had the gall to cite the FBI as the source of the data. The FBI itself *(Uniform Crime Statistics)* reports *86,000* rapes in 1994.[4]

I referred to the work of many experts to provide credibility to the information reported and the conclusions drawn from that information. I also cite a lot of numbers. I did this for the same reason I drew upon the expertise of recognized authorities—to enhance credibility—so bear with the numbers provided since they will make for a much stronger case. Where available, I used recent data and data provided by federal government since they were relatively easy to obtain but, more importantly, probably have fewer axes to grind—were more objective—than data from the private sector. Numerous direct quotes are employed to ensure that the sentiments and opinions of the individuals cited are accurately reflected.

A number of sources proved to be especially valuable in helping me prepare this book. First and foremost was the Bible, God's inerrant word. I drew heavily from Genesis and various books from the New Testament. A wealth of valuable information was found in various publications and institutes/foundations. In the first category are *Reason, Human Events, The Economist, Penthouse, Washington Times, National Review, U.S. News & World Report,* and *Imprimis,* the newsletter from Hillsdale College. In the latter are the Cato Institute and the Heritage Foundation. An unlikely source (I thought) of extremely germane material came from women, women astute enough to look beyond the vitriolic rhetoric of the radical feminists and were dispassionate in their assessment of the male-female milieu. Christina Hoff Sommers' *The War Against Boys* is a compelling read which describes how the female-dominated educational system is discriminating against our sons, humiliating them and trying to feminize them—with your tax dollars. (I am also indebted to her for the idea for the title of this book). Cathy Young is a columnist with the *Boston Globe* and an editor of *Reason;* I referred to several of her articles as well as taking excerpts from an interview with a co-author of hers, Robyn Blumner of the *St. Petersburg Times.* Columnist Ann Coulter's pieces in *Human Events* were a treasure trove. Abigal Kohn is an anthropologist whose article on gun control in *Reason* was a refreshing and enlightening treatment in stark contrast to the usual clap trap one encounters from women about this subject. Betsy Carpenter's article in *U.S. News & World Report* on gender-related aspects of health care was an illuminating discussion of an issue about which most men are ignorant. Two articles by Elaine Donnelly, president of the Center for Military Preparedness, in the *American Legion Magazine* and *Human Events* are excellent reports on the downsides of women in the military. Kudos also to Peggy Noonan and Phyllis Schlafly.

I drew heavily on an article concerning women in religion written for *Commonweal* by Kenneth L. Woodward, *Newsweek's* religion editor. Two of John Leo's editorials in *U.S. News & World Report* proved to be very helpful. Several columns by Thomas Sowell, educator and columnist, in *Human Events* made excellent contributions. Leonard Sax, PhD and M.D., wrote a memorable treatise in *Penthouse* that I referred to in several chapters. Various pieces by Walter E. Williams, economics professor at George Mason University, were right on. Minister C. Russell Yates' newsletter was helpful in crafting material on the relationships between husbands and wives from a Biblical perspective. Focus on the Family's Dr. James Dobson wrote a very enlightening book, *Bringing Up Boys* (Tyndale), that provided insightful material on the physical and psychological differences between boys and girls, men and women. I am especially indebted to my good friend and colleague of 25 years, Dr. James U. McNeal, former professor of marketing at Texas A&M University, who was the only person aware that this book was a work in progress. I thank him for his advice, encouragement, discretion, and sources of information provided.

I am not sure how males will respond to this book. Over the three years that I spent writing it, my emotions ran the gamut from surprise, concern, despair, anger and, eventually, resolve. I am hoping that two of your responses would be concern and anger and that these would be transformed into *action*—action that will address the legitimate grievances that we have, recognize the roles for men and women laid out for them by almighty God, level the playing field, and move our country forward. In order to energize and focus these efforts, specific recommendations are included in the two "what to do" chapters included at the end of this book (chapters eight and nine); they serve as excellent starting points for what needs to be done. In short, we need to shake off the shackles of lethargy and start being proactive.

The terrorist attacks on the World Trade Center and Pentagon have served as a rallying call for action by the United States. In similar fashion, it is hoped that this book will alert American men to the danger they and our nation are facing—a danger that most of us do not even realize as being upon us. It, like the war on terrorism, is a struggle we can not afford to lose.

I wrote this book in my roles as a husband, father, son, brother, and uncle —in short, as a man. As such, I want to be very clear as to what this book is and what it is not. This is a book written for men—a book to inform and energize us and, yes, to uplift us and extol our accomplishments. It is not a book intended to downgrade us and, at the same time, exalt women. There are plenty of books around that do these. If this is what you want—in order to avoid disappointment—go read something else. I make no claims that this effort is an even-handed discussion. It can not be because so many of the major problems facing the United States at the start of the 21st century are indisputably attributable to the female gender.

A brief outline of the rest of the book follows. Chapter Two discusses why it is tough being a man in the environment we are facing today in America. Feminist efforts to emulate men and to feminize us and our sons— what I call the homogenization strategy— is the subject of Chapter Three. Chapter Four describes the increase in power that women have obtained in the United States over the last three decades and Chapter Five shows how this has often occurred through discrimination against men and rank favoritism for women. Chapter Six delineates the decline that has occurred in the U.S. over the last 30 years—a decline that cuts across a wide swath of critical aspects of American life. How women have contributed to this decline is the subject of Chapter Seven. Chapter Eight (political) and Chapter Nine (personal) identify what American men must do to get our country back on the right track.

REFERENCES
1. Cathy Young, "False Diagnosis," *Reason,* May 2001, pp. 22-23.
2. Christina Hoff Sommers, *The War Against Boys,* Simon-Schuster, New York, 2000, pp. 48-49.

3. Christina Hoff Sommers.

4. Leonard Sax, "Guilty Until Proven Innocent," *Penthouse,* December 2000, pp. 123, ff.

TWO

What's It Like Being a Man Today?

"It is hard to be a man. I am certain of it; to be a man in this world is not easy."Peggy Noonan

A good friend and colleague was in my office recently. We got to talking about the usual subjects--families, sports, work, and so on. At the end of our conversation, he made the following statement: "It's tough being a man today." After he left, I reflected on his comment. It is tough being a man today. And, unfortunately, it is probably not going to get any easier.

Consider the large number of important constituencies that men, especially a married man with children, must contend with today:

God	Friends
Children	Work/Bosses
Wife	Church
Parents	Creditors
Siblings	Social Organizations
In-laws	Unions
Grand Parents	Laws
Grand Children	Charities

Although this type of individual has the most constituencies with which to cope, a single man or widower has almost as many.

All of these constituencies have the potential for causing a man problems, so much so that he can feel overwhelmed and stressed out and begin to function less effectively--to the detriment of himself, his family, work, and the other constituencies. How can this occur?

All men have a set of values. This refers to an individual's beliefs, a basic philosophy of life if you will. These values define what a man is and how he acts. They can be instilled in him from a number of sources, including parents, church, friends, teachers, what he reads, and how he reacts to various stimuli. Problems arise when constituencies emit pressures on a man that are at variance with his values, putting him in a quandary: Whatever he does, he alienates either his value system or the constituency, a not altogether desirable situation.

Another all-too-common situation is when two or more constituencies put conflicting pressures on a man such that if his response mollifies one, it antagonizes the other. A classic example is when a wife complains constantly and bitterly about the "long hours" he is putting in at the office--which are required by his job and/or his boss.

The two scenarios described above are much more serious and, therefore, debilitating to the man if the constituencies involved have *power over him*. In the constituency vs. values situation, the man's value system is threatened more if the constituency holds some kind of cudgel over him, such as, being fired from his job if he does not engage in some kind of unethical behavior that is antithetical to his value system. In the job/wife example, both the boss and the wife exert a great deal of power: The boss can fire him, the wife can withhold sex, give him the silent treatment, turn the children against him, leave him, so that whatever he does, he risks alienating a constituency that can cause him a lot of grief.

Let's not underestimate the downsides of this role conflict. If it persists too long and at too high a level, the following disastrous outcomes can result: avoidance, withdrawal, impairment of health, depression, alcoholism, drug addition, and so on. With the number of constituencies indicated earlier—and there may be additional ones that should have been added— the odds are high that a great many men in the United States today are being pressured by a number of constituencies. Let's look at several that exemplify this situation.

It has long been my belief that each partner in a marriage could use one particular weapon in order to gain ascendancy. Wives could withhold sex from husbands and the latter could exercise financial leverage. But look at what has happened in the last three decades. Women, and wives in particular, have been flooding into the work force in even greater numbers. In 1970, 40.5% of wives (18.5 million) were in the civilian work force. By 2000, this percentage jumped to 62%, encompassing 33.9 million working wives, and in 1998, women accounted for about half of the civilian work force. This by itself would erode the man's leadership role in the family, but what has additionally happened is that, compared to men, women are making more money than ever before. In 1963, women on average earned 59% of what men did. By 1998, this figure reached 75%, with some estimates putting the figure at an even higher percentage, Even more telling is that by the end of the 20th century, in approximately one-third of dual-income families, women *out earned men* (really great for the male ego). So husbands' leverage with wives has been severely eroded.

Women are becoming much more sexually aggressive. Whereas the traditional expectation was that wives were obliged to satisfy their husbands, women are now apparently clamoring for the same level of enjoyment generally only attributed to men. Exhibit 2.1 provides the titles of sex-related articles appearing in various women's magazines over the last several years. They clearly show female increased interest in sex, for these magazines would not print such articles unless they were resonating with their readership.

A recent development are medical initiatives to help women

increase their sexuality. These come in the form of medicine and devices. Androstenedione is a supplement that increases the levels of testosterone. Its most famous male user was baseball's home run slugger, Mark McGwire. Soon to be marketed as a chewing gum, one of its target markets was post-menopausal women "looking to increase their sex drives."[1] Agrin Max is designed to increase female blood flow and, thus, heighten sexual desire to increase their level of sexual satisfaction. Some women are trying out Viagra, the pill that has helped men with sexual impotence.[2] One piece of equipment on the market is the Eros Clitoral Therapy Device. Developed by Claire Hovland, an electrical engineer, and sold by UroMetrics (St. Paul, Minnesota), it increases blood flow to the clitoris. It has been approved by the Food and Drug Administration.

The market for these products is likely to be huge, since about 40% of women indicate they have some type of sexual dysfunction, such as, not being able to be aroused, pain during intercourse, or vaginal dryness.[3]

An article in the October 14, 2000 *Spectator* ("Good Vibrations") describes a woman's visit to a feminist sex shop, Erotische Verbeelding, in Antwerp, Belgium. Seemingly a tongue-in-cheek piece, the author (Rachel Johnson), nevertheless, ended up purchasing the Eroscillator, whose label described it as "First appareil to be conceived exclusively for the excitement of female parts" and "can be used in the bath." Another item was an "unfeasibly large bright-blue dildo, purchased by a primary school teacher who chatted amiably with the young female shop assistant while the item was being gift-wrapped."

An interesting perspective on female sexual activity is found in hearings held before the 106th Congress, March 16, 1999. These hearings reported that women who have had multiple sexual partners, particularly at an early age, are much more likely to get cervical cancer than women in general. On the other hand, regular ejaculations for men are known to promote a healthy prostate and may delay or prevent prostate cancer.

EXHIBIT 2.1
SEX-RELATED ARTICLES FROM VARIOUS WOMEN'S MAGAZINES

Title	Magazine and Date
"14 Signs Your Sex Life Is Going Well; 14 Signs it Needs Help."	*Glamour*, November 1998
"Getting Naked Too Soon."	*Glamour*, August 1999
"You Did It Where?"	*Mademoiselle*, December 1998
"Are You Sexually Adventurous?"	*Mademoiselle*, June 1999
"How To Misbehave In Bed & Not Feel Bad One Bit."	*Glamour*, April 1999
"Sin-sational Advice: Passion Pumper Uppers."	*Glamour*, April 1999
"What You And He Are Thinking When He First Sees You Naked."	*Glamour*, June 1999
"What's Your Lovemaking Style?"	*Glamour*, July 1999
"Did Someone Say Orgasm Survey?"	*Glamour*, July 1999
"Doing 'It.' Sex Do's & Don'ts."	*Glamour*, January 1999
"My Two Breast Friends."	*Glamour*, February 1999
"6 Secrets Of Great Morning Sex."	*Glamour*, March 1999
"Who's Better, A New Lover Or A Longtime Lover?"	*Glamour*, June 1997
"Does Size Matter?"	*Glamour*, February 1998
"Could You Pick Your Penis Out Of A Lineup?--Sex And Women: Results of Survey."	*Glamour*, January 1998
"A Month Of Great Sex."	*Mademoiselle*, September 1998
"The Strangest Sex I Ever Had."	*Mademoiselle*, November 1998
"The Worst Sex I Ever Had."	*Mademoiselle*, May 1998
"Your Weird Sex Questions Answered."	*Mademoiselle*, November 1998
"The Sex You Want. . . Is It The Sex You Got?"	*Mademoiselle*, November 1998
	Redbook, September 1998

Jill Conner Browne is a Mississippi-based marketing phenomenon who has gotten as much as $250,000 for a book advance (*Sweet Potato Queens' Bigass Cookbook and Financial Planner*). Her two previous bestsellers were *The Sweet Potato Queens' Book of Love* and the sequel, *God Save the Sweet Potato Queens*. She commands $7,000 a pop for speaking engagements. The 48-year old organizer of the Million Queen March (Jackson, Mississippi, 2001), Browne is an unabashed feminist whose books detail the 'men who may need killing' and the five types of "keeper" men all women need: one to fix things, one to dance with, one to pay for things, one to talk to, and one to have sex with. In order to get men to do what women want them to do, she implores her female readers to "offer The Promise—a pledge to perform a certain intimate physical act—and then *always renege*" (emphasis added; see Victoria Murphy, "Queen for a Day," *Forbes*, July 9, 2001).

More stress is being put on married men because of wives' insistence that they "help around the house." A survey of married, working couples showed that 33.2% of fathers were expected to share *equally* with their spouses in the child care responsibility. For shopping, cleaning, bill paying and cooking, the figures were, respectively, 27.1%, 24.4%, 17.1%, and 12.5%. In some of the surveyed families, fathers had total responsibility for

Bill paying	32.5%
Shopping	11.3%
Cooking	11.3%
Cleaning	5.8%
Child care	5.4% [4]

When both spouses are working, it is perfectly acceptable that husbands assist with domestic chores. Except for child care, it is not appropriate when the male is the only full-time working individual in the house and, for whatever excuse the wife uses, he is required to shoulder these domestic responsibilities. These added obligations will only sap his energy and, for the children, blur the role distinctions between males and females—a most unwelcome outcome. Danielle Crittenden, author of *What Our Mothers Didn't Tell Us*, is disturbed by the "unmanliness of fathers she watches at a playground fussing over young children and cooing at them in 'unnaturally high' voices. She laments that she cannot imagine these new dads in the role of warrior and suggests that their wives must be yearning for "real men." In a similar vein, Norman Podhoretz, writer and former editor of *Commentary*, feels that "Mr. Moms are no better than men who deserted their children" (*Reason*, July 2000).

An undesirable outcome of men being saddled with home chores is the stress that can occur. This can result in "guilt, depression, shoddy work and, still too often, divorce," according to James Levine who puts on seminars for such companies as J.P. Morgan & Co., Merrill Lynch, Texas Instruments, and Goldman Sachs for stressed-out dads torn between work and home. Having to work more hours as he climbs the corporate ladder, the arrival of children and more wives working are the fuel for this stress. The work/ home dilemma is, of course, even worse for single fathers heading households with children, a situation much more common today. In 1979, there were 690,000 such fathers; by 1999, the number had more than tripled to 2.12 million. [5]

If Betty Friedan, feminist extraordinaire, has her way, men will be increasingly responsible for household duties: "As women are now entitled to equal opportunity in the workplace, men should be considered equally responsible for the family" (*NPQ*, Special Issue, 1998).

Men and women in the United States are living longer. This is wonderful, but it does have a distinct downside which puts additional pressure on men. While parents' life spans are, indeed, increasing, they often require time-consuming and expensive care, Alzheimer's being only one example. Men may be forced to look after their own parents, or their wives' parents, reducing the time they can devote to work or to their own families. If parents have not carefully planned financially for their later years, the financial burden placed on children can be enormous; in the late 1990s, the average annual cost to stay at a nursing home was about $42,000 and higher for special care units, such as, those equipped to handle Alzheimer's patients.

Let's not downplay the obligations men have to their parents. Many of us feel grateful to them for the childhood they provided us and the help given during our late teens and early twenties. And this is as it should be. One of the 10 Commandments given to Moses from God says "Honor thy father and mother." Significantly, this commandment is the only one which contains a promise to those that honor it, for the entire commandment reads, "Honor thy father and mother, that thy days may be long upon the land which the Lord giveth thee" (Exodus 20:12).

There has been an unusual phenomenon occurring with children in the last decade or so. More of them are returning to live with their parents. We are talking primarily about children in their late 20s or early 30s who, for one reason or another, are seeking refuge with mom and dad. They may be single young adults who can't make it financially or may be a single mom whose husband has left her. Whatever the scenario, more for the man (and wife) to deal with both financially and relationally.

A different spin involves having to financially help adult children who do not actually move in with parents. Apparently, this is becoming more of a problem for dads and moms. A very informative and best seller, *The Millionaire Next Door*, written by Thomas J. Stanley and William D. Danko, reported on the extent to which millionaires (households with a net worth of at least $1 million) were involved with this type of assistance. For example, 61% provide "forgiveness loans" to adult children, 59% help them purchase a home, and 43% subsidize their adult children by funding tuition for their grandchildren's private school education. While millionaires may be able to afford this type of largesse, what about the strain such benevolence puts on the budgets of less wealthy households?

Since we are on the subject of money, let's take a look at how families are doing economically, particularly since the man is supposed to be the breadwinner. A lot of people have been snookered into thinking that everything is okay because the stock market boomed over the last seven or eight years and the unemployment rate had fallen to about 4%. Every day we are bombarded on television and in magazines and newspapers about the astronomically wealthy *noveau riche*, for example—as I like to call them—the "oligeeks," the *billionaires* like Bill Gates (Microsoft, worth $43 billion in 2002), Paul Allen (Microsoft, $24 billion), Larry Ellison (Oracle, $15 billion), Michael Dell (Dell Computer, $11 billion), and Jeff Bezos (Amazon.Com, $1.8 billion). But what do aggregate data show for people like you and me? They paint a different picture:

1. Tax Day, the day when we stop working for the government and start working for ourselves, occurs later in the year. In 2000, it was necessary for Americans to work from January 1 to May 8 to pay for all federal, state and local taxes. Taxes per capita were $955 in 1970, a whopping $8,000 in 2000. Federal expenditures account for 30% of our gross national product and state and local government taxes add another trillion dollars. [6]

2. Between 1990 and 2000, the level of personal savings in the United States plummeted from $334.3 billion to -$8.5 billion. In other words, we not only did not save in 2000, but had to eat into our savings to pay bills. As a percentage of disposable personal income, we went from a savings rate of 7.8% in 1990 to - 0.19% in 2000. [7]

3. While our savings rate dropped out of sight, debt went through the roof. U.S. families in 1980 had accumulated $350.1 billion of debt, or 8.3% of disposable personal income. By 1998, the figures were, respectively, $1.31 *trillion* and 21.7%. [8] (An interesting aspect of this trend is that it occurred even though the income tax deduction for interest paid on debts other than mortgages was eliminated in the middle 1990s).

4. Given the decline in our rate of savings and the increase in taking on credit, we should not be surprised at what has happened to personal bankruptcies. In 1990, 661,000 were filed. In 1998,

the figure more than doubled to 1,379,000; the figure was 1,240,000 in 2000.[9]

5. In 1990, median family income in 1999 dollars was $38,168. By 1999, it had increased to only $40,816, an increase of only 0.8% a year.[10]

And let's not be lulled into a false sense of security about the level of unemployment having hovered around 4% in 1999 and 2000. This measure of our country's economic health tends to fluctuate, so we can't always assume that it will be the benign figure labor experts are quite content with because they figure many of these unemployed individuals have, on their own, quit a job and are looking for something better. However, in some years during the 1980s and 1990s, the rate of unemployment was much higher than the "acceptable" 4%. In 1982, it was 9.7%, 7.5% in 1984, 6.8% in 1991, 7.5% in 1992 and 6.9% in 1993. [11] In 2002, it hovered around 7.0%

The 1980s and 1990s were the decades in business in America of mergers and acquisitions and downsizing. The result of many of these were mammoth layoffs, for example, IBM (85,000 jobs cut), AT&T (83,500), General Motors (74,000), Sears (50,000), Boeing (30,000), Procter & Gamble (13,000), and Xerox (10,000). There is nothing more damaging to a man's self worth to be without a job and unable to support himself and his family.

Another way that organizations have used to get rid of employees is through early retirement schemes. One of the most notorious of these was the public school system in Pennsylvania that forced out 10 teachers, all of whom had more than 30 years of service to the same school district. They were told that if they did not accept the early retirement scheme, all would be looking at "unfit" evaluations from their principal.

The U.S. economy, which began to free fall before the September 11, 2001 terrorist attack, has been eroded even further by that treachery. Every day, we hear companies reporting failures to achieve profit targets or, worse, losses, accompanied by the inevitable massive layoffs and bankruptcies. One need only follow the saga of our airline industry since September 11, 2001 for high-profile examples.

Our federal government has passed a number of draconian laws in the past 30 years about which most men are not even aware. Unfortunately, the old saying, "Ignorance of the law is no excuse," is applicable and the person caught violating these statutes is in for a rude awakening and, worse, serious jail time and fines if convicted. (If you think the feds are not serious about enforcing these laws, did you know that there are at least 16 federal agencies with over 500 officers who are allowed to carry firearms *and make arrests*, including the U.S. Customs Service, the Immigration and Naturalization Service, the Drug Enforcement Agency, the FBI and, of course, the Internal Revenue Service). Most of the laws discussed below deal with citizens' right to privacy, particularly in the financial realm.

1. The Bank Secrecy Act of 1970. This is a classic example of a misnomer, for the act set out to provide the federal government with access to Americans' banking records. All banks and financial institutions are required to file with the Internal Revenue Service a Currency Transaction Report, or CTR, via Form 4789, on any transaction (deposit, withdrawal, or exchange of currency or other monetary investment) in excess of $10,000. Customs Form 4790 must be filled out whenever cash, negotiable securities or other negotiable instruments are taken outside the United States or are returned to the U.S. Any financial account an American has outside the U.S. must be reported to the IRS. If the sum involved exceeds $10,000, Form 90-22.1 must be filled out; this requires that the nature and location of the account be revealed. So that the financial net is all-inclusive, the Bank Secrecy Act defines a wide range of organizations as "financial institutions," including securities brokers and dealers; investment companies; currency exchange houses; anyone who sells cashiers checks or money orders; anyone who operates a credit card system; all attorneys and accountants; the U.S. Post Office; and automobile, aircraft and boat dealers, as

well as, property dealers and settlement agents. (John Berlau, writing in the November 2003 issue of *Reason*, calls this legislation a "30-year experiment in subverting the Fourth Amendment." John Yoder, director of the Justice Department's Asset Forfeiture Office in the Reagan administration, believes the Act will generate "so much data on people who are absolutely legitimate and who are doing nothing wrong....You have investigators running around chasing innocent people, trying to find something that they're doing wrong, rather than targeting real criminals.")

2. The Comprehensive Crime Bill of 1984. This bill amended the Bank Secrecy Act. Civil penalties were increased from $100 to $10,000 and violations were upgraded from a misdemeanor to a felony. Prison terms of five years were instituted and, if illegal activities are involved, the fine could escalate to $500,000. Wire transfers were now included in the Act and Customs (one of those gun-toting federal agencies) could now search U.S. citizens leaving or reentering the U.S. and their baggage for "probable cause," in other words, without a warrant.

3. Tax Equity and Financial Privacy Act of 1982 (TEFPA). This legislation requires banks and brokerage firms to report interest, dividends and gross proceeds from the sale, redemption or exchange of stocks or bonds. It also enables the IRS to gain access to anyone's financial records through an "administrative summons," which is a written or verbal request from the IRS that allows it to bypass courts for tax cases or criminal investigations.

4. The Deficit Reduction Act of 1984. Form 8300 now requires *any* business that received in excess of $10,000 in cash or monetary instrument to report it to the IRS. Merchants must also report any "suspicious" transaction. Businesses which fail to comply risk the forfeiture of assets as well as prison time. (The IRS visited 5,000 stores in 1991 in order to frighten retailers into compliance).

5.The Money Laundering Control Act of 1986. This legislation outlaws money laundering and allows the government to fine individuals up to four times the amount laundered. What makes this act particularly heinous is that people can be charged even though the funds involved were not derived from any illegal activity. For example, a person wanting to deposit $18,000 would make two $9,000 deposits on consecutive days. The government would view this as money laundering, claiming that each deposit was kept under $10,000 in order to avoid having a CTR filed. In 1991, over 75% of the assets seized under this act were the property of individuals *not* involved in any illegal activity.

6.Anti-Drug Abuse Act of 1988. This act relied on the government's seemingly laudable desire to combat drug usage to further erode our financial privacy. The federal government is now allowed to seize your assets if it believes any of them came from a relative or associate suspected of a drug-related crime. Once your property is seized, you will have to prove it is "clean money," rather than the government having to prove it is "unclean." (Whatever happened to being innocent until proven guilty?). Given the difficulty of proving your innocence, you can probably forget about getting your assets back. Even if successful, you will likely have laid out thousands of dollars in legal fees.

7.The Annunzio-Wylie Anti-Money Laundering Act of 1992. Under this legislation, the federal government put the onus on banks and financial institutions to monitor and report our financial affairs. They are now required to volunteer information about any "suspicious" transaction to the Feds. Conviction as a "money launderer" can result in bank officers being fined and going to jail (up to $500,000 and 10 years) and the bank or financial institution can be taken over and operated by the federal government.[12]

On the horizon is even more troubling restrictions on our financial sovereignty. The United Nations is proposing to create an

International Tax Organization that would force our government to provide other countries with detailed personal and financial information about U.S. citizens (*The Washington Times*, May 20-26, 2002, p. 33).

As a response to the terrorist threat facing our nation after September 11, 2001, the federal government passed far-reaching legislation that gave it expanded powers to invade the privacy of our citizens. This legislation was rushed, to the extent that very little debate was held. Also, most Americans do not realize that President Clinton implemented more executive orders than any U.S. president. Many of these allowed the president and our federal government to gain expanded powers in times of "national emergencies." Because of their nature, these did not have to be scrutinized by Congress. President George W. Bush can rescind these, but as of November 1, 2002, I am not aware that any of Mr. Clinton's executive orders had been eliminated, with the exception of the one dealing with the amount of arsenic that should be in our water supply that Mr. Bush took a lot of heat for.

In February of 2001, Paul Montgomery, President and CEO of Jefferson Coin and Bullion, sent an "open letter" to President George W. Bush. This letter eloquently and perspicaciously addresses the increasing intrusion on our rights by government and the ultimate frightening consequences:

> In the zeal to nab wrongdoers, federal agencies have overstepped the bounds of private sanctity. The banks have been made federal watchdogs, spying on the financial dealings of American citizens. The FBI indiscriminately sorts through our email without due process, whether we've done anything to arouse suspicion or not. Government agencies share our sensitive records with each other (and even sell them to commercial ventures). There has been talk of requiring mandatory DNA printing for every American citizen.
>
> The excuse for all these and other violations of personal privacy is that it's the price we must pay to catch the bad guys. Wrong! I want criminals caught and punished as much as anybody, but if surrendering the right to privacy is the cost, then

the price is too high. I can't get it out of my mind that at least some of the government spying on American citizens has nothing to do with looking for criminals and everything to do with gaining power and control over the citizenry.

The much respected Cato Institute, in its newsletter of January/February 2001, had this to say: "The biggest problem facing America today is a federal government that has slipped its constitutional bounds to become a threat to our lives, liberties and pursuit of happiness."

A man's relationship with God is another significant responsibility. Although God grants eternal life to all who admit they have sinned and recognize the death of Jesus Christ as an atonement for those sins, He does have expectations of those who do repent. Prayer, tithing, fasting, church attendance, patience, turning our problems over to God to work out, forgiving people who have hurt us, fidelity in marriage, and Bible reading are required. However, the most awesome responsibility Christian fathers have is that of ensuring that their children are led to the Lord so that they, too, will have eternal life. Even if a father has an otherwise exemplary record, he has failed his children and his God if his children have not accepted Jesus Christ as their Lord and Savior. Most Christians do so before the age of 18, so fathers are not in a position to procrastinate and pass the buck.

The apostle, Paul, indicates that it is not easy for even Christian men to fulfill God's expectations. In discussing the clash between the new Christian's nature and his old one, he says in Romans 7:15: "For that which I do I understand not; for what I would, that I do not; but what I hate, that I do."

Peggy Noonan, former speechwriter for Ronald Reagan, had this to say in her 2003 book, A Heart, a Cross and a Flag: "It is hard to be a man. I am certain of it; to be a man in this world is not easy. I know what you are thinking, but it's not easy to be a woman either, and you are right. But women get to complain and make others feel bad about their plight. Man have to suck it up and remain good natured, constructive, and helpful...."

REFERENCES

1. Dan McGraw, "A Pink Viagra?," *U.S. News & World Report*, October 5, 1998, p, 54.

2. Stacey Schultz, "When Sex Pales, Women May Need More than Viagra," *U.S. News & World Report*, June 26, 2000, pp. 64-65.

3. Mary Ellen Egan, "The Love Machine," *Forbes*, July 3, 2000.

4. *The American Woman*,1996-1997.

5. Mary Beth Grover, "Daddy Stress: *Forbes*, September 6, 1999, pp. 202-208.

6. Walter E. Williams, "The Legitimate Role of Government in a Free Society," *Imprimis*, Vol. 29, No. 8, 2000, pp. 1, 5.

7. *Statistical Abstract of the United States*, 2001.

8. *Statistical Abstract of the United States*, 2001.

9. *Statistical Abstract of the United States*, 2001.

10. *Statistical Abstract of the United States*, 2001.

11. *2000 Time Almanac*, p. 822.

12. W. G. Hill, *Banking in Silence*, Scope International Ltd., Hants, England, 1996/1997, pp. 49-61.

13. "Nasty Turns in Family Life," *U.S. News & World Report*, July 1, 1996.

THREE

Are Women and Men the Same?

"I believe nature has assigned each sex its particular duties and sphere of action and to act well your part, 'there all honor lies.'" Abigail Adams, wife of our second president.

Over the last 30 years in the United States, women have begun to look more like men and have begun to act more like them. I will first describe the increasingly masculine appearances of women, then show how their actions are becoming more of a mirror image of men's. Some reasons will be offered for the occurrence of these phenomena as will, most importantly, the implications of these trends. We will also take a brief look at the other, more insidious, side of the coin: female efforts to get men to act more like them.

Women Looking Like Men

Let's start at the top and work our way down. A greater percentage of women are electing to wear their hair shorter, such that, based on tonsorial appearance alone, it is hard to distinguish women from men. The most pronounced blurring of gender lines occurs, of course, when women have a "butch" or "buzz" cut—as a greater number of them appear to be doing. Spend an hour or so in any location where there is a great deal of female foot traffic—super markets, airports, shopping malls—and you will be lucky to find 20% of women with hair long enough to even reach their collars. While women will use a variety of reasons to justify short hair—it's easier to take care of, it's the latest style—the Bible essentially denounces short hair by extolling long hair for women: "But if a woman have long hair, it is a glory to her; for her hair is given her for a covering" (1 Corinthians 11:15).

Women's clothing is getting harder to distinguish from men's. Virtually all women in the U.S. wear pants—either all the time or a great deal of the time. Pants are a clothing item for men which women are aggressively adopting as their own but, on the other hand, one does not see men in any great numbers wearing dresses or skirts (traditional garb for women). Whereas women used to be content when they wore pants designed specifically for them, this is no longer the case. Instead, they wholeheartedly began to wear jeans—male outerwear originally conceived to protect men who worked out of doors. We now see women wearing bib overalls, a most ludicrous sight, as the wearers obviously have no intention of doing the rugged work (farming, construction, etc.) usually associated with this type of clothing.

I have noticed in the last decade an increasingly large percentage of women who are wearing baseball hats—formerly a male prerogative. Some females even choose to wear them backwards, signifying (probably unknowingly) that they are ready to take over the most demanding and masculine of all baseball positions: catcher.

Today, it is almost impossible to distinguish men from women based on the type of shoes worn. Both sexes appear to favor the uni-sex type of walking or running shoe put out by the Nikes and Reeboks of the world. And the common type of socks for both sexes are the white, cotton variety.

It is perhaps enlightening to note that when the Russian revolution began in St. Petersburg in 1917, women took to "wearing men's clothes (soldiers' headgear, boots and breeches), as if by re-versing the sexual codes of dress, they were also *overturning the social order"* (emphasis added). [1]

In alarming numbers, women are intruding on another all-male bastion: the wearing of tattoos. Truck drivers, motorcycle toughs and enlisted soldiers and marines were the types of individuals I traditionally associated with tattoos, but not solely anymore due to female encroachment on this former male turf.

Women Acting Like Men

Women's increasingly male-like actions can be categorized into two areas: employment and non-employment.

Employment

There has been a greater incursion by women into occupations formerly dominated by men. For example:

•In 2000, 25.3% of barbers were women.

•In the construction trades in 2000, 2.6% of the work force was made up of women.

•Females in 2000 represented 19.0% of protective service work-ers.

•In 2000, women held 46.9% of sales positions.

•In 1983, females represented 1.4% of total employment in forestry and logging. By 2000, this percentage had increased to 8.4%.

•In 1983, 15.4% of employment in freight, stock and materi-als handling was female; by 2000, it had risen to 22.4%.

• 4.7% of truck drivers in 2000 were female, compared to 3.1% in 1983.

• Women in 1983 accounted for 5.7% of police and detectives in the U.S. By 2000, the figure had more than doubled to 12.1%.

•In 2000, 51.8% of bartenders were women.

•In 1983, 12.1% of farm operators and managers were women, far below the 25.4% figure recorded in 2000. [2]

Military occupations have been aggressively invaded by women. Only 1.4% of the armed forces were female in 1970, but had climbed significantly to 14.4% in 2000. Almost one-fifth (19.0%) of Air Force active duty personnel in 2000 were female, followed by the Army (15.1%), and Navy (14.0%). The Marines brought up the rear at 5.9%. All branches showed sizable gains between 1970 and 2000 (*Time Almanac 2000* and *World Almanac 2001*).

Sports occupations that were male bastions have been assailed by women. Ali, Frazier and Foreman are boxers whose names conjure up their great heavy weight bouts of the 1970s, right? Not any more; each of these pugilistic legends now has a daughter fighting professionally. George Foreman tried to dissuade his daughter from her first bout by offering her $15,000 (her purse), but she refused. And for years, women have been solidly entrenched in professional wrestling.

USA Today (December 13, 1999) reported on efforts to launch a *full contact* football league for women. The league hoped to have six to eight teams by 2000, 12 for 2001. The two current members--the New York Sharks and the Minnesota Vixens--played a Sunday exhibition (December 12, 1999) that drew 300 fans in Uniondale, New York. The Sharks triumphed 12-6. Lynn Lewis, a 40 year-old Sharks tackle was ecstatic after the game. She said: "Out of all the major sports, this is the last one that brought women to its playground. To me, it's the culmination of all sports. I've never had more adrenaline run through me ....This is a place for women to be aggressive." Equally enthusiastic was 26 year-old Vixens defensive end, Christine Szaja: "It's worth it. I was always on the sidelines going 'Oh, it'd be awesome to be out there.'" Natalie Jufer, 30, Sharks running back, adds: "You get such a feeling of accomplishment seeing all those big people trying to crunch each other and you get through."

For over half-a-century, there have been several abortive attempts to organize women's baseball leagues. The movie, "A League Of Their Own," describes one such effort in the 1940s.

Don't look for any decrease in women's efforts to gain employment in male-dominated occupations. Consider the following that appeared in the Bryan-College Station Eagle on September 25, 2001:

Jessica Biel said her character on the WB family drama, *7th Heaven*, will be someone young girls can look up to this season. Biel said her character, Mary Camden, gets an unusual job, but she doesn't want to give away what it will be. 'It's really good for young girls. I'll give you a little hint: it's a profession that there's not too many women in,' she said. She's not a pioneer of the women's movement in this profession, but...it's cool and I think girls will really dig it.'

Non-Employment Arenas

Athletics used to be the domain of men, but not any more. In 1971, only 7.4% of the participants in high school sports were women. Although the number of boys on high school teams remained about the same between 1971 and 1997-1998, the number of female participants exploded from 294,105 to 2,570,330 (nearly 9 times) so that in 1997-1998, 40.6% of high school athletic participants were girls (*Statistical Abstract of the United States*, 1999).

At the collegiate level, there were 64,390 women participants in 1981-1982 in NCAA sports. They accounted for 27.8% of all participants. Their numbers jumped to 145,832 in 1998-1999, resulting in their accounting for 41.2% of all participants at that time. [3]

Women athletes are becoming more of a presence in the Olympic Games. During the first modern Olympics (Athens, Greece in 1896), there were no female participants. In 1972, 14.8% of the athletes in Munich were women. By 2000, the figure about tripled, to 42.0%.

Heather Sue Mercer thought she was going to be the first woman to play Division I football. As a freshman ("freshwoman?") at Duke University in 1995, she kicked a 28-yard field goal in the annual intrasquad game to give her side a two-point victory. She was told by head coach Fred Goldsmith two days later that she was on the team. However, for the next two years she was never allowed to practice or stand on the sidelines during games. As a senior, she filed a federal lawsuit against the University claiming Goldsmith discriminated against her because of her gender.

According to a Duke assistant coach, Fred Chatham, Mercer wasn't good enough to make the team. "The fact is, she just didn't have the talent to kick at this level, as Fred came to see," he said. As a high school kicker she lacked distance, her longest field goal being 33 yards.

When interviewed by *Sports Illustrated*, reporter Michael Bamberger claimed that "her lips quiver and she stares off into space." Eventually, she broke down and cried.[4] On October 12, 2000, Mercer was awarded $2 million in compensatory damages. Now working for Charles Schwab, she intends to use the award to provide scholarships for female place kickers (*Human Events*, October 27, 2000).

Outdoor sports used to be a "guy thing." Not anymore! In 1999, 46.5% of campers were women, 31.5% of fresh-water fishermen were females, 29.3% of salt-water fishermen were women, 42.7% of individuals engaged in motor/power boating were women, 42.2% of canoeists were females, 30.8% of individuals engaged in off-road mountain biking were women, and 42.2% of on-road mountain bikers were women. So much for men as the "great outdoor type." [5]

In a survey of men's and women's participation in various fitness activities in 1999 (see *Statistical Abstract of the United States*, 2000), females accounted for the following percentages of "frequent participants:"

Working out at a club	53.6%.
Bicycling (touring/fitness/training)	44.5%.
Exercise walking	61.9%.
Running/jogging	45.2%
Swimming	53.2%.

Martial arts was a man-thing. In 1997, however, 40.1% of participants were female. Shooting pool was once the domain of men. Not content with this, women are frequenting billiard parlors or pool halls in record numbers such that 37.3% of billiard players in 1999 were female.

There are plenty of non-sports areas where women are blurring the lines between themselves and men. In the 1990s, cigar smoking made a big comeback among men. Cigar sales increased dramatically and hotels began setting rooms aside for cigar smokers. For a lot of men, there is nothing better than puffing on a good cigar—possibly having a brandy along with it—and discussing sports, politics and business with congenial colleagues. Women began smoking cigars, too, and not to be outdone, inhaled them, instead of simply puffing on them. Demi Moore and other high-profile actresses led the way. (I guess Demi wanted to carry on the image she portrayed in the movie, G.I. Jane. I got news for you Demi: Smoking cigars does not prove in the real world you have what it takes to be a Navy Seal. Sorry, Demi, you ain't no Jesse Ventura!).

It used to be a macho thing for guys to drive trucks. Now, I see more of them being "manned" by women—and not small ones either—but bigger ones like Ford F-350s and Dodge Rams. It is most enlightening when the beds of these trucks are examined; in most cases, there are no scratch marks, so the vehicle is not being used for work purposes. My take on this phenomenon is that driving trucks gives females a sense of power because they are so big they can look down on others (especially men) who are driving something much smaller and closer to the ground and, as a result, are more vulnerable should an accident occur. (This suspicion was subsequently corroborated in the January 2003 issue of Reader's Digest. Author Tucker Carlson reports that "A recent commercial for the Hummer promises that women who drive the massive SUV will be able to 'threaten men in a whole new way.'").

Drinking beer is another male prerogative that women are

uslurping (excuse me, I meant usurping). Sharing a six-pack with a few buddies on the weekend at the lake or having one or two on the way home from work in a neighborhood bar or tavern were *modus vivendi* for many of us. This encroachment by women is occurring at increasingly younger ages. I marvel how coeds in their early 20s from my university can wrestle 24-pack cartons into their cars (or trucks) parked in super market lots. Even more amazing, I am sure, is how they can consume the copious amounts that they undoubtedly do.

While not to be commended, off-color jokes and swearing used to be pretty much a guy thing. While I have no data to support this assertion, it appears to me that women are increasingly trying to macho themselves by telling dirty jokes and swearing. I hear middle-aged women use e-mail late at night to exchange off-color jokes, often punctuated with "appropriate" pictures.

During the last 30 years, women became dissatisfied with attending all-women or coed colleges and universities; they wanted admission to exclusively male institutions of higher learning. The barricades fell rather quickly at the high-profile military academies (West Point, Naval Academy, Air Force Academy), but did not come down easily or quickly at the Citadel or Virginia Military Institute. The prohibition against women was dropped at Texas A&M University in the late 1960s under the leadership of president Earl Rudder, famed for commanding the 3rd ranger battalion at D-Day and across Europe.

Efforts by females to gain entrance into male colleges and universities have been quite successful. Below are indicated for 1998 the percentage of women matriculating at various formerly all-male institutions of higher learning:

West Point	14% (572 females)
Naval Academy	15% (603 females)
Air Force Academy	16% (657 females)
Texas A&M University	47% (16,868 females)
The Citadel	6% (116 females)
Virginia Military Institute	4% (53 females)

Many men's clubs and golf clubs were women-free, but female insistence, backed up by anti-discrimination laws that they be gender-neutral, broke down this barrier. One that hasn't given in to female demands is the famous Augusta National Golf Club, home to the Masters golf tournament. Augusta is under attack from the National Council of Women's Organizations. Hootie Johnson, Augusta National Chairman, expects the NCOWO to use boycotts and other economic means but has stated: "We do not intend to become a trophy for their case. We do not intend to be further distracted by this matter" (*Houston Chronicle*, July 10, 2002, p. 6C). Indeed, the NCOWO began putting pressure on the Masters' three sponsors—Citigroup, IBM and Coca-Cola. Mr. Johnson summarily relieved all three of their obligations to sponsor the 2003 Masters and it was televised without commercial interruption.

Why Do Women Want To Be Like Men?

One of the reasons why women want to be like men is their dissatisfaction with themselves and their role in life. Much of this discontent has been fueled by the vitriolic rhetoric of the radical feminists who demean their own gender by making women who submit to their husbands and/or are "stay at home" moms feel inferior.

Some women may act and appear like men because of the childhood they experienced. Perhaps their mothers dominated ("wore the pants" in the family) their spouses and their daughters grew up thinking this was acceptable behavior. Perhaps it is the lure of something exciting, something different, in other words, envy ("the grass is greener" syndrome). In this context, it should be noted that God identifies covetousness as a major sin; it is the last of the Ten Commandments (Exodus 20:17).

Whatever the reason, the desire of women to act and look like men—to homogenize the two genders—flies in the face of common sense and God's purposes. God created two sexes, not one. If he did not want there to be two, why bother to create Eve?

Men and women are not similar. The most obvious difference is physical appearance, but men and women differ in a number of other ways. According to John 0. McGinnis, professor at the Benjamin Cardozo School of Law in New York, men are more aggressive than women, more concerned with status, and more inclined to take risks, while women, again, on average, are more nurturing and empathetic. Mr. McGinnis adds that "Psychological studies also suggest that men and women have different predispositions from *the beginning*" (emphasis added). [6]

Kenneth L. Woodward, Senior Writer at *Newsweek* and that magazine's religion reporter, states " ....I do assume that there are differences between men and women, rooted in biology, and that as a consequence of these differences, every culture makes distinctions between what is masculine and what is feminine ...."[7] Barbara Amiel, writing in *Maclean's* on the physical differences in men vs. women vis-á-vis their ability to serve as firefighters, says:

> But gender differences are real. Feminism started out by maintaining there were no differences between men and women, except perhaps for five-percent upper-body strength. This was orthodoxy in the early years and anyone who departed from it was a reactionary, hurled into the outer darkness. If you were a woman and protested it, the feminists declared you a non-woman, as with Margaret Thatcher, or a raving lunatic, as with me.[8]

Gary Smalley, appearing on the radio show, Focus on the Family (November 29, 1999), asserted that men are better than women at handling conflict in sports, the workplace and in the military, but not as good as women at handling it in the home.

An intriguing study conducted at the University of Pennsylvania Medical School shows a clear physical explanation for the way men and women respond when they are upset. New imaging technology was used to analyze the part of the brain called the old limbic system, a structure humans share with reptiles. Women showed greater activity in the cingulate gyrus, a "higher, more recently evolved part of the brain that humans share with other primates." Commenting on these findings, one observer concluded that men lash out when they get upset—they are "emotional reptiles"—whereas women respond as monkeys: "They sit down and chat about it." Not surprisingly, when Raquel Gur, one of the researchers, presented the findings to a group of *female* medical students, several requested that she not publish her work. [9]

In his book, *Bringing Up Boys* (Tyndale House Publishers, 2001), Dr. James Dobson, founder and host of Focus on the Family, does an outstanding job of explaining the physiological reasons that differentiate boys from girls, men from women. At conception, there is essentially no distinction between boys and girls. But, at about six or seven weeks, male embryos get a "hormonal bath," a flood of testosterone which essentially makes a boy a boy, and differentiates them forever from girls (who do not receive this bath). The brain of boys is altered when this happens. The nerve fibers that connect the two sides of the brain are made less efficient, thereby reducing the number of electronic transmissions that flow from one side to the other. Speech is, as a result, more localized—on one side of the brain—for males than females; for females, speech capability is more evenly distributed on both sides. At puberty, males get another blast of testosterone, resulting in the "sudden appearance of facial and pubic hair, squeaky voices, pimply faces, larger muscles, sexual awakening and, eventually, other characteristics of masculinity."

This extra dosage of testosterone results in males ending up with 15 times the level that females have and explains the following physical and behavioral aspects of men:

1. Men take longer to think about what they believe, particularly if it has an emotional element.

2. Men have more of an interest in such activities as car racing, football, basketball, wrestling, hunting, fishing, guns, and military history.

3. Boys and men are more likely to take risks.

4. Men are more likely to seek wealth, power, fame and status.

5. Boys and men are better at problem solving, math, science,

spatial relations, logic, and reasoning.

Serotonin carries information from one nerve cell to another. It has a number of positive effects, including soothing emotions, controlling impulsive behavior and facilitating good judgment; insufficient levels are associated with depression and suicidal tendencies. Males have less serotonin than do females.

The amygdala is the part of the brain that functions as an "emotional computer;" it is located in the hypothalmus, the locus of emotions. The amygdala is larger in males than in females and explains why boys/men are more aggressive, more volatile than girls/women. However, the amygdala can only respond to what is in its memory bank; as such, it does not think or reason, but reacts—especially to danger by energizing the adrenal glands and other defensive organs.

In addressing the implications of testosterone, serotonin and the amygdala, Dr. Dobson has this to say.

> Would it be better if boys were more like girls and if men were more like women? Should men be feminized, emasculated, and 'wimpified?' This is precisely what some feminists and other social liberals seem to think and want us to believe. As we have seen, some of them are trying to reprogram boys to make them less competitive, less aggressive, and more sensitive. Is that a good idea? Most certainly not. First, because it contradicts masculine nature and will never succeed, and second, because the sexes were carefully designed by the Creator to balance one another's weaknesses and meet one another's needs .... How incredibly creative it is of God to put a different from of dominance in each sex so that there is a balance between the two. When they come together in marriage to form what Scripture calls 'one flesh,' they complement and supplement one another ..... Men ....value change, opportunity, risk, speculation, and adventure. They are designed to provide for their families physically and to protect them from harm and danger. The apostle Paul said, 'If anyone does not provide for his relatives, and especially for his immediate family, he has denied the faith and is worse than an unbeliever' (I Timothy 5:8). This is a divine assignment. Men are also ordained in Scripture for lead-

ership in their homes ....Men are often (but not always) less emotional in a crisis and more confident when challenged.[10]

Anyone expecting anything good from women trying to look and act more like men will be disappointed. This blurring of gender will have serious, negative consequences.

In a nutshell, God made man and woman different—both physiologically and more importantly, psychologically. As such, they are expected in God's economy to fulfill different roles. When women begin looking and, especially, acting like men, they are essentially abdicating their responsibilities and society will suffer; this means women, men and children. The latter, for example, will be unable to differentiate between the roles God has allocated for men and women, thus, increasing the likelihood that boys will become homosexuals and girls will become lesbians.

Some may argue that men should be glad that women are emulating them—that this shows at least a minimum level of respect. Hardly. Emulation often occurs because people are dissatisfied with themselves; and dissatisfied people often feel aggrieved enough to want to "get back" at the people they supposedly respect. This "getting back" often results in activities designed to gain control over the people who are envied—but not in actuality respected.

When women look and act like men, it is a "turn off" (an almost automatic revulsion) for most men, who admire women for their feminity. Another reaction males have to the masculinity of women is fear because they feel threatened. In their minds, men are thinking "I'm not supposed to compete with women. I am supposed to love, cherish and protect them. However, this female is acting like a man. She probably wants to get or take something from me. I'm not going to let that happen."

Even the men who do love, cherish and protect the women in their lives need some time away from them—time to be spent with male companions: sons, dads, friends, colleagues from work. It is a huge mistake for women to resent this and an even bigger one to "masculinize" themselves in order to horn in on what is almost an innate drive for men to spend some time with other men. Such behavior on the part of women will only be resented by men.

The blurring of female and masculine roles brought about by women trying to masculinize themselves results in another negative. One of the basic principles of economics and business is specialization of labor. A firm is more effective if workers are doing one specialized job at which they are most efficient. The same principle can be applied to the family. The family will be more productive if husband and wife perform the tasks they are best suited for. Things go awry when women join the work force and shirk their responsibilities at home, often forcing husbands/fathers to take on family responsibilities that they are not good at doing and do not want to do.

Another economic principle is operative here: sharing fixed costs over a greater number of units yields important benefits. If two people—a married couple—incur one mortgage payment, one utility bill, and so on, the cost per person drops and both are better off. According to Linda Waite, professor of sociology at the University of California, Davis and Maggie Gallagher, Director of the Marriage Project at the Institute of Marriage Values, "just getting married can boost your standard of living by one-third." [11]

There is a dark, other side of the coin. The radical feminists will not ordinarily support women's efforts to look and act like men. Instead, they have a more sinister and diabolical *modus operandi*: Let's get men to be more like women. Of course, they realize that this effort is not likely to be too successful with adult men, so they turn their attention to our sons in elementary schools and day-care centers. Energized by a curriculum guide, *Creating Sex-Fair Family Day Care*, put out by the U.S. Department of Education's Office of Educational Research & Improvement—an organization dominated by women—the principal goal is to get little boys to play with dolls. Included in the 130-page guide—funded, of course, by your tax dollars—are ten photographs. Two show a little boy with a *baby girl* doll; one shows the boy feeding her, the other kissing her. The guide states: "It is important for both boys and girls to learn nurturing and sensitivity, as well as, general parenting skills. Have as many boy dolls available as girl dolls. Boy and girls should be encouraged to play with them."

Such degrading and dangerous social tinkering is founded on a false premise: that there are no biological or psychological differences between boys and girls. (Example: Sandra Lee Bartky, feminist philosopher, says that babies are born bisexual into our *patriarchal* society, and are transformed into males and females through "social conditioning"). As we have seen earlier in this chapter, there are significant differences and many of these have been noted in play environments of pre-school children. When allowed to their own devices, boys will always prefer toys like cars, trucks, airplanes, and G.I. Joes, while girls will gravitate toward dolls and sewing kits. Methods of play have proved to be innately different for boys and girls. In a tumbling room, full of climbing structures, ladders and mats, boys run and climb all the time, with momentary periods of rest, whereas the girls, in the room without boys, quickly lose interest and move on to painting or playing with dolls.[12]

William Bonner, publisher, Agora Publishing, in a promotional piece touting a men's health newsletter, perhaps best describes the implications of women's efforts to feminize men:

> Rembember when a man could be a man? Proud and strong. Rough and ready. A provider for his family. You used to be allowed to admire a beautiful woman. It was okay to like sex, good steaks, and cigars. But those days are long gone, my friend. Rubbed out like a half-smoked cigar in a champagne-soaked ashtray. Now you've got to worry about "correctness" and "feelings." Your testosterone is considered poison. And if you're an average, over-40 male ...you're guilty before you even open your mouth. Modern society is plagued by sensitive "artists" like John Tesh and Yanni...or talk-show hosts like Phil Donahue who encourage other men to cry on camera. Exercise gurus like Charles Atlas have been replaced by Richard Simmons. And our children idolize stars like Michael Jackson, who 'better' themselves with plastic chins and tattooed-on mascara.

One woman who had the right perspective on the male-female

relationship is Abigal Adams, the wife of our second president, John Adams. Abigal was truly a woman to admire. She raised five children, including one who became president, and ran a house in the trying times during the Revolutionary War, while her husband was frequently away, helping to draft and advocate the Declaration of Independence and representing our fledgling nation in France, England and the Netherlands. One of her many letters to her husband contained this line: "I believe nature has assigned each sex its particular duties and sphere of action and to act well your part, 'there all the honor lies.'"[13]

REFERENCES

1.Orlando Figes, *A People's Tragedy--A History Of The Russian Revolution*, Viking, New York, 1996, p. 319.

2. *Statistical Abstract of the United States*, 2001.

3. *Sports Participation In 1997, Series I and II*, National Sporting Goods Association, as found in the *Statistical Abstract Of The United States*, 1999.

4. Michael Bamberger, "No Place For This Kicker," *Sports Illustrated*, September 29, 1997, p. 100.

5. *Sports Participation Index, 1999*, as found in the *Statistical Abstract Of The United States*, 2001,

6. John 0. McGinnis, "Unnatural Selection—The Feminists Unconvincing Biology," *National Review*, April 19, 1999, p. 30.

7. Kenneth L. Woodward, "Gender and Religion—Who's Really Running The Show?," *Commonweal*, November 22, 1996, pp. 9-13.

8. Barbara Amiel, "Sorry Folks, Gender Differences Are Real," *Macleans*, March 15, 1999, p. 11.

9. Christina Hoff Sommers, *The War Against Boys*, Simon & Schuster, New York, 2000, p. 90.

10.James Dobson, *Bringing Up Boys*, Tyndale House Publishers, Inc., Wheaton, Illinois, 2001, pp. 19-27.

11.Linda J. Waite and Maggie Gallagher, *The Case For Marriage: Why Married People Are Happier, Healthier, And Better Off Financially*, Doubleday, New York, 2000 as reviewed in *The Economist*, Books And Arts Section, January 6, 2001, pp. 77-78.

12.Christina Hoff Sommers, pp. 76, 86.

13.David McCullough, *John Adams*, Simon & Schuster, New York, 2001, p. 171.

FOUR

Women and Power

"I want to be the boss of all things." Winsome little girl appearing in a CNBC advertisement for a special on European women business executives.

Over the last 30 years, the level of power attained by women in the United States has expanded dramatically. This expansion has eroded the power base formerly held by men. These trends can be most noted in the following arenas: demographics, work, education, government, military, religion, the home, and wealth.

Demographics

The opportunity for power usurpation increases when one gender outnumbers the other. And, in the United States, women have outnumbered men since 1950 and are predicted to do so in the future by an even greater margin. The outcomes of this phenomenon should not be minimized. Men can be outvoted by women at the polls, more females will be competing with men for jobs, a greater percentage of college and university seats will be occupied by women and not by men, religious institutions will be controlled by women, and so on. In other words, the potential for women to dominate all areas of our society will be inherently greater because of their larger numbers.

Women outnumbered men in 1950 by slightly less than one million. Within 10 years, this figure had essentially tripled, to 2.661 million and almost doubled again to more than five million in 1970. In 1980, 1990 and 2000, there was a plurality of six million in favor of women, and by 2050, it is projected to exceed 7.4 million.

Similar discrepancies in favor of women are noted when the data are examined for the population 18 years of age and older—the age group most likely to be grappling for power. In 2000, it was estimated that there were 8.004 million more women than men in America; by 2050, the figure will rise to 9.559 million (*Statistical Abstract of the United States*, 2001).

Work

In 2000, 69.0% of women were gainfully employed, as compared to 73.5% for men, and women accounted for almost one-half (49.5%) of all workers in the United States. Whereas in 1920, only 9.0% of *married* women were working, by 2000 this figure had reached 62.0%. And frighteningly, 62.8% of married women with children under six years of age were in the work force in 2000 (*Statistical Abstract of the United States*, 2001). Certainly, these data suggest the almost inevitable consequences: neglect of children, husbands and home by working women and the increased opportunity for adulterous liaisons while on the job.

In what kind of occupations are women employed? Suffice to say that they have made great strides in the last 30 years or so, such that, they are now a powerful force in many important occupations. Below are the percentages of women that make up various high profile occupations, all of which were formerly dominated by males:

State and local government employees	44%
Technical, sales, administrative support	41%
Managerial and professional	31% [1]
University teachers	45%
Middle management positions of film studios and television networks	50%
Editors, reporters and technical writers	53% [2]
Finance, insurance, real estate	50%
Management professions	40% [3]
Psychology	more than 50% [4]

Women have been loudly and shrilly complaining that they are underrepresented in top management positions in corporate America. However, significant strides in recent years have been made. In 1999, Catalyst, a New York-based *women's* research organization, estimated that women made up 11.9% of corporate officers in the 500 companies that were studied by the organization. [5] In a study reported by *Business Week* (November 22, 1999), 51 companies were identified that had at least 23.1% of corporate officer positions filled by women; five companies—U.S. West, Pacificare Health Systems, Lincoln National, Avon Products, and Nordstrom—had at least 40% of these positions occupied by females and such icon companies as CBS, Mattel, Merck, Paine Webber, and Southwest Airlines had more than 30% women in top positions. Thirty-six percent of Charles Schwab's executives are female; the figure for Merrill Lynch is 32%, 19% for Bear Stearns, 18% at Lehman Brothers, and 11% for Morgan Stanley Dean Witter and Paine Webber (*Business Week*, October 9, 2000).

Not content with these strides, women still lament that they are being frozen out of the truly top management positions, such as chief executive officer, president, executive vice president, and chief operations officer. The common complaint is that although women may be in management positions, they often do not have bottom line, decision-making authority; instead, they are shunted to heading up such staff areas as public relations and human resources.

I looked at three years of issues of *Forbes, Fortune* and *Business Week* to determine the extent to which women hold high-level executive positions in U.S. firms. I found 135 women in top executive positions who are directly responsible for decisions which impact their companies' operating results. And they are employed by many well-known, large firms, such as, ABC Radio Network (Lyn Andrews, president), Mattel (Jill Barad, CEO), Southwest Airlines (Colleen C. Barrett, president), Bank of America (Amy Woods Brinkley, president), Hewlett-Packard (Carly S. Fiorina, CEO), Paramount Pictures (Sherry Lansing, chair), Xerox (Ann Mulcahy, president), Applebee's (Julia Stewart, chair and CEO), and eBay (Margaret Whitman, CEO). Female executives, contrary to the contentions of various women's advocacy organizations, hold top-level executive positions, not staff positions, directly responsible for decisions which do, indeed, impact their companies' bottom line.

Columnist George Will offers sound explanations as to why women may be *justifiably* under represented in corporate executive positions. Quoting material from "Women's Figures: An Illustrated Guide to the Economic Progress of Women in America," by Diana Furchtgott-Roth and Christina Stolba, Will states that the typical qualifications for such executive positions include 25 years of work experience and an MBA degree, resulting in an *extremely small pool of female* candidates because in the 1970s, women largely eschewed working and pursuing MBA degrees (*Newsweek,* March 29, 1999).

When I was in Russia in October of 2000, CNBC was advertising a special it was going to air on executive women in Europe. Concluding the ad was a shot of a captivating eight or nine year old girl who said, "I want to be the boss of all things." Nowhere in business is this more true than being on the board of directors of major corporations. Boards can hire and fire corporations' top executives and develop product and marketing strategies for their companies. Getting more women onto boards has been a major push in recent years by women's action groups. Besides the power held, board participation can be financially remunerative. *Corporate Board Member* reports that the median pay for board members in 2000 was $100,000 per membership. [6] And you can be a member of multiple boards. Esther Dyson, chairperson of EDventure Holdings, sits on 13 U.S. and Eastern European computer and technology firms' boards. Besides the honoraria paid, board members usually get flat stipends and per diems to attend four to six board meeting annually. [7] Even better, women can use their board seats to further women's careers in business. Karen Hastie Williams, a partner in the Washington D.C. law firm, Crowell & Moring, sits on five boards: Amherst College, NAACP Legal Defense and Education Fund, Continental Airlines, Fannie Mae, and Gannett. She says: "If you see a female executive's compensation package trailing a male counterpart's and she delivers a strong presentation or project, you have the ability to call the CEO's attention to her performance and help her gain recognition." (Note that there is no consideration of the woman's performance compared to that of the man who is out earning her—just go ahead and reward the female).

For obvious reasons, many women may not qualify to sit on corporate boards. And there is no discrimination involved. The high-profile CEO of Cypress Semiconductor, T. J. Rodgers, in a public letter, stated the case most persuasively: "A search for board members who meet the criteria usually yields a male who is 50-plus years old, has a master's degree in engineering or science, and has moved up the management ladder to the top spot in one or more corporations. Unfortunately, there are currently few minorities and almost no women who chose to be an engineering graduate student 30 years ago."[8]

Despite the apparent lack of qualified women, they are gaining more and more board seats. In 1999, almost all *Fortune* 500 companies had at least one woman on their boards, up from 8.7% in 1994,[9] and they hold large proportions of board seats in many high-profile companies, such as, Golden West Financial Group (55.6%), Avon Products (46.2%), Beverly Enterprises (44.4%), and Gannett (40.0%).

Females have been quite vociferous in their allegations that they do not get equal pay for doing the same job as their male counterparts. However, there is strong evidence that the gap is not as great as women would like us to believe. Columnist George Will, writing in *Newsweek* (March 29, 1999), states that between 1960 and 1994, women's wages grew *10 times faster* than that of males. Citing work done by Furchgott-Roth and Stolba, Will writes that in 1999, women 27 to 33 years old who have *never had children* make 98% of what men the same age earn for the same work. Economists Francine Blau and Lawrence M. Kahn of Cornell University estimate that by the *end of the 1980s* (over a decade ago), female wages, when adjusted for differences in education, experience and occupation, were 88% of what men earned.[10] And there is some evidence that, in some professions, women's pay *exceeds* that of men's. Andrew Hacker, in his book, *Money—Who Has How Much And Why*, cited *National Law Journal* findings that in 1994, women law school graduates were paid an average starting salary of $50,000, men $48,000. Hacker also alludes to 1996 Census data that show that women who worked full-time and had never married made $1,005 for every $1,000 earned by a man.

The point is that the compensation gap that the feminists complain about has largely disappeared. While some of the erosion can be attributed to anti-discrimination, affirmative action and passage of the Equal Pay Act in 1963, much of the prior disparity occurred because women were not willing to make the kinds of sacrifices and commitments to their careers that men made.

An analysis of salary and total compensation figures for 48 female executives as reported in *Business Week, Fortune* and *Forbes*, indicated that they are well paid. Their annual salary averaged about $1 million, with total yearly compensation close to $4 million. The highest salary ($7.5 million) was earned by Leslie C. Tortora, Goldman Sach's chief information officer; Heather Killen, senior vice-president of Yahoo enjoyed the highest total compensation package ($32.7 million). *Business Week* (October 27, 2003) reported that, on average, female top executives are compensated "every bit as generously as their male counterparts."

The growing power of women economically can also be noted in the area of entrepreneurship. It has been estimated by the National Foundation for Women Business Owners (NFWBO) that, in 2000, women owned 9.1 million companies, double the number that existed as recently as 1987. They have been starting new businesses at twice the national average, such that, they now own 38% of all U.S. firms. These female-owned companies employ 27 million people, up from 18 million as recently as 1996, and their sales have reached $3.6 *trillion* in 1999, a 56% increase over the $2.3 trillion generated in 1996.[11] And female startups have staying power; 75% begun in 1991 were still in existence three years later as opposed to only 66% for all startups. [12]

Sharon Hadry, NFWBO's executive director, in responding to these data says: "Quite clearly, these aren't women who just want to stay home and start a little something on the side. Their businesses are getting bigger and more substantial." [13]

Female thirst for power can be conveniently slaked through their starting new businesses. They can appoint themselves to their companies' top slots—president, CEO, chairman (or chairwoman?) of the board—and obviously can control the hiring and firing of employees including, of course, males.

Education

In 1970, 58.8% of college and university students were male; 41.2% were females. In only a decade, women became the majority of higher education enrollees (51.4%). By 1998, their share had increased to 56.1%. By 2004, it has been estimated that of 15.9 million men and women in institutions of higher learning, 57.5% will be female. Judy Mohraz, president of Goucher College (Baltimore, Md.), warned that at the present rate, there soon will be no men in college at all and that "the last man to be awarded a bachelor's degree would receive it in the spring of 2067.[14]

Whereas women garnered only 34.2% of all degrees in 1960,

by 1998 they were awarded 56.8%. Similar patterns are noted for various types of degrees. In 1998, women captured 61.0% of associate's degrees, up from 43.2% in 1970. They obtained 56.1% of bachelor's degrees awarded in 1998, up from slightly more than one-third (35.2%) in 1960. About one-third (32.0%) of master's degrees went to women in 1960; by 1998, the figure had jumped to 57.2%. In 1998, it was estimated that women received 42.0% of doctorates awarded to American citizens, compared to only 10% in 1960.

Women are making great strides in obtaining professional degrees. In 1998, they earned 38.2% of the dentistry degrees awarded (D.D.S. or D.M.D.), 41.6% of M.D.s, 38.2% of law degrees, and 26.1%, of theology doctorates (*Statistical Abstract of the United States*, 2001). In 1993-1994, they garnered 49.9% of degrees in optometry and 66.8% of doctorates in pharmacy. [15] And women are accounting for 40% of M.B.A. degrees (Master of Business Administration).

So what difference does it make if lower percentages of higher education degrees are going to men? Plenty! Jobs that men without college degrees go into—and ones avoided by women—plumbers, electricians, construction, auto mechanics, carpenters, welders—are physically demanding and eventually take their toll. So it's less likely that these jobs have as much longevity as other, "softer" occupations, into which female college graduates go.

But the major disadvantage for men not having a college degree is economic. It was estimated in 1999 (*Statistical Abstract of the United States*, 2001) that a male college graduate would earn $57,706 annually, while a male with a high school degree would earn $30,414. If this $27,292 discrepancy were extrapolated over a 40-year career, the man without a college degree would be looking at a shortfall of $1,091,680 and retirement benefits would be much lower even if the male with a high school education were lucky enough to have a pension plan—which many don't. If, on average, a pension plan had a contribution of 15% of the employee's earnings—a typical scenario consisting of contributions from the employee and the employer—the high school graduate, in comparison to the college graduate, would face an annual deficit of $4,094 ($27,292 x 15%). If this $4,094 difference returned an annual yield of 6% over 40 years, the college graduate would have $671,622 more in his retirement fund than would the high school graduate. If the college graduate at retirement withdrew 8% of the principal annually to live on, he would enjoy $53,730 more a year than the high school graduate.

Government

Women have been making increasing inroads into local, state and national governments. At the county, municipal and township levels, about one-fourth of elected officials are women. These are broken down into 22%, 22% and 27%, respectively, for county, municipal and township. According to the *World Almanac*, 2001 there were 88 women mayors of "selected U.S. cities," including Asheville, N.C., Berkeley, CA., Beverly Hills, CA., Boca Raton, FL., Colorado Springs, CO., Erie, PA., Evanston, IL., Gainesville, FL., Greenwich, CT., Kansas City, Kansas and Kansas City, Missouri, Lexington, KY., Long Beach, CA., Madison, WI., Minneapolis, MN., Orlando,FL., Palo Alto, CA., Portland, OR., Sacramento, CA., Sarasota, FL., Scottsdale, AZ., Springfield, IL., Topeka, KS., and Tulsa, OK. In 1969, about 4% of state legislators were female. By 1979, the figure rose to 10%. After the 2000 election, women made up 22% of state legislators. In 2001, five women were serving as their state's governor—the highest figure ever.

Women are gaining increasing powers at the national level. In 1930, there were no female senators and only nine women in the House of Representatives. Little movement occurred with these figures until 1994, when seven women were elected to the senate and 47 won house elections. The 2000 election resulted in all-time highs: 13 senators and 59 representatives, meaning that they made up 13.5% of the Congress in 2000.

But, apparently, women are not satisfied with these numbers. Coretta Scott King, Martin Luther King's widow, writing in the *Time Almanac*, 2000, says:

> This lack of gender balance in government is not only unjust, but goes a long way to explain why children and families are being shortchanged by government policies in the United States and most other nations. Women should continue to overcome sexist stereotypes in the media and society at large. But for improving the quality of our lives, where we really need some more assertive women is in the halls of national, state and local legislatures and in executive offices. As former president of Iceland, Vigdis Finnbogadottir, the first woman elected head of state in a democratic election (1980) and reelected three times, put it, 'Parity democracy means that 50 percent of women should be in the decision making, and 50 percent men. All democratic countries should aim at that. We women of the world, we know that we cannot change it in a day, or in a week, or in a year. But if we have this as an aim, we might get somewhere.

Many women were appointed by Bill Clinton to positions in federal executive departments and agencies. And several of them occupied high-profile positions, including Janet L. Yellen (Chair, Council of Economic Advisors), Charlene Barshefsky (U.S. Trade Representative), Donna Shalala (Secretary, Department of Health and Human Resources), Janet Reno (Attorney General), Madeleine Albright (Secretary of State), Carol M. Browner (Administrator, Environmental Protection Agency), and Aida Alvarez (Administrator, Small Business Administration). An analysis of public documents revealed that 63 women in the Clinton administration headed up various boards, agencies, etc. or occupied the assistant or under secretary positions that are crucial in developing policies at the federal level that *often adversely affect the daily lives of American men.*

While George W. Bush did not appoint nearly as many women to federal government posts, there were still a number of them holding high positions. These include Gale Norton, Secretary of the Interior; Ann M. Veneman, Secretary of Agriculture; Elaine L.

Chao, Secretary of Labor; Condoleezza Rice, National Security Advisor; and Christine Todd Whitman, Head, Environmental Protection Agency.

The Military

There were 30,969 female officers on active duty in the U.S. military in 1998. Most (11,976) were in the Air Force, followed by 10,367 in the Army, 7,777 in the Navy, and 854 in the Marine Corps. This total number of female officers represented about 15% of all officers (211,900) on active duty that year. In 1970, there were only 5,235 female officers on active duty out of a total of 143,704, representing only 3.6% of the total.

Religion

Organized religion in the United States is dominated by women. This in spite of the Biblical prohibitions on women becoming pastors, deacons or elders (see Chapter Seven). Indeed, control of the church by females is so pervasive, even without their holding leadership positions, that we could say the church is being, in large measure, feminized.

On Sunday, in most Protestant churches, 80% of the attendees are frequently women. At other times, church life is even more feminine. Kenneth L. Woodward, religion reporter for *Newsweek*, writes:

> During the week, pastors live in a women's world. Like the suburbs in a John Updike novel, the weekday world of American religion is a world without men. Women dominate church committees, the prayer groups, the Bible study groups, the Sunday schools. You're much more likely to find a women's spirituality group than a men's spirituality group. 'No one told me when I left the seminary,' says William Willimon, a long-time Methodist minister, now dean of the chapel at Duke University, 'that most of my time would be spent with women.' From Monday to Friday, much of a pastor's time is spent in counseling. Many of the counselees are couples, but most are women.[16]

Even though women may not be the pastor in a church, they still hold enormous power. According to Eric Lincoln, a leading black scholar at Duke Divinity School:

> The well-organized black church is an organization of subgroups in which women predominate and wield their own power. Women raise the money and, though men dominate the church board of trustees, it is their wives who effectively determine how it is spent. Among black Baptists, power belongs to 'the mothers,' a group of older women who have been in their congregations for decades and constitute the heart and soul of the church. On Sundays, the Mothers dress distinctively in white and *preside* from a special section of the church—opposite the 'Amen Corner' where the male trustees sit. The minister who has the Mothers on his side is *virtually unassailable* and woe be it to the minister who doesn't (emphases added).[17]

For whatever reason—male lassitude or female zest for control (or both)—roles usually reserved in churches for men have largely disappeared and are now in the hands of women, or the entity no longer exists. These include single-sex male choirs, Sunday school classes for teen-age boys, and the brotherhoods of the Lutheran churches.[18]

On the other hand, church women are not about to let men invade their church groups. Consider the program of the 16th Annual Women & Spirituality Conference held at Mankato State University. The titles of the various sessions appear not to be at all inclusive of men, despite the conference supposedly being "designed for women and *interested men*" (emphasis added). What man would want to sit in on such sessions as "The Crone's Quest," "Loving the Lesbian Goddess Within," "Fairy Godmothers," and "Redeeming and Enhancing Our Aphrodite Nature?"

Although 75% of liberal mainline Protestant clergy are men, this is not likely to continue if current trends are maintained. (Among Universalist-Unitarians, more than half the clergy are already women). The Association of Theological Schools indicated that in 1994, about 40% of students enrolled in a Master of Divinity degree program—which is the track for ordination—were women. Among United Church of Christ, Presbyterian, United Methodists, and Episcopalian seminary students, around half are female. At the prestigious national, nondenominational divinity schools, like Harvard and Yale, women are in the majority and, as noted earlier, 26.1% of theology degrees go to women. [19]

Wealth

Women are well-positioned to accumulate more wealth than are men. A *Working Woman* survey found that two-thirds of women are in charge of family spending and overall finances. Sixth-three percent develop the family budget and 50% head up the family's investment program. In 1997, 39.8% of women were covered with a pension plan, a figure only slightly behind that of men (43.8%).[20] As noted earlier in one third of U.S. families, wives out-earn their husbands. A much greater percentage of men have insurance policies naming their wives as beneficiaries than vice versa and the value of policies on husbands is usually much greater than that on wives.

Women are aggressively investing. According to the Securities Industry Association, there are 220,000 women heading households with incomes exceeding $100,000. This income level is a primary candidate for investments. This number is expected to double by 2010, when this group will control $1 trillion in assets.

Women in 2000 had 1.2 million accounts with the Oppenheimer Fund, up from 270,000 only seven years earlier.[21]

Perhaps the most important factor buttressing women's asset accumulation can be found in U.S. demographic data. Women live, on average, five years longer than do men. This, combined with the fact that wives, on average, are five years younger than their husbands, means that they are much more likely than their spouses to inherit pension funds, social security benefits, houses, automobiles, securities, and cash.

In The Home

It is a "no brainer" that women are usurping the leadership roles of their husbands in the home. Just the fact that many wives are working tends to erode the male power base in households. The slide down the slippery slope is accelerated when the wife makes more money than does the husband and the husband, because the wife is working, is forced to take on various household duties (shopping, washing, cleaning, chauffeuring, etc.) normally performed by wives. The tendency in most families for women to be making the household's financial decisions is another nail in the coffin.

This chapter has clearly demonstrated that women are enjoying increasing power across a number of important fronts. Power is a classic example of what economists like to call a "zero-sum game." That is, one party's gain comes at the expense of the other. Since the level of power for women in the United States is clearly on the rise, then it automatically follows that that of men is on the wane.

What is causing this shift in power? Is it occurring because men consciously defer to women? Is it the result of God's plan for the United States? Is it the culmination of a rational consideration of upsides and downsides? Or, is there something else, perhaps less palatable, that explains the increase of power for women in the U.S. over the last 30 years and the decrease in same for males? The next chapter deals with these questions and the answer is likely to surprise a large majority of readers, particularly those who are male.

REFERENCES

1. *Statistical Abstract of the United States*, 1999.

2. Helen Fisher, "Why Women Will Rule In The New Millennium," *Glamour*, July 1999, p. 116.

3. Cora Daniels, "The Global Glass Ceiling," *Fortune*, October 12, 1998, pp. 102-103.

4. Leonard Sax, "Guilty Until Proven Innocent," *Penthouse*, December 2000, pp. 123-148.

5. Michelle Conlin and Wendy Zellner, "The CEO Still Wears Wingtips," *Business Week*, November 22, 1999, pp. 85-90.

6. *Corporate Board Member*, Winter 2000. p. 72.

7. *Working Woman*, April 1999, pp.65-69.

8. *Working Woman*.

9. *Working Woman,*

10. *Working Woman,*

11. Marci McDonald, "A Start-Up Of Her Own," *U.S. News & World Report*, May 15, 2000, pp. 34-42.

12. Marci McDonald.

13. Marci McDonald.

14. *National Center For Education Statistics, Digest Of Education Statistics*, 1996.

15. *National Center For Education Statistics, Digest Of Education Statistics*, 1996.

16. Kenneth L. Woodward, "Who's Really Running The Show?," *Commonweal*, November 22, 1996, pp, 9.-14.

17. Kenneth L. Woodward.

18. Kenneth L. Woodward.

19. Kenneth L . Woodward.

20. *The American Marketplace*, New Strategist Publications, Inc., Ithaca, New York, 1999, p. 431.

21. Louise Lee, "Brokers Are From Mars, Woman Are From Venus," *Business Week*, December 4, 2000, p. 158.

FIVE

The Ultimate Weapon: Discrimination

"The United States Department of Education spews out over 300 publications on gender equity, none of these aimed at helping boys achieve parity with girls in the nation's schools." Dr. Christina Hoff Sommers

"The federal government spends four times as much on breast cancer research as it spends for research on prostate cancer." Ann Coulter

The previous chapter chronicled the tremendous increase in power women have achieved in the United States across a wide variety of areas over the last three decades. As suggested at the end of that chapter, there is a need to see how this has been accomplished. Unfortunately, as this chapter will clearly show, women's achievements have often occurred through a system of rank discrimination against men and in favor of women which has unfairly tilted the playing field in favor of females. The most glaring of these inequities can be seen in education, the work place, health care, legal system, military, intercollegiate athletics, and the media. It is also instructive to look at demographic figures in order to become aware of an apparent inherent bias against males that affects their longevity. We will also look at a discriminatory practice almost 100% under the control of women that has the same effect but, despite its loathsomeness, is not often recognized as such by males. I am alluding to abortion.

Education

The discrimination that is committed against males begins in elementary school, proceeds through junior high and high school and reaches its zenith in higher education. Because the level of education has such a pronounced effect on the types of careers males can pursue and their lifetime earnings (see previous chapter), it is important to expose the anti-male discrimination which pervades the entire spectrum of education in America.

According to the *2001 World Almanac* (p. 163), there were 1,325,000 male teachers in U.S. primary and secondary schools in 1999, compared to 3,925,000 female teachers. In other words, 75% of these teachers were female. Does this disparity of female to male teachers guarantee a level playing field for boys in school? Certainly not: The evidence clearly shows otherwise.

Consider the disturbing revelations contained in the book by Christina Hoff Sommers (a woman!), *The War Against Boys—How Misguided Feminism Is Harming Our Young Men*, as reviewed by Cherie Harder (another woman!) in *Human Events* (February 5, 2001):

1.Boys are being forced to play with dolls, make quilts, wear high heels and dresses and skirts and role play, taking the part of such women as Etta James, famed blues singer, and Anita Hill, civil rights leader (she of the Clarence Thomas hearings). They are allowed to only play "noncompetitive" tag, their recesses are being eliminated, they are prevented from running, and have to face discipline meted out by "princessipals."

2.The American Association of University Women (AAUW) and "other like-minded organizations have imposed their *strange brand* of *feminism* in the schools, and popularized the notion that girls are being silenced, subdued and subjugated, while boys are the aggressors in waiting who must, for the good of society, be conditioned to be more nurturing and emotive—and *less boy-like*" (emphases added).

3. Girls, on the contrary, are not being shortchanged and demoralized in school. Rather, "it is boys, not girls, on the weak side of an educational gender gap."

4. The emphasis in schools is on "reconditioning" boys. However, since reconditioning never comes easy, boys' resistance must be overcome—often along the lines indicated above.

5. Because efforts to recondition boys flies in the face of human nature—those innate qualities that differentiate boys from girls (see Chapter Three)—the educational system in the United States is a "war *against* human nature, and a *denial* of the Creator" (emphases added).

Dudley Barlow, writing in the March 1999 *Education Digest*, debunks the assertion espoused by the AAUW that schools discriminate against women. How, he asks, can this be since girls get higher grades, outperform boys on standardized reading and writing tests, obtain higher class ranks, get more honors in school, and are far more likely to go to college than boys (see data in Chapter Four). Both boys and girls who sit in classes agree, according to Mr. Barlow: "Schools favor girls. Teachers think girls are smarter, enjoy being around them more, and hold higher expectations of them."[1] Not to be deterred by this evidence, the U.S. Department of Education spews out over 300 publications on gender equity, "none of these aimed at helping boys achieve parity with girls in the nation's schools."[2]

But the discrimination against boys does not end after high school. If anything, its gets even more destructive at the university and college level. It first starts with a concerted, discriminatory effort to pump more women into higher education, while simultaneously keeping young men out of college.

We saw in the previous chapter that about 56% of students in universities and colleges are women and that they are awarded the majority of associate, bachelor and masters degrees, close to half of all doctorates and a majority or close to a majority of most professional degrees. Do these data reflect the fact that women, based on their scholastic achievements in high school, are better candidates for success in college and, thus, deserve more than men the opportunity to attend institutions of higher learning? Hardly.

Acceptance at U.S. colleges and universities is largely determined by applicants' high school grades and their performance on various standardized tests. It is generally believed that girls' high school grades are consistently only *slightly higher* than those of boys.[3] But we get a different picture when we compare boys and girls on the two standardized tests most widely used to predict success (and non-success) in colleges and universities: the SAT and the ACT. Data in the *2004 World Almanac* show that between 1975 and 2003, males consistently outscored females on the verbal sections of the SAT and by a *considerably larger* margin on the math part of this test since 1967. On the composite score on the ACT, since 1990, males and females do about the same. On components of the ACT, women outpaced men on the English portion and on the reading part (but only since 1995), but males consistently outperform women on the math and science reasoning segments (by large margins). Other tests used to evaluate high school students show a clear domination by men in geopolitics and my own research discovered that men consistently do better than women in geography.

Do these findings on high school grades and performance on standardized tests justify the admittance of *1.6 million fewer males* a year into institutions of higher learning in the U.S. (*Statistical Abstract of the United States*, 2001)? I think not. But, I've got news for you: It will probably get even worse. In March of 1997, the Center for Women's Policy in Washington D.C. made the preposterous demand that the College Board, the SAT's sponsor, drop any math questions on which boys get a *higher score than girls*. Diane Ravitch, a Fellow at the Manhattan Institute in New York, points out that boys have outscored girls by about 35 points annually on the math portion of the SAT over the last 30 years even though girls have taken as many math courses in high school (algebra, geometry, precalculus, and calculus) as boys and get about the same grades in these courses. Ms. Ravitch sarcastically concludes: "Why stop at dumbing down the SAT? Why not eliminate math altogether? Then, we can be sure of equal results." [4]

Unfortunately, Ms. Ravitch got it only half right. In March, 2001, Richard Atkinson, former head of the National Science Foundation and presently president of the prestigious nine-campus University of California system, called for *total elimination* of the SAT as a diagnostic tool in college admissions. His rationale: It discriminates unfairly against poor and minority students (blacks and Hispanics). Perhaps a more insidious reason that Mr. Atkinson and others would like to see the SAT go is that it would wipe out a major advantage that males have in getting into college. In commenting on Atkinson's call, *The Economist* (February 24, 2001), says that the SAT is better at predicting college students' grades than are high school grades. "It cannot be entirely coincidental that American SAT-backed universities are the envy of much of the world, whereas many of its high schools, without any national testing, are dreadful..."

Had enough? Sorry, there's more. A 1992 report put out by the American Association of University Women *(How Schools Short-change Girls)* decried the 'persuasive inequalities in our schools' and was successful in getting many schools to establish single-sex math and science classes in order to "eliminate the male voices, aggressiveness and male-student favoritism by teachers."[5] Here's another example of how our educational system screws our boys. The Preliminary Scholastic Assessment Test (PSAT) is used to identify prospects for the highly prestigious and lucrative National Merit Scholarships. The Office of Civil Rights in the U.S. Department of Education demanded that the PSAT be changed because the test resulted in more boys getting National Merit Scholarships, 56% to 44%. The PSAT caved in; a new version contains a greater emphasis on writing skills on which girls are guaranteed to do better than boys.[6] (The Office of Civil Rights, dominated by women, was headed up by Norma V. Cantu). Not satisfied with discriminating against boys by meddling with the PSAT, Ms. Cantu has looked beyond that test to take aim on both the SAT and the

ACT. In 1999, her office decreed that the "use of any educational test which has a significant disparate impact on any particular race, national origin or *sex* is discriminatory" (emphasis added). Because boys, as explained earlier, do better on these tests, in general, than girls, you can bet who the gender targets are of this guideline which, according to *The Chronicle of Higher Education,* had college and university officials "reeling;" they only had four days to prove that if they used these tests for admissions and financial decisions, the tests were not discriminatory.[7]

The attempts to thwart the educational goals of gifted males is particularly reprehensible. It is a generally accepted fact that there is more variability in male intelligence than there is for females. In other words, greater percentages of males, in contrast to women, will be found at high IQ levels. The flip side, of course, is that greater percentages of males will be in the lower IQ categories and will be "academic duds." [8] After analyzing 32 years of standardized test results, it was reported in 1995 in *Science* magazine that University of Chicago researchers found that boys outnumber girls three to one in the top 10% in mathematics, seven to one in the top 1%.[9]

The proof of male superiority in math and science is found when analyzing Nobel prize winners over the last 50 years, when women have been enrolled in colleges and universities in increasing numbers. Gosta Wrangler, professor emeritus in electrochemistry at the Royal Institute of Technology in Stockholm Sweden, found that of 102 laureates in Physics in the last half century, only one was female. Only one was a Chemistry laureate (out of 83 awarded), only six out of 120 were recipients of the Nobel prize in medicine and none of the 38 winners in Economics was a woman. Mr. Wrangler concludes, "With only 8 women (2.3%) out of 343 Nobel laureates in Science and Economics in the last 50 years, we can safely assert: For research in its highest power, testicles are, as a rule required." [10]

In 1997, the U.S. Health and Human Services Department, headed up by Donna Shalala, launched Girl Power! to "raise public awareness about the needs of America's *demoralized girls"* (emphasis added). The National Science Foundation, under another female, Rita Caldwell, allocated millions of dollars annually to help these "demoralized" girls improve their science and math skills. But there was no such help for boys: To the contrary, in 1994, Congress passed the Gender Equity in Education Act which identified girls as an "under served population," to take their place with discriminated-against minorities, opening the door for millions of dollars of grants to study their plight. And to top it off, our delegation to the United Nations Fourth World Conference on Women in Beijing, China in 1994 called the "educational and psychological deficits of American girls a *pressing human rights issue"* (emphasis added).[11]

There is a saccharine advertisement that has played on the radio for about three years. It shows that the female movement in the United States will engage in a variety of weapons, besides overt discrimination against males, to get more girls into science and math curricula at institutions of higher learning. A woman claiming to be a forensic scientist in the state of Delaware crime lab tells us that math and science led her into a "life of crime," a "girl can be any kind of scientist," and "turn your daughter onto math and science." The advertisement is sponsored by the Ad Council and the Women's College Coalition.

For about 30 years, there has been an aggressive campaign by women, buttressed by affirmative action legislation, to force all-male colleges to open their doors to females. And the walls (ivy-covered) came tumbling down: the service academies (West Point, Naval Academy, Air Force Academy), Virginia Military Institute, and the Citadel being the high-profile examples. But there were plenty of others that succumbed to the pressure, such as, Boston College, Notre Dame, Franklin and Marshall. A perusal of enrollment data contained in the *2000 Time Almanac* reveals that there are only three colleges or universities in the United States that are still all male. These are Morehouse College, Atlanta, Georgia; Wabash College, Crawfordsville, Indiana; and

Hampden-Sydney, Hampden-Sydney, Virginia—all well-respected private institutions, with Morehouse generally regarded as the second-best school for Blacks, behind Spelman (see *2000 Time Almanac,* p. 885). On the other hand, there are 19 all-women's colleges which have not opened their doors to men, including such prestigious institutions as Barnard, Mount Holyoke, Simmons College, and Wellesley.

Apparently, the feminists can't figure out what they want—coed or single-sex colleges. After pushing for 30 years for the coed option, the American Association of University Women (not them again!) reported in two studies (1991 and 1994) that girls did not fare well in coed institutions of higher learning; "they are not called on by their teachers as often as men, they are sexually harrassed, and they are crippled with self-esteem problems." Eventually, eating disorders and self-mutilation was added to the list.[12] But in 1998, the AAUW did another flip-flop: Even though single-sex schools raised girls' math scores, encouraged them to take risks, and raised their self-confidence levels, they were not the answer because they promoted "sexist stereotypes." [13]

Wellesley is an *all-female* (discrimination against men?) liberal arts college in Massachusetts which has such graduates as Hillary Rodham Clinton (the college insists on including the maiden names of their alumnae) and Madeleine Albright. In describing a celebration of its 125th anniversary, *The Economist* (April 28, 2001) says that returning alumnae were greeted like "rock stars, a sure sign that the sting still remains in feminism." Drawing the most cheers were statements by speakers that they had succeeded *in spite of their husbands.* Speakers like Martha McClintock, professor of biology and psychology, thanked their alma mater for giving them a level of ambition and confidence impossible with men around. (Mrs. McClintock is famous for discovering that when women live together, they menstruate at the same time).

Boston College is the venue for a bizarre twist on the single-sex class controversy. Mary Daly, a professor at this Catholic college for 33 years, refused to admit a man, Duane Naquin, into her all-female class on feminist ethics. Instead, she provides males with a private tutorial , using the same texts and materials. The Washington, D.C. Center for Individual Rights has sued on behalf of Mr. Naquin, causing Ms. Daly to call them "dickheads," a not surprising epithet since Ms. Daly, in her books on theology, philosophy, myth, prophecy, and history advocates the deconstruction of what she calls, "phallocracy."[14]

Maybe the feminists can't agree on the type of colleges they want for women, but there is unanimity that the curricula should be feminized. This can take a variety of forms. In many colleges and universities, courses related to women have been added. What kind of courses? My own university, Texas A&M University, is illustrative. Some of our courses in "Women's Studies" include Introduction to Women's Studies; Introduction to Gender and Society; Psychology of Women; Sociology of Gender; Women in Politics; Gay and Lesbian Literature; Women in the Bible; Women Writers; Women and Culture; Women, Minorities and the Mass Media; Women and Work in Society; Employment Discrimination Law; History of American Women; Women and the Law; History of Modern American Women; Studies in Women Writers; and Women in Modern European History. (In all, 24 separate courses are listed). Texas A&M University does not require that any of these courses be taken as part of its core curriculum that all students, regardless of their major, must take, but they are included as options in the Humanities and Social and Behavioral Sciences areas. At other schools, they are required. The men who take them are often subjected to male bashing by female professors who, at best, are vehement feminists and, worse, lesbians.

There is some pressure for single-sex courses, as well. Michael Schage, writing in *Fortune* (August 16, 1999) says that "top business schools, like Harvard, MIT and Stanford, will offer single-sex advanced management programs." No doubt, this will be fueled by the fact that many of the top business schools have women's groups on campus. Columbia's Graduate School of Business has Columbia Women in Business, Stanford's Graduate School of

Business has Women in Management, University of California at Berkeley's Haas School of Business has Women in Leadership, and the Women's Business Association flourishes at Northwestern University's Kellogg Graduate School of Management.

What kind of preferential treatment do female MBA students at these high-profile B-schools get? Plenty! At Columbia, there are "brown-bag" lunches and annual conferences co-sponsored by the Committee of 200, a high-powered women's networking group. At Stanford, local business leaders mentor women students. At Ohio State, women are matched with successful executives through the MBA Corporate Mentoring Program. Virginia's Colgate Darden Graduate School of Business Administration provides facilities for the national MBA women's organization, Graduate Women in Business.[15]

Then there is Boston's Simmons College. The Simmons Graduate School of Management, founded by two female management professors from Harvard, is the only all-female business school in the United States. (Can you imagine the hue and cry if a similar, all-male venture were started?). Gushes Patricia O'Brien, the School's dean: "People (I guess she means women) learn better when they can identify with the teacher." (Obviously, she means *female* teacher, but isn't it rank discrimination to not have any male professors?). She goes on: "This is a place where a woman can find her *own voice*" (emphasis added).[16]

This use of the term, "voice," is especially interesting. Carol Gilligan, Harvard's first professor of gender studies, has used this theme in several books, *Different Voices* (1982) and *In A Different Voice (1993),* to contend that girls are silenced in school and not listened to. Here's how Ms. Gilligan defines "voice:"

> When people ask me what I mean by voice and I think of the question more reflectively, I say that by voice I mean something like what people mean when they speak of the core of the self. Voice is natural and also cultural. It is composed of breath and sound, words, rhythm, and language. And voice is a powerful psychological instrument and channel, connecting inner and outer worlds. Speaking and listening are a form of

psychic breathing. This ongoing relational exchange among people is mediated through language and culture, diversity and plurality.[17]

New England is also the venue for a far-reaching power grab by radical feminists. Initially promoted at the University of Massachusetts, Amherst by Ann Ferguson, Director of Women's Studies, the presidents of the Universities of Vermont, New Hampshire and Maine have endorsed the following and want to take it *nationwide:*

•Curricula would be transformed according to guidance from an *autonomous* women's studies site.

•*Every academic department* would have to hold an annual seminar on gender issues.

•Gender would have to be part of *all* pertinent programs of institutional research.

•Faculty would be held accountable if their teaching styles were not "woman-friendly."

•Teachers who do not comply would be denied promotion, raises and other benefits.

•Departments with high female drop-out rates (probably in science and math fields) would be penalized.

•Overrepresentation of males in the curriculum would not be allowed. For example, a course on Renaissance Art would have to involve 50% of such female artists (an impossibility because there probably were only a handful of female Renaissance artists).

John Leo, editor of *U.S. News & World Report* (January 19, 1998), in discussing this absurdity, calls it "stupefying" and refers to women's studies programs as "part therapy group, part training grounds for feminist cadres to fight the patriarchy."

If young men believe that the discrimination against them in the educational arena is going to abate once they are on campus, they are in for a rude awakening. A study conducted by *Men's Health* identified 10 "male friendly" and 10 "anti-male" colleges. Author Laurence Roy Stains, in presenting the 10 "male friendly" institutions, says "We think guys will be able to feel a real difference in the air. There is less *overt* hostility and the traditional male point of view is appreciated socially and academically" (emphasis added), suggesting, of course, that he is apparently comparing these schools to the "anti-male" ones, which include Antioch College (the first all female college in the United States), Bates College, Brown University, Columbia University, Dartmouth College, Georgetown University, Oberlin College (the first to admit women), University of California at Santa Cruz, University of Massachusetts (Amherst), and the University of Michigan.[18]

Should male students be concerned about anti-male bias on college campuses? You bet. Consider what one of these schools, Columbia University, is doing. In 1999, it established a sexual misconduct policy that "guarantees the conviction of any accused male, whether innocent or guilty," because the accused is forbidden to exercise his constitutional rights, namely, he will be tried in absentia, not allowed to be represented by an attorney and prevented from cross-examining hostile witnesses. Furthermore, the penalties meted out will be increased if he lines up favorable witnesses or reveals the identity of his accuser—because he has violated Columbia's "rule of secrecy." Such an abrogation of rights is so heinous that it caused University of Pennsylvania professor, Alan Charles Kors, president of the Foundation for Individual Rights in Education, to write Columbia University's president about Columbia's version of the Nuremburg Laws" (the 1933 laws that took away the rights of Jews in Nazi Germany).[19] And consider what happened at Penn State University. Students there were forced to pay nearly $10,000 to fund a radical feminist gathering called "C— Fest." The conference featured giant papier-mâché statues of female genitalia, full-nudity, and *storytelling about killing men.*

Male university faculty are not immune from such practices if they do not toe the feminist line. Jared Sakren was a professor of theater at Arizona State University who was fired because he would not put on plays that feminists wanted. Professor Sakren objected when his department wanted him to adopt a more "politically correct, feminist approach." He refused, and was fired, despite having impeccable academic credentials; he had taught at the Juliard School and Yale University. Instead of producing such "politically correct plays as Betty the Yeti, in which a female Sasquatch seduces a conservative, gun-toting logger and turns him into a sensitive, enlightened environmentalist," Sakren emphasized plays by Shakespeare. To which, one of his accusers, a female teaching feminist courses, said: "The feminists are offended by the selection of works from a sexist European canon that is approached traditionally."[20]

The Work Place

The tide of pro-female, anti-male discrimination is just as deep in the work place as it is in the education arena. Under affirmative action guidelines, employers are forced to hire females in order to meet federally imposed quotas. Often, females are hired over men even though they are less qualified than male applicants. And it makes little difference what kind of job is involved, or whether the public interest is threatened. For example, I know of a case where a female applicant for a fire fighter's job was hired over better-qualified male applicants—even though she did not meet the strength and endurance requirement, thus, failing the physical, whereas all of the male applicants had passed the physical part of the tests. Did this rank favoritism do the community a favor? Of course not. In fact, it may have jeopardized peoples' lives in the future.

Colleges of Business at universities all across America are under increasing pressure to hire more female teachers because over 50% of their students are women and the overwhelming majority of their existing faculty are males. In order to hire females, special dollars earmarked solely for hiring them, particularly if they are minorities, suddenly become available from hitherto "resource poor" central administrations. In order to entice them, these females are often given salaries higher than male full professors with 30 or more years experience and possessing outstanding research records. The "goody pie" is sweetened further for these women, with brand-new PhDs and no research track record, by their getting lighter teaching loads and summers off with pay in order to "develop their research programs," while productive males instruct more courses and have to teach in the summer for additional compensation—and are, at many institutions of higher learning, forced to beg for these summer teaching assignments.

While on the job, women are demanding and getting preferential treatment. For example, the vice-president of merchandising at a billion-dollar retailer was allowed to work at home for the rest of her pregnancy and for a post-natal period—about six months in all. Several of the company's board of directors who were not consulted—the CEO made a unilateral decision—wondered if a work-at-home request from a male would have been granted. Women are also angling for higher pay even though, as was seen in the previous chapter, the slightly higher pay for males—when it exists—is justified on a rational basis. In Bill Clinton's 1999 State of the Union address, he said: "And let's make sure that women and men get equal pay for equal work by strengthening enforcement of the equal-pay laws." Seizing on the opportunity, the AFL-CIO has begun a drive for equal pay in 24 states. Returning to the subject in a Saturday radio address, Clinton urged Congress to pass the Paycheck Fairness Act, sponsored by Tom Daschle, at that time senate minority leader, and the liberal representative from Connecticut, Rosa DeLauro.

At Virginia Commonwealth University, women faculty complained that they were discriminated against pay-wise. The weak-kneed administration agreed—after doing a regression analysis that excluded *all notions of merit* (scholarly articles, books, student evaluations, etc.)—and awarded an across-the-board pay raise to *all women teachers* (Ann Coulter, "Keep Your Laws Off My Judiciary, *Human Events,* May 21, 2001).

In their zeal to improve female pay and not caring if it comes as the expense of men's compensation, the above troika (Clinton, Daschle and DeLauro) "conveniently" forgot that pay equality has already been in force through the 1963 Equal Pay Act. They also ignored the fact that in the last five years, only 1.5% of all complaints brought before the Equal Employment Opportunity Commission involved charges of unfair low pay for women and it found probable cause in only 4% of these instances.[21]

We saw in the previous chapter that women have been increasingly successful in moving into top management positions in the corporate world. Such accomplishments have often been supported by overt efforts on the part of companies to make it easier for them, regardless of their capabilities compared to those of male personnel who would also like the pay, prestige, responsibilities, and perks associated with these positions. Some of the more blatant pro-female initiatives along these lines include:

•Coopers & Lybrand links part of its partner bonuses to their performance on diversity issues. Chairman and CEO, Nicholas Moore, in a June 21, 1997 memo, stated that "30% of new partners would be women," an increase of one-sixth over the previous year.

•J.C. Penney, Motorola, Colgate-Palmolive, and Dow Chemical have committed "serious resources and credibility to setting women on the right track.... and are devising *novel* succession strategies" (emphasis added). According to David T. Buzzelli, vice-president and board member at Dow Chemical: "We are not going to get to where we need to get to with diversity issues unless we push it." (Dow wants women to account for as many promotions as men).

•At Motorola, top managers are asked to put the names of likely successors into three categories; the women or minority closest to being qualified for the job must be included in the third-priority group. These individuals are to be given preferential treatment because they are to be provided the experience needed for promotion. "As a result, women have moved into the first or second slots for approximately 75 of the company's 300 *most prized* slots" (emphasis added).

•Hoechst Celanese is pushing a goal by 2001 of 34% of its top managers being women and minorities, up from 20% and 14%, respectively, who are currently in middle management positions. Hoechst pairs senior men with these fast-track women and minorities. They are exposed to the company's decision makers, "while the mentors learn to be more comfortable working outside *all-male cliques*" (emphasis added).

•J.C. Penney wants 46% of its managers to be women, up from 26.6% and 18.9% over the figures existing in 1990 for middle and senior managers. "Women tapped as upper-management candidates regularly have lunch and roundtable discussions with senior managers."[22]

Females often support their demands for top jobs by asserting that they perform better on factors critical for success at top management levels. One such set of findings was reported in *Business Week*.[23] Women were judged to be better than men on "motivating others," "fostering communication," "producing high-quality work," and "listening to others." They were on a par with men on "strategic planning" and "analyzing issues." (These findings supposedly came as a surprise to the researchers; they "stumbled on them while compiling and analyzing performance evaluations").[24] Rosabeth Moss Kanter (professor, Harvard Business School), who wrote *Men And Women Of The Corporation* 20 years ago, claims that "women get high ratings on exactly those skills needed to succeed in the Global Information Age where teamwork and partnering are so important."[25]

But let's take an objective look at these findings. Except possibly for "producing high quality work," the factors women supposedly outpace men on are "soft" issues not directly related to performance; "hard" measures are not included in the study. For example, "ability to make effective decisions" is not included, nor are measures of output, profit, sales, company stock price, value of the company, etc. And "producing high *quantity* of work" may be a better indication of performance than "producing high quality work." After all, employees might be better able to produce "high quality work" because the *quantity* of their work is low. Finally, the authors admit in the article that on those factors on which females outperform men, the differences are slight.

Don't expect the head-long rush to add females to corporate boards of directors to decrease soon. Korn/Ferry International, one of the largest head-hunter (recruiting) firms, reported in its annual board of directors study for 2001 that "seeking more women and minorities" was the most frequent answer that current board members gave when indicating what extra efforts they were making to attract high quality outside directors.

The last chapter discussed women's increasingly prominent role as entrepreneurs. Much of this upsurge can be attributed to start-up capital being earmarked solely for female-controlled ventures. In 1999, such venture capital firms as Aurora Ventures, Women's Growth Capital Fund, and Capital Across America began targeting female entrepreneurs. At the federal level, the Small Business Administration specifically earmarked $1.7 billion for *women's* startups in 2000 or 16.4% of its total budget: 21.0% of all SBA loans went to women-owned businesses. Such focus will undoubtedly continue as the SBA's office of advocacy states that it "will continue to pursue its part in the U.S. Small Business Administration's mission to facilitate women moving into the economic mainstream (*SBA's Woman in Business*, 2001, p.22).

Due to a number of factors, the pro-female, anti-male bias that is getting more pronounced in the work place will certainly continue in the future—and probably at an accelerated pace. For one thing, politicians will court female voters by pushing this agenda. For another, women are still in favor of affirmative action. A 1999 study by *Working Woman* (July 1999) found that 48% of women felt there was still a need for affirmative action, 56% believed that it has helped shape the world, 57% said such fields as engineering, law enforcement and construction—that according to them have in the past typically excluded women—should "encourage more recruitment of women." Finally, industry is convinced that females are better qualified to work in the "new information age."

I have not noticed in the last five years or so much of an outcry by males against the discrimination encountered in the work place.

One explanation is that the economy was especially buoyant during the latter years of the 1990s. What will the response be by men as our economy continues to tank, fueled by dismal earnings reports, the September 11 terrorist attack, misconduct by corporate executives and massive layoffs, and the unemployment rate starts hitting 7% or 8%? At these levels, the anti-male discrimination is likely to be more noticeable and more harmful. Is it fair for women to be given preferential treatment under these conditions? Is it fair for a man, who is the sole bread winner for his family, to be unemployed while married women who are only the second income producer in the household, or just want to work so that they can "self-actualize," are given preferential treatment?

Mortimer B. Zuckerman, editor-in-chief of *U.S, News & World Report,* wrote an insightful editorial (December 10, 2001) on the state of the U.S. economy. In almost dirge-like fashion, he lists the factors that he believes will push the unemployment rate to 7%: falling annual capital spending (15% to 20%), shrinking industrial output, 52% decrease in corporate profits in the second quarter of 2001, an 18-year low on help-wanted ads, and 1.5% lower retail sales for the Thanksgiving weekend.

Health Care

Women have vociferously claimed that they are being short chanced medically when, in truth, men are the health care second-class citizens. The author, using data from *Scientific American* (September 1996), made some calculations which show the wide disparity in favor of women on research expenditures for the two types of cancer that are the most lethal for men and women. The total expenditures for breast cancer was almost five times (4.8) that for prostate cancer. And the expenditures per case and per death also showed a large bias in favor of women, $1,813 to $224 (expenditure per case) and $7,556 to $1,713 (expenditure per death). Ann Coulter *(Human Events,* February 18, 2000) exposes the bias against men in cancer·treatment with her data: The rate of prostate cancer for men is 147 for every 100,000 men. The rate for breast cancer is 113 per 100,000 women. Each type of cancer has about the same mortality rate. The federal government spends four times as much on breast cancer research as it spends on prostate cancer research.

Similar data from *Cancer Statistics Review* and *U.S. News and World Report* (April 3, 2000) show that although the gender gap has narrowed somewhat, there is still a wide bias in favor of women; research expenditures per case and expenditure per death still favor women about 2-1. And lest men think these results augur for a diminished bias in favor of women, consider what happened when the post office issued a breast cancer and a prostate cancer stamp. The breast cancer stamp cost 40¢ with seven cents going to breast cancer research. The first run of 200 million quickly sold out, providing $14 million for breast cancer research, and an additional run of 80 million was authorized. The prostate cancer stamp cost 33¢ with *no proceeds* earmarked for prostate cancer research; "demand for the 78 million stamps printed has been lackluster."[26]

If it weren't for Michael Milken, funding for prostate cancer research would be even more bleak. Milken, billionaire junk bond dealer who spent time in prison for insider trading, developed prostate cancer. Through aggressive intervention, Milken beat the disease; his $50 million contribution for prostate cancer research was a God-send and has attracted additional funding.

On March 16, 1999, hearings were held in Congress on the subject of cervical cancer. Witnesses indicated that cervical cancer kills 5,000 women annually in the United States, but far below the number of men who succumb yearly to prostate cancer. Nevertheless, based on the Breast and Cervical Cancer Mortality Act of 1990, as amended in 1993, Congress in 1999 allocated $159 million for early detection of cervical and breast cancer. Congressman Gene Green from Texas recommended that the Act be expanded to include treatment and that the budget be doubled in size.[27] (The ironic aspect of cervical cancer is that women who have had multiple sexual partners, particularly at early ages, run a much higher likelihood of contacting the disease. It almost appears that women are being rewarded for their immorality).

In one of his election speeches, then vice-president Al Gore guaranteed *women* the *right* to a second opinion if they were diagnosed with cancer. In none of his speeches were men guaranteed the same right.

In the early 1990s, female scientists and female politicians and various women's advocacy groups began an aggressive push for more health-care research dollars for women. In addition to achieving the expanded resource commitments, several other objectives were also obtained. The National Institutes of Health now requires that all scientists receiving NIH funding must include women in their research. In addition, "there's a women's health office in *every major* federal agency to keep it *focused* on *women's* interests" (emphases added),[28] but none exist for men.

Several popular magazines annually rate various hospitals and HMOs in the United States. An overall score is obtained from the ratings on a number of factors. The *Newsweek* (November 8, 1999) evaluation of HMOs lists six components: "Access & Services," "Child & Adolescent Care," "Getting Better," "Member Satisfaction," "Qualified Providers," and, you guessed it, "Women's Health." "Men's health" is not considered important enough to be included by *Newsweek*, nor by *U.S News & World Report* when it ranks hospitals.

Millions of school-age boys are being medicated with the drug, Ritalin, because they supposedly have "Attention Deficit Disorder," or ADD. Many critics of this procedure, however, feel that these boys are exhibiting normal patterns of male aggressiveness and exuberance. The drug is supposed to have a calming effect. Even so, there is concern about its side effects. There are some experts who claim that the drug will turn boys into homosexuals by the time they are 15 years old. Dr. Joel Wallach, a leading proponent of natural supplements, has long been opposed to the use of Ritalin. Both an M.D. and D.V.M. —he has performed thousands of autopsies on animals while working with Marlin Perkins (Mutual of Omaha's famous Wild Kingdom television show) and hundreds of autopsies on humans—believes that ADD can be effectively treated by taking 90 essential nutrients and sticking to a diet that minimizes sugar intake. Sadly, parents may be prevented from doing what Dr. Wallach recommends. Courts, public schools and child protective services are charging parents who refuse to put their sons on Ritalin with *child abuse.*

Legal System

The anti-male discrimination that exists in the U.S. legal system is truly frightening. This bias results in trials over trivial matters that should never go to trial but, more significantly, often lands *innocent men behind bars.* The legal system in the United States so favors women that, contra to the U.S. Constitution, men are often considered to be *guilty until proven innocent.* A spate of laws favorable to women, and unfavorable to men, gives women an unfair advantage in civil and criminal trials; a similar body of pro-male legislation does not exist to balance the scales of justice. Judges frequently exhibit blatant anti-male bias in both civil and, more importantly, criminal trials by limiting evidence that would be favorable to male defendants, admitting evidence that is prejudicial to males, and rendering decisions and imposing sentences that clearly do not square with the facts of the case.

Cathy Young writes for the *Boston Globe.* Robyn Blumner is a columnist for the *St. Petersburg Times* and the Tribune Media Services. Ms. Young has also written *Ceasefire! Why Women And Men Must Join Forces To Achieve True Equality.* Both were interviewed by *Penthouse* (January 2001) and made some comments which clearly reveal the bias against men that exists in our legal system. Following an opening statement by the interviewer, "On issues ranging from domestic violence to sexual harassment to divorce, the women's movement wants the law and society to view men as villains and women as victims," here are some of the interviewees' comments:

. Ms. Blumner: "Feminism has shifted from a movement about equality to one which seeks to give women a legal advantage. I think that's because some women found equality to be a difficult prospect. It's not easy competing every day in a workaday world. And equality doesn't guarantee happiness; it just offers opportunity."

Ms. Blumner: "Victim feminists want gender to be taken into account so women can be preferred in such matters as child custody cases, hiring decisions, and domestic violence disputes."

Ms. Blumner: "Now, unfortunately, with much prompting by today's feminists, the scales are tipping in favor of gender-based preferences—for example, rape-shield laws that keep the sexual history of the alleged victim out of sexual-assault trials but allow the defendant's past to be brought in. There is also the tendency in society, in general, to protect the woman's identity in cases of alleged rape, but not the man's."

Ms. Young: "The problem we have today is that for the most part it's acceptable for women to vent their frustrations with men in a way that is not acceptable for men to vent their frustrations with women."

The true real-life experiences that will now be described provide ample evidence of how the U.S. legal system is tilted against men.

Patrick Griffin was director of internal medicine at St. Luke's/ Roosevelt Hospital in Manhattan. He did his undergraduate work at Columbia, obtained his M. D. from Columbia and did a fellowship at Harvard. Dr. Griffin's patients loved him. He provided help to patients who could not pay. National Public Radio did a piece on him (AIDS and health care).

In November, 1994 a patient he had been treating for stomach problems, 43 year-old Christine Jeffreys, asked him if he would testify on her behalf in a $2 million lawsuit against a former landlord who had evicted her three years earlier from her apartment, claiming that the eviction was the cause of the stomach malady. Dr. Griffin refused. Three months later, Jeffreys claimed to the police that Dr. Griffin had sodomized her during tests he had conducted. Wearing a wire provided by detectives, Dr. Griffin could be heard vigorously denying her allegations. Nevertheless, in July, 1995 he was arrested, handcuffed and taken to a holding cell.

The New York City District Attorney's Sex Crime Unit ran ads on the radio and in newspapers asking women to call an 800-number if they had ever been harassed or assaulted by Dr. Griffin. Two called in—one claimed her hair had been mussed during a procedure, the other asking help in recovering a ring she believed she had lost in the doctor's office.

During the trial, judge *Marcy* Kahn stacked the deck against Dr. Griffin. He was not allowed to indicate that he had refused to participate in the law suit, that Ms. Jeffreys had instigated other frivolous law suits and was deeply in debt, that the drugs used during the tests conducted by him often caused memory loss and induced sexual fantasies, and his lawyer was not allowed to thoroughly cross examine the plaintiff. Not surprisingly, Dr. Griffin was sentenced to three and one-half to ten years.

Upon appeal in 1998, the New York Supreme Court reversed the decision and a new trial was held. This time (April 2000), Dr. Griffin was acquitted. However, his license to practice medicine was revoked, his wife divorced him, he is $500,000 in debt and still had to face Ms. Jeffrey's $10 million civil lawsuit. Having lost his luxurious apartment on the upper west side, he now sleeps on the couch at his great aunt's home in Queens, driving a truck for a horse farm.[29]

Tony Morrison was a freshman scholarship football player at Virginia Tech. At 2:00 A.M. on the morning of September 21, 1994 a knock awoke Morrison and his roommate, James L. Crawford. Christy Brzonkala and Hope Handley, freshmen (or is it "freshwomen?") had stopped by to "get acquainted." After a few moments of conversation, Crawford and Handley left the room and Morrison and Brzonkala proceeded to have sex.

Eight months later, Brzonkala alleged she had been raped by Morrison and Crawford. A grand jury refused to indict either man. Undaunted, Brzonkala hired an attorney, Eileen Wagner, who convinced her to go after Morrison under the 1994 Violence Against

Women Act (VAWA), which allows women to sue men for monetary damages for any "gender-motivated" crime, from sexual harassment to sexual assault, to rape, even if the man has not been convicted in criminal proceedings. In the civil court proceedings, the plaintiff only has to prove that it is "more likely than not" that what the plaintiff alleges has occurred. Thus, it is much easier to win in a civil trial under VAWA than in a criminal proceeding.

A federal court ruled that VAWA was unconstitutional. That decision was upheld by a federal appellate court. Ms. Brzonkala appealed to the U.S. Supreme Court. The Supreme Court ruled that VAWA could not be used to sue in *federal* court, but was okay in *state* courts. [30]

In Chapter One, we were introduced to Tom. In this chapter, we will give additional information about Tom because his situation involved child sexual abuse charges, an area that the legal system is terribly biased toward men, resulting in many of them going to jail and their lives ruined even if they avoid jail.

Tom, 34, an air force veteran, was a pilot for one of the major airlines. Separated from his wife, Sybil, he had filed for divorce and custody of his five-year old son, John. In Texas, there is no provision for alimony, so it was to Sybil's benefit to get custody of John so that she could rake in child-support payments until John turned 18. As might be expected, the dispute became increasingly bitter.

Several weeks after Tom had told Sybil he was dating another woman, who was present with Tom during one of John's visits with his father, Sybil went to police and accused Tom and his friend of sexually abusing John. The alleged perpetrators were stunned but were relieved when Child Protective Services in Texas, the first step in the legal process, informed them that the charges were being dropped.

Soon after, CPS changed its mind because now John, not only Sybil, was articulating the charges. (This new development occurred three weeks after a CPS official told Sybil that nothing could be done unless John, himself, verbalized the abuse). Both Tom and his friend took lie detector tests and submitted to detailed psychiatric testing, both of which proved that they had not, even could not, commit the alleged crime. Nevertheless, CPS decided to turn the case over to the police.

As the police investigation unfolded, Tom's civil rights were trampled. None of his references were consulted. At a court hearing, he was prevented from calling witnesses, including a doctor who was prepared to testify that a physical examination of John had not revealed any sexual abuse. In defiance of a court order, Tom was denied access to the Child Protective Service's report and was not allowed to discuss his side of the case with CPS beyond the initial hearing. Tom was forced to listen to Sybil's threats, curses, ranting, and raving over the telephone, but was not allowed to call her to discuss such mundane issues as visitation times. Sybil, on numerous occasions, refused at the last minute to have John available for court-mandated visitations.

Fortunately, the prosecuting attorney did not take the case to a grand jury because Tom could have been sentenced to five years in prison. However, Tom suffered extreme mental anguish—he truly loved his son and the false allegations would forever damage this relationship—and his savings were depleted because he had to pay not only for his attorney, but *Sybil's as well,* along with an *ad litem* attorney for John, various psychologists, therapists and doctors for his son, the polygraph and psychiatric tests for himself and his friend, and a court appointed supervisor to monitor him during the visits with his son. The financial strain was worsened by Sybil having clandestinely removed $50,000 from their joint bank account while they were still married, leaving him with only $10,000. (Sybil's lawyer had magnanimously advised her not to take all of it).

Women will be well-positioned in the future to continue their assault on men through the legal system. According to *U.S. News & World Report* (April 9, 2001), about half of law school admittees are women. And female law school students have clamored for more "relevant" courses so that topics like rape, violence against women, sexual harassment, and personal injury involving "discussions of how female injury victims should be compensated for reproductive medical problems and the value of lost work in the home as well as on the job" are standard fare. What should be disturbing to men, however, is the statement in the article by Leslie Bender, professor of law at Syracuse University, that the recent scholarship of female law professors has 'persuaded lawyers to make new claims *on behalf of women* and encouraged judges *to find in their favor*' (emphasis added).

Child Custody Battles

Here is an area of the legal system where the cards are definitely stacked against men. In 1990, there were 18,684 instances in which children were awarded to men, 132,692 in which women were granted custody and 29,754 joint-custody decisions. In other words, 88% of the single-parent rulings were in favor of women. In 1997, out of the almost 14 million custodial arrangements, only 11.4% involved children living with their father (*Statistical Abstract of the United States*, 2001).

Such a bias in the courts is reprehensible, particularly as it affects boys assigned to live apart from their fathers and to society as a whole. Psychology professor, David Lykken (University of Minnesota), says, "More than two-thirds of incarcerated delinquents, of high school dropouts, of teenage runaways, or abused or murdered babies, and of juvenile murderers were reared *without their biological fathers*" (emphasis added). Sociologist David Blankerhorn states, "Here is the rule. Boys raised by traditionally masculine fathers generally do not commit crimes. Fatherless boys commit crimes." [31]

Sexual Harassment

The courts are increasingly expanding the scope of what constitutes sexual harassment. Once almost confined to instances of sexual discrimination—quid pro quo discrimination ("sleep with me or you lose your job") and intimidation against female workers—the following is now considered by the courts to involve sexual harassment: sexual innuendoes; comments or bantering; humor or jokes about sex or females in general; touching a person; giving a neck or shoulder massage; leering or oogling (such as "elevator eyes"); calling women "hot stuff" or "cutie pie;" sexual graffiti; laughing at or not taking seriously someone who is experiencing sexual harassment; describing a randy TV show; paintings that supposedly embarrass females; having a picture of your wife in a bikini on your desk; complimenting a woman on her blazer; and downloading risque jokes from the Internet onto office computers.[32]

Here's an incident that shows how the system is biased against males. Several years ago, the National Basketball Association (NBA) ruled that female reporters had the right to be in players' locker rooms after a game to interview the players. On February 27, 2001 a female employee of the Toronto Raptors was in the Raptors' locker room gathering post-game quotes. Chris Gatling, Raptors' forward, mentioned in a joking manner that "I thought there was a double standard that women are allowed in men's locker rooms and men are not allowed in women's locker rooms." Mr. Gatling was fined $10,000 by the league office and forced to send a letter of apology (*Bryan-College Station Eagle,* March 2, 2001).

Companies are becoming increasingly intolerant of sexual harassment violations and are, accordingly, developing explicit and far-reaching anti-sexual harassment policies and appointing enforcers to reduce the danger of being sued. So men, you need to watch your step. You can be fired for violating company sexual harassment guidelines and you will have little chance of winning a wrongful termination suit.

Violence Against Women Act

We saw previously in discussing the Tony Morrison case that the Supreme Court of the United States has ruled that civil suits at the state level can be brought by women alleging rape and other violent felonies as defined by state law. This law is a license for men to be sued by women without their having been brought to trial and convicted in a criminal court; as such, males will face a higher probability of being found guilty. And it is a law that never should have been passed, notwithstanding the Court's refusal to apply it at the federal level. Justice David Souter used outdated or greatly disputed facts in writing his opinion. Anita K. Blair and Charmaine Yoest (notice: two women) state that "the deceitful data that appeared in the legislative history of VAWA now reappear in the legal briefs, as if continued reliance on false statements and nonexistent studies somehow give VAWA credibility."[33]

Hate Crime Legislation

Under a Hate Crimes bill being pushed by senate Democrats in 2002, hate crimes protection would be extended to racial minorities, the handicapped, homosexuals, lesbians, and women. Did you notice a significant omission? Of course: white heterosexual-able-bodied men, or WHAMS. They are excluded because they are automatically assumed to be the perpetrators, never the victims. Look at the rank discrimination here. If a wife maims her husband, it is not a hate crime, but it is if a husband beats a wife.

In addition to the frightening bias of this legislation, it is yet another example of power grabbing by the federal government at the expense of the 50 states. By federalizing hate crimes, Congress conveniently ignores the fact that appropriate laws already exist at state levels.

Child Abuse

Men are overwhelmingly accused of committing child abuse and many end up in prison because of these charges, particularly for those allegations involving child sexual abuse, of which there were close to 100,000 cases in 1998.[34] But, before you rush to judgment, consider the following:

• Richard Gardner, a clinical professor of child psychiatry from Columbia University, wrote in the *Wall Street Journal* (February 22, 1993) that the child-abuse witch hunts of recent years represent the "third great wave of hysteria" in U.S. history, following the Salem witch trials of 1692, which saw 19 hanged, and the McCarthy persecutions of the 1950s. "Our current hysteria," Gardner said, "is by far the worst with regard to the number of lives that have been destroyed and families that have disintegrated." Gardner was attacking what he rightly called the "child abuse establishment," a network of social workers, psychiatrists, psychologists and its legal buttress, the Child Abuse Prevention and Treatment Act of 1974, the perversion of which has led to monstrous persecutions of day-care workers, also the use of wild allegations in vicious child-custody cases (*The Nation,* April 5, 1993). Gardner, writing in *Readers Digest* (April, 1993) says "we've reached the point where an accusation is almost tantamount to a conviction."

• In virtually all cases in which allegations of criminal conduct are made, police investigate and make arrests. Yet when the charge is child abuse, social workers call the shots, and the system doesn't hold them accountable. What's worse, once parents are accused, the burden is on them to prove their innocence, unlike in a criminal trial, where the burden of proof is on the accusers (*Readers Digest,* April, 1993). The immunity from lawsuits that caseworkers enjoy invites systemic abuse. Police can be charged with crimes and hauled into court. Child protective agencies should not be treated any differently (*Readers Digest,* April, 1993).

• Regarding false allegations of child abuse in divorce and custody proceedings, Schetky and Green (*Child Sexual Abuse: A Handbook For Health Care And Legal Professionals*) cite a psychiatric paper on child custody and visitation cases involving preschool children seen at conciliation court. Sexual abuse could be substantiated in less than 30% of the cases reviewed. Similar documentation abounds in the professional literature (*Society,* September/October, 1991).

• Evidence is mounting that children, particularly those who have been extensively coached, give inaccurate testimony far more often than previously imagined. Both research studies and courtroom experience are causing many psychiatrists to question their views of the reliability of what comes from the mouths of babes *(Time,* March 4, 1991).

• Child custody disputes are often the trigger for youngsters' unwitting lies. Suspicions can cause parents to launch what legal scholar Douglas Besharov of Washington D.C.'s American Enterprise Institute calls the "atomic bomb" of child custody suits—the charge of sex abuse. In these stressful situations, children quickly discover what adults want to hear and can offer lies or distortions in order to please an anxious parent or social worker *(Time,* March 4, 1991).

Restraining Orders

The increasing use of court-issued restraining orders that prevent fathers from contacting their children and spouses is yet another example of anti-male bias occurring in the United States. How discriminatory are these restraining orders? Consider the following:

1. An article by a judge in the *New Jersey Law Journal* in 1995 identified restraining orders as 'probably the most abused piece of legislation that comes to mind.'

2. Liberal judges often issue restraining orders on *uncorroborated* allegations by wives and ex-wives.

3. Massachusetts attorney, Gregory Hessian, says 'The restraining order is one of the most unconstitutional acts ever passed.'

4. Restraining orders can be issued without a hearing, resulting in dads being kicked out of their own homes, not being allowed to see their children again and taking their money. Absurd rulings which, unfortunately, still damage men greatly, abound. One father was arrested for putting a note in his son's suitcase notifying the mother that the boy had been sick during a weekend visit. Another went to jail for sending his son a birthday card!

5. Elaine Epstein, former president of the Massachusetts Women's Bar Association, says that 'allegations of abuse are now used for tactical advantage' and are 'doled out like candy.'

6. In a most chilling example of how men's right are being violated, New Jersey municipal judge, Richard Russell, told fellow judges at a 1994 legal seminar: 'Your job is not to become concerned about the constitutional rights of the man that you're violating as you grant a restraining order. Throw him out on the street, give him the clothes on his back and tell him, see you around .... We don't have to worry about the rights' (Stephen Baskerville, "No Restraint On Restraining Orders," *Human Events.* August 5, 2002, p. 16).

Military

There have been two showcase trials involving the military which received nationwide attention and unambiguously demonstrate the bias men in the military are facing. Both involved charges of sexual misconduct.

Command Sergeant Major Gene C. McKinney, the Army's highest-ranking enlisted man (and an African American) was accused by six female soldiers of sexual misconduct. On March 13, 1998, a military jury acquitted McKinney of all charges of sexual misconduct, but found him guilty of one charge of obstruction of justice by contacting a *potential* witness. On the latter charge, tapes clearly showed that McKinney did not improperly coach this person; in addition, the government manipulated McKinney into calling her, and she had been allowed by the government to lie to McKinney about previous contact with investigators.

Two of McKinney's accusers, upon cross examination, admitted acts of adultery. One of these, an officer (major) described several adulterous affairs, fraternization with enlisted personal under her command (a criminal act) and "indecent assault" on an enlisted man under her command. Both of these females had been granted immunity in the Army's zeal to nail McKinney.

Major General Robert Foley was the officer who decided that McKinney should be tried. Calling this the most weighty and important decision he ever had to make, he admitted that he never bothered to read the 6,000-page verbatim transcript of the preliminary hearing.

The trial was covered by a gaggle of feminist reporters. They were tremendously interested in the daily media briefings provided by a young military lawyer who had a vested interest in "spinning" the evidence because he was assigned to the district's staff judge advocate, the military's equivalent of a district attorney. The interest of the female reporters and their attendance at these briefings noticeably waned as the defense started shredding the testimony of the military's witnesses. [35]

Charges of sexual misconduct swirled around the Aberdeen Proving Grounds in Maryland. On trial were black drill sergeants who were accused of raping five, young female privates. At the trial, however, they admitted that they had been pressured, cajoled, coerced, and intimidated in an effort to get them to cry rape. All five said that they had had consensual sex with their drill sergeants. Of course, consensual sex is a no-no, but it isn't rape. Even the female privates who engaged in the consensual sex had committed an illegal act and that's where the Army's Criminal Investigation Division was able to exert leverage: If you say you were raped, we can drop the consensual sex charge.[36]

Then, there's the almost humorous Claudia Kennedy episode. Ms. Kennedy was the *highest ranking female officer* in the Army, a Lt. General (three stars). She accused a *lower ranking* (at the time of the alleged incident) male general of groping her. The incident was reported months after it supposedly happened. It later came out that the accused general had received an assignment coveted by General Kennedy, but it was probably too late to stop the accused's reputation from being tarnished.

In 1970, total military strength of the U.S. was 3,026,228; by 2000,under the downsizing of the military prompted by the "peace dividend" resulting from the breakup of the former U.S.S.R., it was 1,375,961. What is noticeable in these numbers is the *increase* in the number of females in the military when total strength was *being reduced by 55%.* In 1970, there were 41,479 females in the military, accounting for 1.4% of total strength. By 2000, the number had increased almost five times to 198,138 over the 1970 figure, accounting for 14.4% of all military personnel .[37] Do these numbers indicate discrimination? I'm not sure, but what is certain was the all-out effort by the Clinton administration to feminize the military and, in so doing, discriminate against male members of our armed services and, at the same time, reduce the effectiveness of our fighting forces.

In 1991, Congress, in response to such feminists as Rep. Pat Schroeder (D-Colo.), voted to allow women in combat aviation roles and established a commission to explore the implications. After months of hearings, the commission recommended that women should continue to be exempt from most combat assignments. It based its recommendations on two assumptions: physical differences between female and male soldiers and "putting women in combat would signal acceptance, and even encouragement, of deliberate violence against women" [38]

Clinton, through his Secretary of Defense, Les Aspin, ignored the commission's recommendation. As a result, the Pentagon dropped rules that exempted women from assignments close to battle areas; women were soon put in hundreds of occupations that could put them in harm's way. And, in furtherance of the feminist agenda, women were allowed to be deployed on combat ships. And they were permitted to serve on air cavalry helicopters, which "routinely deploy with artillery and armored units and virtually guarantees that women will be shot down, killed, or captured as prisoners of war."[39]

But the radical feminists wanted even more, that is, to change the culture of the male-dominated military. Men had to undergo sensitivity training and, except for the marines, there would be co-ed basic training and barracks.

When it was discovered that female trainees are 50% to 60% less strong than males and have 25% to 30% less aerobic capability for endurance, the feminists—never daunted—came up with a simple solution: "dumb down" the requirements. Physical aspects of proficiency tests were given less weight and those parts on which women do well, such as map reading and first aid, would be given more importance. The feminists and the military leaders who caved into their demands justified these capitulations on the basis of their measuring "equal effort," instead of results.[40] In other words, the feminists and their dupes feel it's more important to coddle female recruits than it is to have a military capable of defending our country.

Another tack taken has been the use of the old standby, "sexual harassment." A female marine recruit complained of sexual harassment because she claimed a three-mile, morning run was "demeaning" to women. Top brass suspended the exercise while the charge was being investigated.

Colonel James Hallums was removed from his position as chairman of the Department of Behavioral Sciences at West Point due to charges of sexual harassment brought by female faculty. One of his offenses: After exercising, he walked through the department wearing shorts and a sleeveless shirt. Col. Hallums had been appointed to this position because of the school's "deteriorating military and disciplinary standards." (See Paul Craig Roberts' discussion of Howard S. Schwartz's book, *The Revolt of the Primitive: An American Inquiry Into The Roots Of Political Correctness,* Praeger Publishers, 2001 as found in The *Washington Times,* October 22-28, 2001).

Mr. Roberts' review of Howard Schwartz's book revealed an even more egregious use of the sexual harassment ploy by female military personnel. Admiral Stanley Arthur was the commanding officer of the U.S. Air Force in the Gulf War and in line to become commander of all forces in the Pacific. Unfortunately, this appointment was denied him because he refused to reinstate a female lieutenant who had washed out of helicopter school. The lieutenant blamed her failure on sexual harassment, a charge that Admiral Arthur rejected after a careful and thoughtful review of the lieutenant's performance record. Unfortunately, his decision ran counter to that of Senator David Durenberger (R-Minnesota) who the lieutenant enlisted for help. The Senate successfully blocked the admiral's promotion.

Intercollegiate Athletics

An amendment to the 1964 Civil Rights Act, Title IX, was passed in 1972. This law prohibits discrimination on the basis of sex in federally funded education programs. Much of the application of this law has occurred in athletic programs of colleges and universities that have accepted federal funds.

The law was passed under the assumption that women were being discriminated against, that colleges and universities were favoring males when it came to fielding inter-collegiate varsity athletic programs.

Title IX designated three ways that institutions of higher learning could comply. (If they are found to be non-compliant, they could lose their federal funding which, for many colleges and universities, would be millions of dollars). They could show proportionality in the number of male and female athletes. This proportionality would be determined by the percentage of men and women enrolled at the college or university. Thus, if 60% of an institution's students were female, 60% of its athletes would have to be female and 60% of its athletic scholarships would have to be given to women. The Clinton Office of Civil Rights, located in the female-dominated Department of Education, has warned schools that not even a 1% deviation in the male/female ratio in scholarships would be tolerated.[41] The other ways to be in compliance are to successfully show that the college or university has a "history of expansion designed to accommodate women" and that, numbers aside, the "interests of women athletes are being met."[42]

Unfortunately—but as might be expected—the Office of Civil Rights, which enforces Title IX, has seen fit to ignore the second and third options, in order to concentrate on the quota system. .What are the results of this decision? Essentially, overt discrimination against male athletes in favor of female athletes as schools struggle to comply. Consider the following:

•Limited budgets prevent colleges and universities from expanding women's athletic programs, so they cut back on men's sports. Over 350 have been dropped since 1992.[43] An NCAA survey in 1998 showed that Division I male varsity rosters had to be reduced by 20,000 participants, Division III by 9,000 (and these students rarely receive athletic scholarships).[44] Particularly hard hit are men's wrestling, swimming and diving, gymnastics, and even golf which has been enjoying a recent surge in popularity. Possibly hit hardest has been UCLA. Its swimming and diving team, which had produced 26 NCAA champions and 10 Olympic gold medalists during the last two decades, was eliminated, as was its world-class men's gymnastic team.

•As women are added to intercollegiate varsity teams, they put on marginal performers who detract from the teams' overall competitiveness. At the same time, bona fide varsity male athletes are prevented from participating because there are fewer slots available for them.

•In order to comply with Title IX, institutions of higher learning are forced to add marginal sports for women. In 1996-1997, 42 NCAA schools fielded women's fencing teams; 22 had ice hockey, 182 lacrosse, 97 rowing, 40 skiing, 26 squash, and 23 water polo.[45] (Swarthmore even had a women's badminton team). In 1999, Texas A&M University hailed the creation of two new women's sports, archery and equestrian. In making the announcement, athletic director, Wally Groff, said: "We needed to offer more opportunities for female student-athletes for us to achieve compliance with proportionality rules under Title IX." The archery program will offer up to five scholarships and have about 20 participants. Only two other Division I schools—James Madison and Barnard College—have varsity archery programs for females. The equestrian team will consist of 75 girls with no scholarships *initially.* Only five other Division I Schools have female equestrian teams: Fresno State, Oklahoma State, South Carolina, Cornell, and College of Charleston. [46]

This insanity has now spread to the Olympics. Women's *wrestling* has been added, so the number of weight classes in men's

Greco-Roman wrestling had to be reduced.

Demographics

Between 1985 and 1999, there have been more male babies born each year in the United States than female babies (on average, about 51.2% of babies born are males; 48.8% are female). This continues a pattern that has been occurring in the U.S. for decades. And yet, population data show consistently that, in any year, there are more women in the United States (*Statistical Abstract of the United States*, 2001).

What's causing this seeming anomaly? Obviously, the answer must be in the death rates for males and females. Between1970 and 2000, males perished at higher rates than did females. And the higher death rate for men results in their having a lower life span than women (see *Statistical Abstract of the United States*, 2001), about 73.9 to 79.4 for women.

But more insightful data are obtained when the death rates for males and females are examined by age. These clearly show that the death rates are significantly higher for males across all categories, but the real discrepancy occurs in the 15-24 age category where the death rate for men is almost *three times* higher than it is for girls.

These results lead inexorably to the next question: What are the causes of death for boys in the 15-24 age category? Fifteen to 24-year old males are six times more likely as girls to die from murders and homicides. But the real shocker occurs in the suicide category which most people do not usually think of as a leading cause of death. Suicide was the third most important reason as to why males15-24 perished in 2000; they were about six times more likely than girls to commit suicide. In absolute numbers, this means that 3,532 boys/young men died by their own hand, compared to 603 girls/young women.

The Social Security system discriminates against men because of males' lower levels of longevity. For Americans born before 1960, full social security benefits are available at age 65. If you were born after 1960, the age is 67. Individuals who die before obtaining these threshold ages obviously forego these benefits; there is no return at all from being forced to pay into the system over a life time of work.

What is the likelihood that a male will die before reaching age 67—the new cut-off figure for benefits? A study by the Heritage Foundation estimated that 29.6% of single males employed in manufacturing jobs would die before age 67, as would 18.9% of married males. The similar figures for single females and married females were only 18.4% and 11.6%, respectively. Definitely, the cards are heavily stacked against males not receiving a dime from social security.[47]

How much of a loss are we talking about? Plenty! Assume a male worked 40 years at an average salary of $50,000. He would have paid 6.2% a year, based on the current figure, to social security on that income, or $124,000. If he could have invested this $3,100 a year payment over 40 years at a 6% return, he would have around a $500,000 nest egg. Because we, under the current system, are not allowed to invest these contributions, the income actually lost is the loss of an annual stipend. In 2001, the highest level of Social Security payout per month was around $1,800 per month, so the annual loss would be $21,600.

Abortion

It is estimated (see Chapter Six) that there were 41,221,400 abortions in the United States between 1970 and 2000. If it is assumed that 51.2% of all abortions involved males, 21,105,356 boy babies were murdered, compared to 20,116,043 female babies. In other words, there were almost *one million* (989,313) more males exterminated than females. Thus, males suffer more from *females'* decisions to abort babies than do females, but I certainly would not want this finding to, in any way, denigrate the 20+ million female babies that also lost their lives.

There is another aspect of abortions which receives scant attention. A fetus has both a mother *and a father.* What about the father's right to have a say in the abortion decision? The female advocates of abortion talk all the time, *ad nauseum*, about *their* bodies and *their* rights to decide whether to allow the fetus to be born, but shouldn't fathers have a say? By giving all of the decision-making authority to women, men are shut out of the process. It's as if men are assumed automatically to not be interested in having a son or a daughter. The height of female contempt for men as a possible parent is manifested when women—*married or single*—never tell the father that they are pregnant and slink off to have an abortion, leaving the man without even the knowledge that he had fathered a child and certainly not soliciting his input as to what should be done.

The Media

We noted earlier that the media are dominated by women. Thus, it should not surprise anyone at the extent to which men are discriminated against by the media. James Dobson, in his book, *Bringing Up Boys,* presents a number of these instances in a chapter entitled, "Men R Fools:"

1. There are the "dumb-guy" advertisements. For example, "the stupid guy is so taken with a gorgeous woman that he pours his Heineken beer on his pants."

2. The Internet is rife with anti-male jokes. For example: "Don't imagine you can change a man—unless he's in diapers."

3. Greeting cards demean men. One of Hallmark's says: "Men are scum... .Excuse me. For a second there I was feeling generous." An even more heinous one by American Greeting Cards stated: "Men are always whining about how we are suffocating them. Personally, I think if you can hear them whining, you're not pressing hard enough on the pillow."

4. Post-it notes marketed by 3M said: "Men have only two faults: every thing they say and everything they do." [48]

Men, as you watch your favorite TV shows, be on the look out for the number of times we are demeaned, humiliated and embarrassed. You'll be surprised at the pervasiveness, especially on the sit-coms. Of course, as Dr. Dobson so aptly says, how long would men get away with doing the same thing to women? I certainly don't need to answer a question with such a self-evident answer!

Even the Readers *Digest* is getting into the male-bashing act. Under *Marriage Encounters* in the December 2001 issue we read:

> While I was visiting my sister one evening, I took out a candy dispenser that was shaped like a miniature person. 'How does that thing work?' she asked. As I turned the figurine's arm to pop candy out, my sister laughed. 'I see ... it's a lot like my husband,' she said. 'You have to twist his arm to get anything out of him.'

If the United Nations has its way, the United States would sign the Elimination of All Forms of Discrimination Against Women protocol. It would give women preferential treatment in a wide number of areas. For example, Article 1 would abolish discrimination against women in political, economic, social, cultural, civil, and other fields. Article 2 outlaws discrimination against women by "any person, organization or enterprise," including all "public institutions," thereby, justifying the presence of women in our military. Article 10 would eliminate any stereotyped roles of men and women, such as, those found in textbooks and in teaching methods (remember the discussion in Chapter Three of female efforts to homogenize the genders?). Articles 11 and 16 would essentially legislate equal pay for woman and their "right" for abortion on demand.[49]

REFERENCES

1. Dudley Barlow, "AAUW Gender Equity Research: Scholarship Or Partisanship?," *The Education Digest*, March 1999, pp. 46-50.

2. Christina Hoff Sommers, *The War Against Boys*, Simon & Schuster, New York, 2000, pp. 38-39.

3. Dudley Barlow.

4. Diane Ravitch, "Showdown At Gender Gap," *Forbes*, April 7, 1997, p. 68.

5. Dudley Barlow.

6. Dan Seligman, "Gender And Brains, II," *Forbes,* April 20, 1998, pp. 52-53.

7. John Leo, "The Feds Strike Back, *"U.S. News & World Report,* May 31, 1999, p. 16.

8. Dudley Barlow.

9. Michael Schrage, "Why Can't A Woman Be More Like A Man?, *Fortune,* August 16, 2000 p. 184.

10. Gosta Wrangler, "No Belles: The Second Sex," *National Review,* November 11, 1996, p. 34.

11. Christina Hoff Sommers, p. 23.

12. "Feminists Will Be Feminists," *National Review,* April 6, 1998, pp. 17-18.

13. "Feminists Will Be Feminists."

14. Maria Karagianis. "Quite Contrary," *MS.,* June/July, 1999, pp. S6-S9.

15. Nancy Henderson, "Class Acts," *Working Woman,* October, 1998.

16. Nancy Henderson.

17. As quoted in Christina Hoff Sommers, p.114.

18. Brady Creel, "Magazine Rates A&M Pro-Male." *The Battalion,* September 22, 2000.

19. Paul Craig Roberts, "Columbia Targets Heterosexual Males," *Human Events,* November 17, 2000.

20. Randy Wayne White, "Man Crushed By Bigfoot," *Men's Health,* June 1999, pp. 56-58.

21. Kate O'Beirne, "Equal Time," *National Review,* April 5, 1999, p. 26.

22, Linda Himelstein and Stephanie Anderson Forest, "Breaking Through," *BusinessWeek,* February 17, 1997, pp. 64-70.

23. Pallavi Gogoi, "As Leaders, Women Rule," *Business Week,* November 20, 2000, pp. 75-84.

24. Pallavi Gogoi.

25, Pallavi Gogoi.

26. Susan Brink, "Prostate Cancer: Kinder Cuts Mean Sharper Dilemmas," *U.S. News & World Report,* April 3, 2000, pp. 58-60.

27. *Women's Health: Raising Awareness of Cervical Cancer,* Hearing Before The Subcommittee On Health And Environment Of The Committee On Health And Environment Of The Committee On Commerce, House of Representatives, One Hundred Sixth Congress, First Session, March 16, 1999.

28. Betsy Carpenter, "Her Turn," *U.S. News & World Report,* November 10, 1997, pp. 82-84.

29. Leonard Sax, "Guilty Until Proven Innocent," *Penthouse,* December 2000, pp. 123, ff.

30. Leonard Sax.

31. Leonard Sax.

32. Lee Rosen, "In Defense of Gender Blindness," *The New Republic,* June 26, 1998, pp. 25-27; John Cloud, "Don't Try This At The Office," *Time,* April 13, 1998, p. 51; and John Leo, "Every Man A Harasser," *U.S. News & World Report,* February 16, 1998, p. 18.

33. Leonard Sax.

34. *Statistical Abstract Of The United States,* 2001.

35. Charles W. Gittins, "Show Trial," *National Review,* May 4, 1998, pp. 28-30.

36. Eric Felten, "Sex And The Single Soldier," *National Review,* April 7, 1997, pp. 21-22.

37. *2001 World Almanac.*

38. Elaine Donnelly, "Women In Combat—Time For A Review," *The American Legion Magazine,* July 2000, pp. 12-16.

39. Elaine Donnelly.

40. Elaine Donnelly.

41. Jeremy Rabkin, "Gender Benders," *The American Spectator,* April 1999, pp. 58-59.

42. Pete Du Pont, "Men's Athletic Programs Dumped To Satisfy Quotas," *Human Events,* September 3, 1999.

43. Pete Du Pont.

44. Jeremy Rabkin.

45. *Statistical Abstract Of The United States,* 1999.

46. *Bryan-College Station Eagle,* September 17, 1999.

47. Terence P. Jeffrey, "Bush Targets Other Death Tax," *Human Events,* March 12, 2001, pp. 1, 6-7.

48. James Dobson, *Bringing Up Boys,* Tyndale House Publishers., Inc., Wheaton, Illinois, 2001, pp. 161-171.

49. Phyllis Schafly, "President Should Reject Global Feminists' Agenda," *Human Events,* June 24, 2002, p. 14.

SIX

What Hath Woman Wrought?

"In 2000, the World Health Organization ranked the quality of health care systems in 191 countries. The United States ranked 37th." *USA Today.*

"The crime-drop party is over." James Alan Fox

We saw in Chapter Four that women in the United States have gained an increasing level of power, but we noticed in Chapter Five that much of this power was achieved through wide-spread discrimination in favor of them and against men. What has been the result of this expanded role for females across a wide swath of American society? Do these results justify their being achieved often through unfair means? In other words, has America become a better nation over the last three decades?

On The "Killing Fields" Front

Women were given the legal right through Roe vs. Wade to decide if they wanted to complete a pregnancy or murder their unborn child through abortion. There could not have been a more clear-cut case of an individual having to choose between good and evil. Unfortunately, evil won.

Look at Exhibit 6.1. Since 1970, approximately 41,221,400 babies were aborted by women in the United States. Overall, 26.5% of all pregnancies were terminated in this fashion. Between 1979-1984, almost one-third of pregnancies were aborted. The steep rise in abortions can be seen after 1973 when Roe vs. Wade was decided. Ignoring women who have had multiple abortions, these data mean that over one-fourth of women in the United States who became pregnant since 1970 murdered their unborn children.

Is abortion part of God's plan for women? Of course not. God gave women the responsibility for child bearing : "Unto the woman he said, I will greatly multiply thy sorrow and thy conception; in sorrow thou shalt bring forth children" (Genesis 3:16). It makes no difference that God put this responsibility on women as punishment for Eve's disobedience in the Garden of Eden. Genesis l: 27-28 says: "So God created man in his own image, in the image of God created he him; male and female created he them. And God blessed them, and God said unto them, Be fruitful, and multiply and replenish the earth...." Exodus 20 (the Ten Commandments) provides the ultimate prohibition against abortion: "thou shalt not kill" (Exodus 20:14).

If God's admonitions are disobeyed, the transgressors will suffer. Many women are haunted for a lifetime by their decision to terminate a pregnancy. They wonder what the child would look like at certain ages and what their personalities might be. They speculate as to what their interests might be, what careers they might have chosen. They bemoan the companionship that might have been, the good times, being able to teach and instruct the child as he or she matures. Many sink into depression.

What are the national implications of abortions? What future leaders, teachers, lawyers, doctors, engineers, scientists, and entertainers has our country been deprived of through abortions? How much richer culturally would America be? Many economists, such as the late Julian Simon, feel that a slowing or declining population is one of the greatest threats facing our country, a sentiment

EXHIBIT 6.1
ABORTIONS IN THE UNITED STATES, 1970-2000

Year	Abortions	Pregnancies	Percentage Of Pregnancies Resulting In Abortions
1970	500,000[1]	4,231,000	11.8
1971	500,000[1]	4,056,000	12.3
1972	586,760[2]	3,844,760	15.3
1973	744,600	3,881,600	19.2
1974	898,600	4,058,600	22.1
1975	1,034,200	4,178,200	24.8
1976	1,179,300	4,347,300	27.1
1977	1,316,700	4,643,700	28.4
1978	1,409,600	4,742,600	29.7
1979	1,497,700	4,991,700	30.0
1980	1,553,900	5,165,900	30.0
1981	1,577,300	5,206,300	30.3
1982	1,573,900	5,254,900	30.0
1983	1,575,000	5,214,000	30.2
1984	1,577,200	5,246,200	30.0
1985	1,588,600	5,349,600	29.7
1986	1,574,000	5,331,000	29.7
1987	1,559,100	5,408,100	29.0
1988	1,590,800	5,500,800	28.9
1989	1,566,900	5,607,900	27.9
1990	1,608,600	5,766,600	27.9
1991	1,556,500	5,667,500	27.5
1992	1,528,900	5,593,900	27.3
1993	1,500,000	5,500,000	27.3
1994	1,431,000	5,410,000	26.5
1995	1,363,690	5,263,690	25.9
1996	1,365,730	5,256,730	26.0
1997	1,365,730	5,260,730	26.0
1998	1,365,730	5,253,730	26.0
1999	1,365,730	5,261,730	26.0
2000	1,365,730	5,264,730	25.9
Totals	41,221,400	155,759,500	26.5

[1] Author's estimates for 1970 and 1971
[2] Abortion data, 1972-2000, based on research published by the Alan Guttmacher Institute, the special research affiliate of Planned Parenthood Federation of America, the nation's largest provider and promoter of abortion. Estimates for 1997-2000 are based on trends from previous years.

echoed by Pat Buchanan in his *Death of the West*. How have abortions contributed to this possibility?

Consider the case of Celine Dion, the popular singer. Her mother came close to aborting her. Already the mother of 13, she was told by her Roman Catholic priest not to do it. Fortunately, she listened to him. [1]

Many righteous individuals point their fingers at the genocide committed by Adolph Hitler and the Nazis and Joseph Stalin and the Soviet Communists. These pale in contrast to the level of infanticide perpetrated by our abortion death mills. And, unfortunately, it probably will not get any better. On September 28, 2000 the Food and Drug Administration announced that it had approved the drug, mifepristone (RU-486) which induces abortions. (If the drug were unsuccessful in inducing abortion, a surgical abortion would be required). And three powerful leaders of our new administration—President Bush, first lady Laura Bush and Attorney General John Ashcroft—have not publicly stated that they want to eliminate a woman's right to commit murder through the abortion process, despite the Republican party having had a pro-life plank in the 2000 election platform. On the contrary, both Laura Bush and John Ashcroft have publicly stated that they are not in favor of the repeal of Roe vs. Wade.

I don't want to sound like a doomsdayer, but I wonder how long a loving, yet sovereign and just God, will wait to bring retribution to our nation because we did nothing to stop the murder of innocent children?

On The Health Front

Wives/mothers are supposed to be providing their families (and themselves) with nutritional, well balanced meals. This is one of their major responsibilities. Apparently, they are failing this mandate big time. In 1960-1962, 24.4% of men and women were overweight, 22.9% of males and 25.6% of females.[2] In 1998, 63.6% and 47.1% of males and females, respectively, were overweight and 20% of both sexes were considered to be obese.[3] Even more alarming is the assertion by the Institute of Medicine of the National Academy of Sciences in 1998 that "about *two-thirds* of us are too heavy for optimum health" (emphasis added).[4]

Think two-thirds is awful? Try *three- fourths*, a figure from a 1996 study that indicated that proportion of Americans that "exceeded their maximum recommended body weight."[5] The problem with being overweight is that it increases the probability of your having heart disease, high blood pressure, certain types of cancer, and the disease for which obesity is the greatest risk factor, diabetes.

Let's look at some data on diabetes. Seven percent (16 million) of Americans have this disease. Long a malaise associated with middle age, there was a scary 70% increase between 1990-1998 for persons in their 30s. More frightening yet is the increasing incidence of the disease in children: According to the American Diabetes Association, 45% of the new diabetes cases discovered in children are of the adult onset type, the variety almost exclusively formerly found in overweight middle-age persons. Heretofore, almost 100% of children who contacted diabetes had Type 1, a lifelong autoimmune disorder.

So what's the problem with having diabetes? "The complications are horrific. Diabetes is the leading cause of both blindness and kidney failure. Diabetics are two to four times more likely to suffer from heart disease and stroke than is the general population, and nerve damage in lower limbs leads to 56,000 amputations a year."[6]

In 1997, it was estimated that one in five white women in the United States and one in two black women have genital herpes, a particular type of sexually transmitted disease (STD).[7] Ann Wald, medical director of the Virology Research Clinic at the University of Washington (Seattle), says "Herpes has become a major public health problem."[8] Besides the uncomfortable itching and painful blisters that develop, there are more ominous aspects of genital herpes. One-third to one half of babies born to mothers with the disease acquire it; herpes may attack infants' brains, causing blindness, deafness, mental retardation, or even death. Studies have shown that herpes sufferers are potentially nine times more likely to contact HIV and women can infect their male sexual partners. (Men are just as likely to be affected with herpes by a female partner as women are likely to be affected by men).[9] To make matters worse, there are no reliable diagnostic tests available for the disease.[10]

How good is health care in the United States? Not so good! In 2000, 12 countries had higher levels of life expectancy and lower infant mortality rates— two crucial measures of a nation's health— than we do. But, you argue that these results occur because we spend less on health care than do these other countries. Wrong! We spend the most on health care as a percentage of gross domestic product than any country in the world (14.0%) yet they have better vital statistics than we do (*Statistical Abstract Of The United States*, 2001).

Here's another shocker. In 2000, the World Health Organization ranked the quality of health care systems in 191 countries. The United States finished 37th. Thirty-seventh! (First was France, second was Italy).[11]

Here are some indications as to the extent to which Americans suffer from mental health problems (as reported by the National Institutes of Mental Health):

1. The International Labor Organization estimates that 200 million working days are lost annually to work-related mental health difficulties and we spend as much as $44 billion annually on treating depression.

2. Around 19 million adult Americans suffer from various kinds of depression. It is considered by the World Health Organization, World Bank and Harvard University as being the leading cause of disability.

3. 2.3 million adults suffer from bi-polar illness; as much as 20% of those afflicted commit suicide.

4. More than two million U.S. adults are afflicted by schizophrenia. Most suffer throughout their lives. Ten percent commit suicide. Over $32 billion annually is spent on the treatment of schizophrenia.

5. 16 million adults 18 to 54 years of age suffer from anxiety disorders, costing the U.S. around $50 billion annually. Panic disorder affects 2.4 million, often resulting in agoraphobia in which

individuals become afraid of being in a place or situation where escape might be difficult or help unavailable in the case of a panic attack. Obsessive-compulsive disorders harm 3.3 million Americans, costing us $8.4 billion in 1990. Post-traumatic stress disorder (PTSD) affects 5.2 million adults. The disease is especially likely to afflict men and women who have spent time in war zones. Around five million of us have social phobia, which is often accompanied by depression and frequently results in alcohol or drug abuse. Attention deficit hyperactivity (ADHD), affecting 3% to 5% of school-age children, can lead to low levels of success at school, work and socially.[12]

On The Education Front

In inflation adjusted dollars, the U.S. spent $3,372 in 1965 per pupil on education. By 1998, this figure had skyrocketed 234% to $7,896. The Federal government spends about $54 billion a year on education through 39 different agencies;[13] state governments spend $167 billion annually and local governments lay out $145 billion. As a result of this spending, pupil-teacher ratios have declined from 21.4 in 1960 in public schools to 14.4 in 1998.[14]

What has been the result of this mammoth investment on education— an industry made up of 75% of females? Succinctly put, taxpayers are being taken to the cleaners and our children are getting a third-rate education. Examinations of Scholastic Achievement Test (SAT) scores in math and English, 1967-2003, show a distressing pattern: Scores in English have dropped over that three-decade period, from 543 to 507 in 2003 on the verbal part, up slightly in math, 516 to 519. More evidence that U.S. students are woefully educated: For 1996 and 1998, the U.S. Department .of Education presented data on the percentage of fourth and eighth grade students who scored at or above the "proficient level" on national tests. In 1998, only 29% of fourth graders met or exceeded the proficiency level in reading; 62% did so for math. For eighth graders, 31% met or exceeded the standard in reading; in 1996, 61% did so for math, but only 27% met or exceeded the proficiency level for science.

Okay, so Johnny and Jane can't read, add or do a science experiment. But Johnny and Jane do all right in other disciplines, don't they? Wrong! Let's consider geography, keeping in mind that, according to Gilbert Grosevenor, president of the National Geographic Society, geographical knowledge is the key factor needed to effectively market products in an increasingly competitive world.[15] Only one-third of college students in North Carolina knew that the Seine River was in France. Ninety-five percent of freshmen at St. Mary-of-the-Woods College in Indiana could not correctly identify the nation of Vietnam on a map. In 2000, only 15% of high school seniors knew the difference between longitude and latitude.

I got first-hand knowledge of the woeful level of college students' geography knowledge in 1989 when 116 junior and senior business students taking my International Marketing course were provided a map of the world that contained the outlines of 152 unnamed countries and were asked to identify as many of them as they could. The average number of correct identifications was only 17, or 11% of the 153 nations. I had students in the same course repeat the exercise a decade later. The results were a little better, but still appalling; 252 students correctly identified, on average, 28 of 167 countries (16.8%). A 1988 study conducted by the Gallup organization revealed that, out of 10 nations studied, United States 18-24 year-olds ranked last in that age group in identifying 16 places on a world map *(National Geographic,* December 1989). With results like those described here, it is no wonder that James Vining, Executive Director of the National Council for Geographic Education, laments: "We have a situation where Johnny not only doesn't know how to add or read, he doesn't even know where he is."[16]

Oh, well, so Johnny and Jane don't know where they are, but they certainly know where they came from. Wrong again! William Bennett, former Secretary of Education under president Reagan, and author of such best-seller books as *The Book of Virtues* and *The Death of Outrage,* stated that 25 million students in America reach the 12th grade without knowing the essentials of U.S. history. [17] So why is history so important? What good does it do to memorize all those dates and names? According to famed historian, Edward Gibbon, author of the monumental *Rise and Fall of the Roman Empire,* "Those who fail to know the lessons of history are bound to repeat its mistakes." Diane Ravitch, historian and education professor at New York University states "Our ability to defend intelligently and thoughtfully what we as a nation hold dear depends on our knowledge and understanding of what we hold dear" *(USA Today,* May 10-12, 2002, p. 1).

When I teach business majors international marketing and international logistics, I tell the students that if they don't remember anything else about me, I want them to remember me as "Mr. History" and "Mr. Geography" because these disciplines are so important in understanding these two subjects. You can imagine my reaction several years ago when, after carefully delineating the geographical/ German logistics reasons for the surrender of General Paulus' German Sixth Army to Russian troops at Stalingrad during World War II, one student said, "Dr. Hise, do we have to know this? After all, this all happened before we were born."

We have already seen how U.S. students stack up against foreign students on geography. How well do they measure up against foreign students in other areas? In a nut shell, terribly. In 1996, the U.S. Department of Education reported the results of a study in which U.S. eighth graders and students taking their final year of secondary school science and math were compared to similar students in other countries. Our eighth graders in science scored significantly above the international average, but still trailed eight other countries, such as, the Czech Republic (first), Netherlands (second), Slovenia (third), and Austria (fourth). However, U.S. students in their final year of secondary school science scored *significantly lower* than the international average, trailing 15 countries. U.S. eighth grade mathematics students tested around the international average, but were behind 14 other nations. The older students—those in their final year of secondary school math—scored significantly lower than the international average—well behind 17 other nations.[18]

This lack of educational competence in science and math is likely to have undesirable consequences down the road. Stanford University economist, Paul M. Romer, warns that the United States is turning out too few college-trained scientists and engineers and that, as a result, the U.S. is likely to be facing decreased returns from technological innovations.[19]

Oh, well you say, our schools can't be good at everything. So maybe our children aren't learning anything in our schools but, at least, they are places where our children can go and be safe. Right? Wrong! A study by Columbia University found that 60% of American high school students were attending schools where illegal drugs were taken, kept or sold. The cost to American tax payers from dealing with this problem: A "paltry" $41 billion annually *(The Economist,* September 8, 2001). And let's not forget the high profile shootings that have occurred. What is not widely known, however, because teachers and administrators want to keep their jobs, are the beatings, intimidation and threats that pervade our schools' cafeterias, hallways, playgrounds, rest rooms and, yes, the class rooms themselves.

On The Crime Front

When crime data from 1979-1999 are examined, a clear-cut pattern in the number of crimes committed emerges. For the two major categories—violent crime and property crime—there was a consistent upward trend from 1979 until the middle of the 1990s when a downward trend began. And the same pattern is evident for five specific types of crime reported, that is, murder and non-negligent manslaughter, forcible rape, robbery, burglary, and larceny-theft. For property crimes, murder and non-negligent manslaughter, robbery, and burglary, the number of crimes committed are lower than they were for 1979.

For all these seven categories of crime, the incidence of crime—

as measured by the rate per 100,000 people—also showed increases until the middle of the 1990s, then a drop off. Sizable decreases between 1979 and 1999 are noted for property crimes (down 25.4%), murder and non-negligent manslaughter (down 41.2%), robbery (down 31.2%), and burglary (down 49.0%).

Before we start leaving our doors unlocked and start walking in strange neighborhoods after dark and turning in our weapons of self-defense, we need to be aware of several caveats. Crime Stoppers in Texas estimates that 64% of all *major crimes* are not reported, so the level and incidence of crimes may not have slowed as much as the "official" figures show. If there was a drop in crime, it has not resulted from a change in heart of the American people—an improvement in morality, if you will—but is largely attributable to the greater numbers of people who have been incarcerated. There were 182,288 people in jail in 1980. By 1997, it had skyrocketed to 557,974, a 3.06-fold increase. In 1997, 1,185,800 persons were in prison versus 319,598 in 1980, up 3.7 times. By the end of 2001, it is estimated that two million Americans will be behind bars. (In other words, with 5% of the world's population, we will have 25% of the world's inmates).[20]

Parole and probation figures are also meaningful. The ratio of parolees (685,033) in 1997 compared to those on parole in 1980 (220,438) is 3.1 and the probation ratio is 2.9 (1,118,097 on probation in 1980 versus 3,261,888 in 1997).[21]

The major problem is that there are over 500,000 inmates who are due to hit the streets in a few years and with the projected rate of recidivism—The *Economist* (May 5, 2001) asserts that recidivism rates have not changed in decades—two-thirds of convicts will be rearrested within three years of release and 40% will go back behind bars. James Alan Fox, criminologist at Northeastern University in Boston, states flatly! "The crime-drop party is over."[22] More gloom and doom is added by Columbia University's Jeffrey Fagan: "Throughout our history, each recurring cycle of crime has been worse than the last."[23]

The fact that the age group that commits the most crime—14

to 17 year-olds—is increasing in size is another reason why crime is expected to rise, not to continue dropping off. [24] In 1980, juveniles (10-17 year olds) committed 77,220 *violent* crimes. By 1997, it had jumped to 99,342. For this group, weapons law violations were up by 84% and manufacturing and sale of drugs leapt 135.6%.[25]

Another important development. In 1978, there were only 9,555 incarcerated women, but it surged to 83,000 in 1999. In 1999, women accounted for 6.0% of all inmates.[26] And yet another disturbing report. The level of crime is increasing at our nation's colleges and universities. In 1999, reports of sexual offenses, robberies and hate crimes increased. (It should be noted that many institutions of higher learning, such as the University of California and the University of Pennsylvania, have been notorious for under-reporting crimes on their campuses even though a 1990 law mandates that all 6,000 colleges and universities which receive federal funds must do so).[27]

On The Military Front

The Economist reported in its issue of February 17, 2001 on the strength of the U.S. armed forces in 2000, compared to what it was in 1990. Instead of the 18 active Army divisions in 1990, only 10 existed in 2000. Army reserve brigades declined from 57 to 42. The Navy has suffered similar declines in strength: 11 aircraft carriers, compared to 15; 10 active air wings, instead of 13; 55 attack submarines, down from 91; and 116 surface ships, instead of 206. Overall, the Navy had fewer than 200 ships in 2000, compared to almost 600 when Ronald Reagan left office in 1988.

The Air Force has also suffered. Twenty-four active fighter wings in 1990 were reduced to 12 in 2000. Whereas 12 reserve fighter wings existed in 1990, only seven were available in 2000. Reserve air defense squadrons were decimated from 14 to 4 and bombers were sliced to 190 from 277. A radio newscast that the writer caught on May 2, 2000 indicated that 115 of 330 Air Force units were not combat ready, the lowest level in 15 years.

Only the Marines escaped unscathed from this bloodletting, retaining all three of their divisions in the 10-year period. But, overall, the level of armed forces personnel dropped to about one million in 2000, down from around 1.9 million in the early 1990s.

Another deficiency that has become apparent recently is the shortage of equipment that forces the use of already existing equipment well beyond its intended, operational life span. But perhaps the most serious deficiency of all is American's lack of an antimissile defense system which, thank God, President George W. Bush seems adamant about our having.

The Senate Armed Services Committee held hearings after the U.S.S. Cole was attacked in Yemen in October, 2000. Those hearings produced this comment by Senator Jim Inhofe (R-Okla.): "Readiness—or our lack thereof—is now clearly an issue." The director of the CIA went further: "The U.S. is about the most vulnerable it has been since becoming a nation" because of downsizing and the damage that has been done to military readiness. In October of 2000, General Norman Schwartzkopf told the Republican National Committee that military readiness had suffered under president Bill Clinton.

A survey of 12,000 servicemen as reported in *American Military Culture in the 21st Century*, published by the Center for Strategic and International Studies, dramatically revealed the low level of morale existing among U.S. servicemen:

1. Only 35% of servicemen agreed with the statement, "When my service's senior leaders say something, you can believe it's true."

2. Only 44% of the Army's junior officers believed that "my service's senior leaders have the will to make the tough, sometimes unpopular, decisions that are in the best long-term interest of the service."

3. Only 51% and 36%, respectively, of the Navy's officers and enlisted men expressed satisfaction with the Navy's overall leadership. These figures in 1996 were 63% and 41%, respectively.

4. Between 1996 and 1998, the level of Army officers' satisfaction dropped from 72% to 57%; enlisted men's satisfaction fell

from 52% to 45%.[28]

Given the lower levels of morale expressed, it is hardly surprising that attrition rates for first-term, four-year enlistees are rising. A General Accounting Office report indicated that it was 36% for all services, with the Army's highest at 39%. The attrition rate for women was 45%, including 26% who separated because of pregnancy. On the other hand, attrition rates for the Marine Corps continued to decline. Elaine Donnelly, President, Center for Military Readiness, says: "The volunteer force is losing experienced people and recruiters are hard-pressed to meet their goals. This is the only military we have, and our national security depends on it." [29]

When the "peace dividend" was declared, the Clinton administration seized the opportunity to also decimate our intelligence operations. As the aftermath of the terrorist attacks on New York's World Trade Center and the Pentagon unfolds, our intelligence arms—National Security Agency, FBI (domestic terrorism responsibility) and the CIA (international terrorism responsibility)—bear much of the blame for not recognizing the threat and preventing it. Consider the following:

1. A Senate committee in the Spring of 2001 indicated that terrorists had weapons of mass destruction.

2. In a June 23, 2001 interview with a British journalist, Osama bin Laden and his top aides indicated that they were coming after the United States—and soon.

3. The Mossad, the Israeli intelligence arm—and arguably the best in the world—notified the U.S. in August, 2001 that they had overwhelming evidence that Moslem terrorists were planning a major strike on the U.S. soon.

4. Airline identification cards and uniforms were stolen in Rome about eight months before the New York and Washington D.C. attacks. Apparently, our intelligence people could not connect the dots to September 11, 2001.

5. Several of the hijackers were already on watch lists, but these were not made available to airport security personnel.

6. *After* September 11, the U.S. advertised for help from people who could speak either Arabic or Farsi.

7. The FBI, at the time of the attacks, was looking for two of the hijackers, but *could not find them.*

8. Intelligence operatives could not make the connection from terrorists blowing up planes to hijacking them and plowing them into buildings. They apparently ignored the fact that Moslems believe that in fighting "infidels" through a "jihad" (holy war), they would immediately go to heaven when they die and that there was an obvious precedent: Japanese kamikaze pilots during World War II that deliberately crashed their planes into U.S. ships (that history thing again).

On The Family Front

Over the last third of the 20th century, there has been an almost total collapse of the family in America.

Exhibit 6.2 shows the number of divorces and the rates of divorce that have occurred from 1970-2001. The data clearly portray the dramatic increase in divorces that occurred in the U.S. Close to 35 million divorces were granted, or about an average of one million families a year torn asunder. The divorce rate reached its zenith during the 1980s and, thankfully, dropped somewhat during the 1990s.

Make no mistake about it, divorce has cruel implications. For the spouses involved, there is hurt, depression, anger, fear, and reduced standards of living since two households now have to be maintained. In many cases, loving parents—especially fathers, because they are less likely to be granted custody— may be denied a desired level of contact with their children because the ex-spouse has moved somewhere else, or the divorce decree gives them only minimal visitation rights.

But the real harm is done to the children of divorce. Studies show that deep emotional scars remain even after 10 years. One of the long-term effects is self-blame, even though they are in no way responsible for the breakup. They sense a lack of love; after all, if my parents truly loved me, they would try to work things out. They feel resentment; they have a deep sense of loss. Insecurity sets in. Low self-esteem often occurs. [30]

There are especially grievous consequences when divorce deprives children of their fathers; daughters can suffer as much as sons. (A recent study revealed that 50 percent of children of divorce had not seen their fathers during the past year and only 16% saw them regularly).[31] Divorced children are twice as likely to drop out of secondary school. Girls are twice as likely to become teen-age (usually unmarried) parents. Children of divorce are 1.5 times more likely to be idle rather than gainfully employed.

Without fathers, even girls from otherwise advantaged homes are at risk. Social scientists Sara McLanahan and Gary Sandefur assert that 'the chances that a white girl from an advantaged background will become a teen mother are five times as high, and the chances a white child will drop out of high school are three times as high, if the parents do not live together.'[32]

On The Morality Front

Between 1990 and 1999, there were, on average, 500,000 births annually to teen-age mothers.[33] In 1999, it was estimated that 12,708,000 unmarried women ages 15-44 had intercourse in the previous year.[34] In 1999, about one third of all children born were born out of wedlock; in 1990, it was 27%.[35]

In 1995, the National Center for Health Statistics published the results of the National Survey of Family Growth. One of the questions dealt with the number of sexual partners women ages 15-44 had in their lifetime. Of the 10,847 women interviewed, 53.7% admitted having three or four and 15.5% claimed 10 or more. The same survey found that 41.1% had cohabited *outside of marriage*. About 10% had never married, 23.6% had cohabited before their first marriage, 7.3% after their first marriage, and 7.0% were currently cohabiting. [36]

Sexual promiscuity among teen-age women is rampant. Over half (56%) have had sex by their 18th birthday.[37] A 1999 PBS

EXHIBIT 6.2

NUMBER OF DIVORCES AND RATES OF DIVORCE
(1970-2001)

Year	Number of Divorces	Divorce Rate (Per 1,000 Population)
1970	708,000	3.5
1971	773,000	3.7
1972	845,000	4.0
1973	915,000	4.8
1974	977,000	4.6
1975	1,036,000	4.8
1976	1,083,000	5.0
1977	1,091,000	5.0
1978	1,130,000	5.1
1979	1,181,000	5.3
1980	1,189,000	5.2
1981	1,213,000	5.3
1982	1,170,000	5.1
1983	1,158,000	5.0
1984	1,169,000	5.0
1985	1,190,000	5.0
1986	1,178,000	4.9
1987	1,166,000	4.8
1988	1,167,000	4.8
1989	1,157,000	4.7
1990	1,182,000	4.7
1991	1,187,000	4.7
1992	1,215,000	4.8
1993	1,187,000	4.7
1994	1,191,000	4.6
1995	973,000	4.1
1996	1,150,000	4.3
1997	1,163,000	4.3
1998	955,000	3.5
1999	1,145,000	4.1
2000	1,186,000	4.2
2001	1,140,000	4.0

Source: Statistical Abstract Of The United States, 2002.

documentary, *The Lost Children of Rockdale County,* covered a story about an outbreak of syphilis in teenagers living in the white, affluent town of Conyers, Georgia. The show revealed that 50 teenagers engaged in sex with 20 to 50 partners in which the only clueless people were the parents. Groups of 12 and 13 year olds mimicked the sexual behavior they had seen on the Playboy channel.[38]

Extra-marital sex on our college and university campuses is

occurring at unprecedented levels. Wendy Shalit, a 24 year-old graduate of a private liberal arts college, says in her book, *A Return to Modesty,* that sex is exchanged as casually on campus as their parents shook hands when they were in college. She feels that sex on campus is about as personal as "two planes refueling." Indeed, the phrase used is "hooking up." In hooking up, both partners are supposed to adhere to the unwritten code: The liaison is based solely on physical attraction and neither partner has the obligation to date the other. The availability of large quantities of alcohol helps to shed any vestiges of inhibitions.[39]

Child abuse and neglect increased from 691,000 cases in 1990 to 862,000 in 1998. Around one-half of the incidents are neglect, one-fourth physical abuse, six percent are emotional maltreatment, 2.4% involve medical neglect, and 11.5% of the cases involve sexual abuse. About 50% of the victims are female and 50% are male. Around one-fourth of the victims are ages two to five, one-fourth are 6-9 years old, one-third are 10-17, and 14% are one year or younger.[40] *U.S. News & World Report* (April 9, 2001) estimated that child abuse costs the U.S. $94 billion a year, with large chunks spent on hospitalization, mental health and health care, child welfare, juvenile delinquency, and adult criminality. In addition, there are the personal burdens that abused children must bear, including greater likelihood of doing poorly in school and becoming teen parents, abusing drugs and alcohol, chronic health problems, and committing crimes.

On The Political Front

The eight-year term of President Bill Clinton was a nightmare for the United States. Only an unprecedented economic surge—which, by the way, started in the last year of George Bush's administration and begun to unravel during the last year of Clinton's second term (Clinton's Department of Commerce "overestimated" how well the economy was doing then) —served to mask the incalculable damage he did to this country. And, unfortunately, because he is still relatively young, we probably have not heard the last of him or his wife, now the junior senator from New York who, in the final analysis, may be an even bigger threat to this nation than her husband was or will be.

About Mr. Clinton's character, consider what Mark Helprin, a contributing editor to the *Wall Street Journal,* had to say. Mr. Helprin, who was educated at Harvard and served in the British Merchant Navy and Israel's Army and Air Force, stated the following in an address at Hillsdale College's first annual Churchill Dinner (December 5, 2000):

> I believe we are in the wilderness, that we are in the wilderness because of too many lies told and too many lies believed and that, if left unchecked, this habit of untruth will destroy us. Virtually all of his arguments were founded upon lies. It was a lie that he did not perjure himself. It was a lie that he did not conceal evidence. It was a lie that he did not conspire to intimidate witnesses. It was a lie that all these things were personal mistakes. It was a lie that the assemblage of raw FBI files on 900 Republicans was not for the purpose of blackmail. It was a lie that these files came to the White House by mistake. It was a lie that Mrs. Clinton did not benefit from guaranteed transactions in commodities trading. It was a lie that this was not a bribe. It was a lie that the president did not receive millions of campaign dollars from China. It was a lie that he did not personally intervene to aid the transfer to China of military technology that China intends for potential use against the United States. It was a lie that these two actions were unconnected. It was a lie that the grounds for impeachment were not mystifyingly narrow. It was a lie that the Senate could not try on political rather than legal grounds. There were so many lies that they were like sand in a sandstorm. They got into everything. You could not see the ground in front of you for all the lies that swirled in the air like brown dust. [41]

Mr. Clinton is vitally concerned with his "place in history." On December 22, 2001 he announced from his Harlem office that he had assembled an advisory group to help preserve his legacy. Here is the actual legacy that the "spin masters" will be trying to make us forget about:

•The Clinton administration botched the opportunity to help Russia become a democratic society with a free market economy after the fall of Communism in 1991. As a result, the Russian people suffered severe economic deprivation in 1998 when the government had to default on its international loans and the ruble was devalued; corruption is rampant and the Russian government is cozying up to such rogue nations as Iran, Iraq, Libya, and the People's Republic of China diplomatically, economically and militarily.[42]

•Clinton and Gore imperiled the security of the United States by aiding and abetting the transfer of nuclear and missile technology to the People's Republic of China.[43]

•The federal register of regulations quintupled in size during "Slick Willy's" regime. Over 700 new crimes were added to U.S. statutes.

•The Federal government consumed 21% of our gross domestic product in taxes, leaving us with the greatest tax burden since World War II. Since 1992, tax revenues grew at an annual rate of 7.6%, three times faster than the rate of inflation.

•Our national defenses steadily declined.

•Clinton issued more executive orders than presidents Bush and Reagan combined.

• Americorp's paid "volunteers" proved to be a $500 million boondoggle. The "volunteers were barely competent... for any task more complex than picking up beer cans along a highway."

• In contrast to the supposed friendlier and more customer-oriented IRS, during the Clinton administration it seized more than 12 million bank accounts and checks, put liens on three million homes, confiscated homes and cars from more than 100,000 people, used audits to punish persons and groups critical of Clinton's administration and squeezed billions of dollars from taxpayers that they didn't owe.[44] Most shockingly, it stalked single women. According to the Government Accounting Office, the IRS wrongfully prosecuted 50,000 female ex-spouses a year for taxes they didn't owe. "Alone and unlikely to reconnect with their former mates, they represent the perfect target for a government that shakes them down for more than they'd owed together." [45]

• Even the ultra-liberal American Civil Liberties Union (ACLU) criticized Mr. Clinton, condemning his actions to restrict habeas corpus, efforts to censor the Internet and his intention to create databases on all Americans. [46]

Mr. Clinton's female appointees have been a disaster, starting with Janet Reno. Here's what the much-respected Cato Institute had to say about Ms. Reno: "The so-called Justice Department under the truly abysmal management of Janet Reno has been the most politicized in this century. From its refusal to seriously investigate the many misdeeds of this administration to its own thuggery at Waco and in the Elian Gonzalez case, to its attacks on Microsoft and the firearms industry, to its complicity in establishing a tobacco cartel, the Reno Justice Department has consistently denigrated the concept of the rule of law." [47]

Then there is Madeleine Albright, erstwhile Secretary of State. In addition to her involving the United States in various, unneeded military interventions around the world—Kosovo being the major one—she championed the ill-advised policy of forcing Israel, under prime minister Ehud Barak, to make concession after concession to Yasser Arafat's militant Palestinians who want nothing other than the total destruction of Israel. These concessions did little but to seriously compromise Israeli security and spark the bloody Palestinian uprising in the fall of 2000. Even more costly blunders, in light of the September 11 terrorist attacks, were made by Ms. Albright in 1995 and 1996. As reported by Oliver North in *Human Events* (October 15, 2001), in 1995, intelligence officers for the Sudan offered U.S. officials information on Osama bin Laden's activities in that country. Ms. Albright turned down the offer. In 1996, Sudan offered to turn over bin Laden himself to the United States, along with two terrorists Sudan thought were involved with the bombings of our embassies in Kenya and Tanzania. Incredibly, another "no" from Secretary of State Madeleine Albright.

And let's not forget Doris Meissner, former head of the Immigration and Naturalization Service (INS) under Clinton and Gore. Ms. Meissner and Janet Reno filed false arrest and search warrants to allow the raid on the relatives of Elian Gonzalez, which resulted in that little boy being returned to Communist Cuba. Ms. Meissner and Ms. Reno are being sued by Elian's relatives and, in an effort to manipulate testimony before the court, recently announced awards for the "FBI thugs who gassed and assaulted Elian's family and neighbors."[48]

As bad as the Elian Gonzalez situation was, it pales in comparison with another Meissner misdeed. She collaborated with the Clinton-Gore administration to grant amnesty to hundreds of thousands of immigrants illegally in the United States—immigrants who were predominantly disposed to vote for *Democratic* candidates. Furthermore, background checks on these individuals were either waived or rushed, allowing thousands of individuals with *criminal records* to remain legally in the United States.

And who could forget Jocelyn Elders, Clinton's Surgeon General, who retired to Arkansas to pursue a life-long dream—writing a book on masturbation.

Let's not ignore those liberal, female members of Congress that have harmed our country. Three, in particular, come to mind: senator Diane Feinstein (D-Cal.), senator Barbara Boxer (D-Cal.) and representative Pat Schroeder (D-Colo.). Ms. Feinstein has vigorously pushed for a national identity card to be issued by the federal government. Ms. Feinstein's remarks in the *Daily Washington Journal Roll Call:*

> I believe that a new, phone- or machine-readable card that all job benefits applicants would be required to verify their work or eligibility for assistance deserves careful consideration. As the Senate Subcommittee on Immigration heard from representatives of the State Department, INS, FBI, Social Security Administration, Secret Service, state, and motor vehicle authorities, counterfeit-resistant cards that incorporate 'biometric' data are available and in use today. Whether the card carries a magnetic strip on which the bearer's unique voice, retina pattern, or fingerprint is digitally encoded, or whether it incorporates a

digitized photo and signature integrated into the plastic card itself, it is clear to me that state-of-the-art work and benefits eligibility IDs can and must replace the Dinosaur Age documents now being used.

In commenting on the national identity card, a computer software entrepreneur has concluded that it is a dire threat to civil liberty because it has the potential for a despotic government to extrapolate its use beyond the benign goal of tracing missing children (a ploy often used to sell Americans on the idea of a national identity card):

> Why not use it, at virtually no additional cost, to track convicted child molesters as well? Who would dare object? Why not then also track the movements of convicts and murderers? And rapists. And drug dealers, and felons in general. And fathers behind in child support. And tax-evaders. And 'political extremists.' Members of 'religious cults.' Drug addicts. AIDS carriers. Gun owners. Each turn of the political cycle, left and right would add their favorite batch of social enemies to the surveillance list.[49]

Pat Schroeder has been the champion of weakening our armed forces by pushing for higher levels of involvement by females, regardless of whether they can do the job or the effect on the morale of male soldiers.

Barbara Boxer is a fervent advocate of the power of big labor, higher taxes and burdensome regulations.

A little-known ambassador to Iraq, April Glaspie, made one of the most colossal diplomatic blunders of all time. On July 25, 1990 Ms. Glaspie told Saddam Hussein that the U.S. would not take sides in Iraq's border dispute with Kuwait. Emboldened by her statement, Iraq attacked Kuwait only eight days later (Terrence P. Jeffrey, "Do We Need Another War With Iraq?" *Human Events,* October 29, 2001).

On The Business Front

Women and women's rights groups have pushed hard for women to get higher pay, more executive positions and more seats on corporate boards of directors. Let's see how well women who are the leaders of various high-profile companies are doing.

Anne Mulcahy is president of one of America's icon companies, Xerox. Unfortunately, Xerox is in a lot of trouble. On October 5, 2000 it announced that it was expecting a loss of 15 cents to 20 cents a share for the third quarter, instead of making a profit as previously expected. There was also the possibility that the dividend might be lowered. These ominous warnings plunged the company's stock to $7 in March 2001 from a high of $64 in May of 1999, taking $38 billion of stockholder wealth with it.

There was speculation that Xerox would be forced to sell off some of its assets in order to improve its financial position (it has $7 billion of corporate debt). Likely candidates include the financing operation, its 50% interest in Fuji Photo Film and its low-end inkjet and copier business which, in total, could fetch $5 billion to $8 billion. [50] In October 2000, Mulcahy astonished business analysts by saying that Xerox had an "unsustainable business model" *(Business Week* March 5, 2001).

Under Mulcahy's watch, there was even more startling revelations about Xerox that came out in the summer of 2002: Xerox admitted that it had overstated its revenue by $6.4 billion over the last five years.

Jill Barad was CEO and chairman of Mattel for three years. During her tenure, the toy company purchased Learning Co. for $3.5 billion in an effort to break into the CD-ROM game market. Unfortunately, the Internet craze dried up the CD-ROM market and the company's stock crashed. Ms. Barad was fired. Not to worry, though, she received a *$50 million* severance package which included a $1.2 million annual pension. Mattel would have to sell 600,000 more Barbie dolls annually for 10 years to cover just her yearly stipend.[51]

In 1998, German car maker, Daimler-Benz, acquired Chrysler Corp. In the last two quarters of 2000, Chrysler lost close to $1 billion. One of the Chrysler executives fired on November 17, 2000 by Daimler-Benz's CEO and chairman, Jurgen E. Schremp, was Kathleen M. Oswald, the firm's chief administrative officer.[52]

Another auto executive to lose her job was Karen Francis, of General Motors' Oldsmobile division. GM CEO, Richard Wagner, announced on December 12, 2000 that the entire division was to be axed. Ten percent of GM's salaried workers were sacked—6,000 in the United States and 1,700 in Europe.[53] After a rocky two-year tenure, Cynthia Trudell, head of GM's Saturn division, resigned.

Another female executive in danger of losing her job is Linda Wachner, chairman, president and CEO (from all of her titles, it certainly looks as though she wants to be the "boss of all things") of Warnaco Group, Inc., a clothing manufacturer. Ms. Wachner, known in the Seventh Avenue fashion houses for her aggressive manner and mouth—Calvin Klein called her a "cancer" and her language, "disgusting"—has presided over the firm as its shares slid from $44 in mid-1998 to 39¢ just two years later. Angry stockholders place much of the blame on Linda who received $2.5 million in salary and a total compensation of $7.2 million in 2000, along with 3.3 million additional stock options,[54] and a *$44 million* golden parachute.

Pat Russo was executive vice-president for corporate strategy and operations at Lucent Technologies. On April 11, 2001 she was named President and CEO at Eastman Kodak. Ms. Russo's timing was impeccable. In mid-April, Lucent filed for bankruptcy. In August 2001 Deborah Hopkins, Lucent's Chief Financial Officer, was rewarded for her ineptness with a $5 million severance package.

What better job could anyone have than to be CEO of Sotheby's, the famed auction house—to be well compensated, to rub shoulders with the rich and famous, travel extensively, and move in a world of rare paintings, antiques, and other objects d'art? This was the life of Diana D. Brooks, who no longer holds this position and, instead, faced a jail sentence.

Ms. Brooks and Sotheby's each pleaded guilty to a single count of conspiring to violate U.S. antitrust laws on October 5, 2000. The former CEO admitted meeting with Christopher Davidge, the CEO of Sotheby's arch rival, Christie's, to fix the commissions charged sellers between 1993 and 1999. Ms. Brooks alleges that she was acting on orders from Alfred Taubman, the former chairman of Sotheby's and her boss.[55] Her testimony against Mr. Taubman, who vigorously denies her allegations, got her six months home detention, which probably will be served in her $4 million waterfront property in exclusive Hobe Sound, Florida. On the other hand, Mr. Taubman received a one-year prison sentence.

Carly Fiorina is America's highest profile female CEO because she heads up the largest firm led by a woman executive—Hewlett-Packard ($34 billion in annual sales). This 60 year-old company, founded in a garage in Palo Alto by the legendary Bill Hewlett and David Packard, was famous for its decentralized management style. Not anymore. Carly has centralized operations, collapsing 83 formerly autonomous units into two "back-end" divisions—one developing scanners and printers, the other computers—which report to the "front-end' groups which market and sell the products. This reorganization involved changing HP's strategy, structure, culture, and compensation scheme all at once—a daunting task for any company, but particularly so for tradition-rich HP.

Carly took over in mid-1999. On November 13, 2000 she announced fourth quarter earnings of 41¢ a share, 10¢ less than expected. Not surprisingly, the company's stock dropped 14% and 1,700 marketing personnel were laid off. At the same time, a proposed $18 billion acquisition of consulting firm, Price-Waterhouse Coopers, was announced—a potential deal that was eventually squashed.

Undaunted by all of these negatives, Ms. Fiorina informed analysts that HP was raising its projected sales increases from 15% to 17%. Her rationale: "In blackjack, you double down when you have an increased probability of winning. And we're going to double down."[56]

In April 2001, the *Econmist* reported that HP "would not match expectations." As a result, 3,000 more employees were axed. In its August 25, 2001 issue, The *Economist* reported that due to poor results, "Carly Fiorina, the computer giant's glamorous chief executive of the past two years, might go." However, she may have literally "bought" herself a two- or three-year grace period. In September 2001, Hewlett Packard announced its intention to pay $20 billion to acquire Compaq. Carly will become chairman ("chairwoman?") and CEO. The market reacted negatively to the news; HP's shares dropped 24%, reducing shareholder value by another $6 billion in one day *(The Economist,* September 8, 2001). And the proposed merger ran into stiff opposition from the heirs of Bill Hewlett and David Packard who control sizable blocks of HP shares. Walter Hewlett announced to the press in March of 2002 that Carly would split $115 million with her Compaq counterpart if the merger vent through *(The Economist,* March 2-8, 2002).

On the Economic Front

The U.S. seemingly had a buoyant economy over about the last decade. Unemployment dropped to less that four percent, personal incomes rose, the housing industry boomed, interest rates were low, and half of Americans were investing in the stock market as the Dow and Nasdaq surged to record levels.

But astute, albeit in-the-minority economists, began pointing to some disturbing aspects of the U.S. economy. Many of the high-flying technology firms enjoyed increasing stock prices, but weren't making any money. Some of these were floating initial public offerings that made investors overnight millionaires (some billionaires). Many ill-advised mergers or acquisitions were consummated. People who know little about the stock market were investing and growing accustomed to—and expecting—20% or more in annual appreciation. Bankruptcies hit all-time highs, whereas savings rates sunk to miniscule levels and, in some months, were even negative. Debt surged to record levels. The result, according to Wynne Dodley, distinguished scholar at the Jerome Levy Economic Institute: "Private spending is growing faster than income, and it cannot continue forever." Britain and Japan experienced such private sector deficits in the 1980s and eventually suffered prolonged and severe recessions.[57] The U.S. continued to run up sizable trade deficits, hitting a record $435 billion in 2002, more than four percent of gross domestic product. And here's a real stunner: It was estimated that the average household in the U.S. had only a $10,000 net financial worth and this figure *included retirement funds.*

Even as the stock market went south in the first half of 2000, we were told not to worry because corporate earnings were still strong. But, as 2000 marched on and eventually 2001 was here, company after company reported less-than-expected earnings, or even deficits, and the inevitable occurred: Corporations began to shutter operations and lay off personnel. On January 24, Lucent Technologies laid off 10,000. Whirlpool sent 6,000 packing. Five days later, Daimler-Chrysler cut 26,000 jobs. On December 12, 2000 General Motors announced it was closing down production of oldsmobile, involving 15,000 jobs. Technology leaders Motorola and Cisco cut 18,000 and 8,000 jobs, respectively. J. C. Penney was closing a number of stores, costing 6,000 jobs; Stage Door was shuttering 250 of its Bealls, Palais Royal and Stage Door department stores. Montgomery Ward closed all of its stores. General Electric, considered by many experts to be the world's most successful firm, announced layoffs of *75,000* personnel over a two-year period.

Another sign of a troubled economy are inventory buildups. In early 2001, General Motors dealers had 101 days of cars and trucks on their lots instead of the usual 80 for this time period. Cisco's inventories jumped $800 million in just six months, to $2 billion by January 2001. Georgia Pacific, Guess Jeans, Levis, Burlington Industries, and LTV all have reported inventory gluts causing financial problems. LTV, for example, had to file for bankruptcy and Guess Jeans had to restate fourth-quarter earnings.[58]

On The Drug Front

It is apparent that the so-called "War on Drugs" has been an abject failure. Although drug seizures and arrests are increasing, drug usage has escalated significantly.

In 1990, the combined efforts of the DEA (Drug Enforcement Agency), the FBI, Customs Service, the U.S. Border Patrol, and the U.S. Coast Guard resulted in the seizure of 1,704 pounds of heroin, 235,891 pounds of cocaine, and 483,353 pounds of marijuana. In 1998, almost twice as much heroin (3,384 pounds), 12% more cocaine and 3.6 times more marijuana (1,762,734 pounds) were seized.

There has been an alarming increase in the rate of arrests for possession of drugs in the last decade. In 1990, there were 295 such arrests per 100,000 U.S. inhabitants. By 1997, it had essentially doubled to 594.

Here is more disturbing news about the war on drugs:

•In 1965, the average age at which marijuana was tried for the first time was 18.8. It was 16.4 in 1996.[59]

•Heroin use is on the increase. There were an estimated 68,000 users in 1993, but the figure more than tripled to 216,000 in only three years.

•Indications are that methanphetamine usage is on the upswing.

•Stimulants, such as "Ecstasy," are in common usage among teenagers. [60]

•New designer drugs are constantly appearing. Case in point: OxyContin, a morphine-like substance that is known as the "poor man's heroin." It is a derivative of Oxycodone, a breakthrough pain killer which users use to get high on. [61]

•The increasing number of women who are being jailed for drug usage puts an incredible strain on family relationships. Many of the children involved have to be placed in foster homes.

•In 1999, there were 555,000 drug-related emergency room admissions. Illicit drugs cost the U.S. $300 billion a year in lost productivity, crime and health-care outlays (Don Feder, "Is Bush Neglecting Drug War?" *Human Events,* March 12, 2001).

On The Religious Front

Church attendance is at an all-time high, yet a Gallup poll

indicates that people saying they need to experience "spiritual growth" rose from 54% in 1994 to 82% in late 1998.

Since 1993, Gallup's "Religion in America" index has been heading upward. There are all kinds of examples: a million people attending Catholic retreat centers each year or seeking spiritual information guided by spiritual directors, recent movies or TV programs with a spiritual emphasis (Dead Men Walking, The Prince of Egypt, Seven Years in Tibet, Touched by an Angel), and the explosion of New Age sections in book stores which deal with angels, near-death experiences, reincarnation, astrology, and other paranormal claims. [62]

During the 1990s, a number of high-profile cases of Catholic priests engaging in pedophilia occurred. Indications of homosexuality among Catholic priests also bubbled to the surface. These tended to obscure the exploding number of instances in which male, Protestant clergy were guilty of adulterous relationships with women often married to a member of the clergy's congregation. [63]

On The Male-Female Relationship Front

I am probably not fully aware of the nature and extent of male-female relationships in the U.S., but what I have noticed is a trend in the last decade or so is a decrease in rapport between men and women. This decrease can take many forms—none of which are positive—less caring, less spontaneity, less sharing, less openness, less empathy—all because men are choosing to reduce the level of contact with women, i.e., withdrawing as the psychologists would say. And this phenomenon is occurring across a wide swath of venues: in the office, in the home, in public. This is a sad commentary on the current state of affairs between men and women as we head into the 21st century; it signifies a slippage in the richness of American society.

In summary, this chapter has shown that over the last three decades, the moral, physical and mental fabric of the U.S. has severely deteriorated. All of this occurred as women were gaining an increasing level of power.

It is important to note that this deterioration has occurred internally, not as a result of external factors. Historians note that rot and decay within are the usual causes for the decline of various civilizations. Tom Osborne, famed University of Nebraska football coach and currently in the U.S House of Representatives, recognized this phenomenon in a speech that was covered on C-Span, October 20, 2003. In explaining the demise of Rome and Great Britain, and the potential for the same in the United States, Osborne pointed to our decline in values, divorce rate, fatherless homes, drug usage, and rise in juvenile crime.

What has caused what can only be frankly called the decline of the United States over the last one-third of the preceding century? This question will be analyzed in the next chapter, with careful attention paid to the role played by women.

REFERENCES
1. *Human Events,* January 22, 2001.
2. National Center For Health Statistics, *Health, United States,* 1993.
3. *Statistical Abstract Of The United States.,* 1999.
4. Jacob Sullivan, "Fat Chances," *Reason,* February 1998.
5. Jacob Sullivan.
6. Catherine Arnt, "Taking The Sting Out Of Diabetes," *Business Week,* February 19, 2001.
7. Betsy Carpenter, "The Other Epidemic," *U.S. News & World Report,* November 10, 1997, pp. 78-82.
8. Betsy Carpenter.
9. *Statistical Handbook On Women,* p. 238.
10. Betsy Carpenter.
11. *USA Today,* July 21, 2000.
12. National Institutes of Mental Health as found in *2000 Time Almanac* and *International Herald Tribune,* October 11, 2000.
13. Matthew Robinson, "Bush Ed Plan Has Pluses, Minuses," *Human Events,* February 5, 2001, p. 4.
14. National Education Association estimates.
15. Gilbert M. Grosvenor, "What Happens When America Flunks Geography," *Vital Speeches Of The Day,* June 15, 1985, pp. 533-535.
16. Lucia Solorzano, "Why Johnny Can't Read Maps Either," *U.S. News & World Report,* March 25, 1985, p. 50.

17. Heritage Foundation's *Members' News,* Summer 2000.

18. National Center For Education Studies, *U.S. Department Of Education Third International Mathematics And Science Study,* 1996.

19. Gene Koretz, "The Economy's Achilles Heel," *Business Week,* November 13, 2000.

20. Sebastian Mallaby, "Two Million Behind Bars," *The World In 2001, The Economist,* 2001.

21. U.S. Bureau Of Justice Statistics, *Correctional Population In The United States.*

22. Kevin Johnson, "Party Is Over As Decline In Crime Hits Bottom," *USA Today,* December 19, 2000.

23. Kevin Johnson.

24. Kevin Johnson.

25. Kevin Johnson.

26. Toni Locy, "Like Mother, Like Daughter," *U.S. News & World Report,* October 4, 1999, pp. 18-27. *USA Today,* October 16, 2000.

27. Statistical Abstract of the United States, 2002."

28. See Scott Park, "Clinton-Era Morale Crisis Grips U.S. Military," *Human Events,* January 21, 2000.

29. Elaine Donnelly, "Women In Combat—Time For A Review," *The American Legion Magazine,* July 2000, pp.12-16.

30. Bill Stephens, "Divorce—How It Affects Children," *Answer Magazine,* October 1999, pp. 2-3, 6.

31. Bill Stephens.

32. Jonathan Rauch, "When Did You See Your Father Last?," *The World In 2001, The Economist,* 2001.

33. *Statistical Abstract Of The United States,* 2001.

34. *Statistical Abstract Of The United States,* 2001.

35. *Statistical Abstract Of The United States,* 2001.

36. *Statistical Abstract Of The United States,* 2001.

37. *Sex And America's Teenagers,* The Alan Guttmacher Institute, 1994.

38. Paula Rinehart, "Losing Our Promiscuity," *Christianity Today,* July 10, 2000, pp. 32-39.

39. Paula Rinehart.

40. *Statistical Abstract Of The United States,* 2001.

41. The full text of Mr. Halperin's speech is available in Hillsdale College's *Imprimis,* January 2001.

42. *Russia's Road To Corruption,* Speaker's Advisory Group On Russia, U.S. House Of Representatives, Washington D.C., September 2000.

43. The Christopher Cox Report On China, U.S. House Of Representatives, 1999.

44. *Claremont Review,* Fall 2000.

45. Matthew Robinson, "Clinton-Gore Caused Our Pain," *Human Events*, October 6, 2000.

46. *Publications And Events*, Cato Institute, September, October 2000.

47. *Cato Memorandum*, May 8, 2000.

48. *Judicial Watch*, October 2000.

49. Jack Van Impe, *2001: On The Edge Of Eternity*, Word Publishing, Dalls, 1996, pp. 77-78.

50. John Hechinger and William Bulkeley, "Weakened Xerox To Sell Assets To Strengthen Balance Sheet," *European Wall Street Journal*, October 5, 2000.

51. Dean Foust, "CEO Pay: Nothing Succeeds Like Failure," *Business Week*, September 11, 2000 and "Let's Talk Turkey," *Business Week*, December 11, 2000.

52. Christine Tierney, "Can Schrempp Stop The Careening At Chrysler?," *Business Week*, December 4, 2000.

53. David Welch, "GM: 'Out With The Olds,' Is Just The Start," *Business Week*, December 25, 2000.

54. Diane Brady, "Who Does Linda Wachner Answer To?," *Business Week*, August 7, 2000, p. 37.

55. Laurie P. Cohen, "U.S. To Face Obstacles In Effort To Prosecute Taubman," *European Wall Street Journal*, October 9, 2000.

56. Peter Burrows, "Can Fiorina Reboot HP?," *Business Week*, November 27, 2000 and Peter Burrows, "The Radical—Carly Fiorina's Bold Management Experiment At HP," *Business Week*, February 19, 2000.

57. Steven Butler, "Fueled By Debt, The Economy Roars On," *U.S. News & World Report*. September 18, 2000.

58. Andy Serwer, "Glut Check," *Fortune*, March 5, 2001.

59. SAMSHA, Office Of Applied Studies, *National Household Survey On Drug Abuse*, 1994-1997.

60. National Institute On Drug Abuse.

61. Gary Cohen, "The Poor Man's Heroin," *U.S. News & World Report*, February 12, 2001.

62. David G. Myers, "More Age Of Plenty," *Christianity Today*, April 24, 2000.

63. Kenneth L. Woodward, "Gender & Religion—Who's Really Running The Show?," *Commonweal*, November 22, 1996.

SEVEN

Why?

"It is even more the case now that radical feminists have succeeded in making some women feel that they have a moral obligation to hate men with the same intensity that Nazis felt for Jews and Communists for the bourgeoisie." Paul Craig Roberts

"Certainly, there is a suspiciously close correlation between the rise in women's employment and their earning power relative to that of men, on the one hand, and the rise in marital breakdown on the other." *The Economist.*

"It is seldom that liberty is lost all at once." David Hume

Why has the U.S. gone down the slippery slope toward mediocrity, or even worse? While many of our problems can be attributed to the attitudes and actions of the female *majority* in America over the preceding three decades, men are also culpable.

The average man is involved with two major areas of life: his work and his family. In setting these priorities and, in an effort to be successful in both arenas, he has to give up something. That something is often the time to reflect on, and adjust to, the changes in our society—in its culture, politics, religion, and so on. In other words, his work-and-family "tunnel vision" causes him to not be aware of many of those forces which strongly impact his world and that of his family.

The changes that do get through his filter are often viewed as inconsequential because he has ignored their cumulative effect. This latter failing is quite analogous to the frog example that is familiar to many of us. A frog is placed in an aquarium with water which is added to incrementally with ever-increasing temperatures. Because each additional dousing is only slightly hotter than what the frog's body has gotten used to, he doesn't realize he is in danger until he is boiling to death. In a speech at Hillsdale College (Michigan), Walter E. Williams, the economist who is the John M. Olin distinguished professor of economics at George Mason University, aptly captures this concept when discussing the increasing power of the federal government: "If you take tiny steps toward a goal, one day you will get there, and the ultimate end of this process is totalitarianism, which is no more than a reduced form of servitude." Williams solidifies his point by quoting philosopher David Hume: "It is seldom that liberty is lost all at once."

So, many men, in their preoccupation with work and family, do not have a clear idea as to the peril they and their loved ones face. This is a classic example of sins of omission. While bad enough, it pales against the sins of commission committed by women. Let's see what these have been over the last 30 years.

✳ Women Break God's Laws

God has promulgated laws to help us, not to punish us by not letting us have fun. Some of these laws are physical, others—our concern here—deal with cultural issues, especially the relationship between men and women. Whatever the type of law, God's warning is clear: When His laws are broken, the law-breaker suffers as, unfortunately, as do often those persons affected by the sin.

Let's see what the Bible has to say about the relationships between husbands and wives, and men and women in society, with the understanding that if we follow God's ordinances we and our society will flourish; if we don't, we will have to suffer the consequences.

A good place to always start is at the beginning—in the book of Genesis. It is clear that God first created man (Adam), *then* the woman (Eve), and that Eve was created to be a companion for Adam and that she was created in order to *help* Adam: "And the Lord God said, It is not good that the man should be alone; I will make him an *help meet* for him"(Gen. 2:18) (emphasis added). The *World Book Dictionary* defines "help meet" as "help mate," and "help mate" is defined as a "companion and helper." The "help mate" definition states that it is "perhaps an alteration of help meet." The New International Version of the Bible is much less equivocal than the King James Version; it simply says "The Lord God said, "It is not good for the man to be alone. I will make a *helper suitable for him.*" I think that it is important to note, additionally, in the NIV translation that God is providing man with a "suitable" helper; the *World Book Dictionary* defines "suitable" as "fitting" or "appropriate." In other words, God was not shortchanging man but, rather, was truly interested in his well being by providing him with a person *uniquely qualified* to assist him.

Genesis contains a description of Adam being put into a leadership role by God; there is no example in Genesis of Eve being given a leadership responsibility. Genesis 2: 19-20 tells the story of God asking Adam to name *"every living creature"* (emphasis added) that God had created. "And Adam gave names to all cattle, and to the fowl of the air, and to every beast of the field" (Gen. 2:20). How well did he do? Apparently, very well, for Gen. 2:19 tells us "and whatsoever Adam called every living creature, that was the name thereof."

Additional light is shed on the relationship between man and woman in the telling of their fall in the third chapter of Genesis. The serpent (Satan) is described in Gen. 3:1 as being "more subtle than any beast of the field which the Lord God had made." *Webster's Universal College Dictionary* defines subtle as "characterized by or requiring mental acuteness, penetration, or discernment; cunning, wily or crafty; insidious in operation; skillful, clever or ingenious." Given these characteristics of Satan, it is likely that he carefully planned his assault in order to maximize the potential success of his mission which was to get Adam and Eve to disobey God by eating of the tree of the knowledge of good and evil, which God had forbidden them to do (Gen. 2:16-17): "And the Lord God commanded the man saying, of every tree of the garden thou mayest freely eat: But of the tree of good and evil, thou shalt not eat of it: for in the day thou eatest thereof thou shalt surely die".

Isn't it obvious that Satan would approach the weaker of the two in order to attain his nefarious objective? He chose Eve, she succumbed, and got her husband to also eat the forbidden fruit. The fact that Eve was approached first, capitulated before Adam, and then ensnared him in no way lessens Adam's guilt and failure as the *leader* of his family. As the designated leader by God, he had the obligation to make sure that his wife so understood the gravity of God's warning that she would not be beguiled by Satan. Also, even though Eve had sinned, Adam should not, himself, eaten of the fruit. Adam's sin was actually more grievous than Eve's because although she was deceived, Adam was not; he apparently knew precisely what he was doing. I Tim. 2:14 says "And Adam was not deceived...." In fact, it is *Adam's sin* which is blamed for the sinful, fallen state of all mankind: "Wherefore, as by *one man* sin entered into the world, and death by sin, and so death passed upon all men, for all have sinned" (Rom. 5:12) (emphasis added).

When God commanded that the fruit from the tree of knowledge of good and evil not be eaten, doesn't it make sense that he would be certain to get this message to the person in the leadership role? Look carefully at Genesis 2:16 as indicated above. God commanded *the man* not to eat of the forbidden fruit. In fact, if verses 16-22 are in chronological order—and they appear to be— Eve was not created until *after* Adam had received this stern admonition from God. This chronology is strongly suggested as one reads I Tim. 2:13-14: "For Adam was first formed, then Eve. And Adam was not deceived, but the woman, being deceived, was in the transgression." A major responsibility of Adam's, then, would have been for him to have articulated this warning in no uncertain terms to Eve.

After committing this sin, Adam and Eve, for the first time, realized that they were naked. And so they clothed themselves in fig leaves. Upon hearing the voice of God, they hid themselves. When God became aware of what Adam and Eve had done— eaten of the forbidden fruit—the person addressed was *Adam, not Eve:* "And the Lord God called *unto Adam,* and said *unto him,* where art thou" (Gen. 3:7-9; emphasis added)? As befitting Adam's leadership role, he was called on the carpet first.

The most direct indication in Genesis of what male and female responsibilities are in society is contained in the verses which describe the punishment for the two transgressors. Genesis 3:16 says "Unto the woman, he said, I will greatly multiply thy sorrow and thy conception; in sorrow thou shalt bring forth children; and *thy desire shall be to thy husband, and he shall rule over thee"* (emphasis added). This relationship is succinctly and strongly reiterated in the New Testament: "Neither was the man created for the woman; but the *woman for the man"* (emphasis added; 1 Cor. 11:9). In both the *Schofield* and *Ryrie Study Bible,* the reader, when confronting this passage, is referred to Genesis 2:18: "And the Lord God said, It is not good that the man should be alone; I will make him an *help meet* for him"(emphasis added).

It is important to note, in meting out punishment, that God did not open up the notion of women working by referring to them having to work by the sweat of their brow; this was specifically reserved for man (Genesis 3:19: "In the sweat of thy face shalt thou eat bread . . ."). The child bearing dictum at least, implicitly, places women in the home-making role, not working outside the home.

Let's take a look at another husband-wife account in the Bible, an account that has had almost as tragic consequences as the Adam and Eve scenario. This is another example of what happens when wives attempt and succeed in taking a leadership role in the household through husbands' caving in to their wishes which are contrary to the will of God. Abraham had no male heir. However, God told him that he would have an heir and he, Abraham, would be the father of many: "Look now toward heaven, and count the stars, if thou be able to number them: and he said unto him, so shall thy seed be (Gen. 15:5). Abraham believed what the Lord had told him and "he counted it to him for righteousness" (Gen. 15:6).

Sarah, his wife, however, became impatient (a common trait of wives and women in the United States in the 21st century) and devised a scheme that would supposedly satisfy *her* longing for children. She advised Abraham to take her Egyptian handmaid, Hagar, for a wife and have children by her. Sarah's words were; "I pray thee, go in unto my handmaid; it may be that I may obtain children by her" (Gen. 16:2). And, unfortunately, Abraham listened to his wife and, in so doing, disbelieved God. Hagar conceived and bore Abraham a son, Ishmael. Whereupon, Sarah perceived that she was despised in Hagar's eyes (a classic case of be careful what you wish for because you may get it?).

Later, God told Abraham that his posterity, which involved the lineage to Jesus Christ, would not come through Ishmael but, instead, through his son, Isaac, eventually born to him and Sarah as God had promised. Ishmael and his mother were taken by Abraham as ordered by God and abandoned in the wilderness of Beersheba. At that time, a merciful and just God supplied all of their needs and, in time, as promised by God, Ishmael became the father of a great nation himself. And, in fact, this has, indeed, occurred. Ishmael is the father of the Arabs and, of course, Isaac is the father of the Jews, Abraham the father of both.

I am sure that I do not need to describe for the reader the fallout from the enmity which has existed between the Arabs and Jews for the last 3,500 years; the papers everyday are filled with it. Making the situation even more volatile is the fact that Mohammed, the founder of the Moslem religion, is a descendant of Ishmael. And, today, we are all aware of the impact on the United States from the world of Moslem extremists. All of this grief because Sarah attempted to usurp Abraham's God-ordained leadership role—and succeeded—because Abraham acquiesced; he did not exercise leadership as God had ordained him to do.

The New Testament provides further confirmation of what the relationship between husbands and wives is supposed to be. Ephesians 5:22-24, 33 says, "Wives, submit yourselves unto your own husbands, as unto the Lord. For the husband is the head of the wife, even as Christ is the head of the Church; and he is the savior of the body. Therefore, as the Church is subject unto Christ, so let the wives be to their own husbands in everything" (Eph. 5:22-24). "And the wife, see that she reverence her husband" (Eph. 5:33). While these admonitions are directed to wives in general, similar instructions are reserved for older wives: "Likewise, teach the older women to be reverent in the way they live, not to be slanderers or addicted to much wine, but to teach what is good. Then they can train the younger women to love their husbands and children, to be self controlled and pure, to be busy at home, to be kind, *and to be subject to their husbands*, so that no one will malign the word of God (Titus 2:3, emphasis added).

It is critical to note that these commands are *not conditional;* they do not come with a promise of a reward. Wives are not supposed to submit if they feel like it, their husbands make $500,000 a year, they grant their wives their every wish, they take them out to eat five nights a week, or the husband does all of the housework and child rearing. Nor is it suggested that wives will become wealthy or happy or exalted if they subject themselves to their husbands.

In clearly recognizing what the Bible has to say on the subject, the Southern Baptists endorsed a statement at their 1998 convention that "wives should submit graciously to their husbands." After asserting that the husband is the provider, protector and *leader* of the family, the statement reads: "A wife is to submit graciously to the servant leadership of her husband even as the church willingly submits to the headship of Christ." Mary Mohler, wife of Southern Baptist Theological Seminary president, R. Albert Mohler, Jr., feels that submitting to her husband's authority is "my duty and my glad responsibility," a sentiment endorsed by Dorothy Patterson, wife of Paige Patterson, the newly elected president of the Southern Baptists, who takes it one step further when she said: "As a woman standing under the authority of scripture, even when it comes to submitting to my husband when I know he's wrong, I just have to do it," (*Bryan-College Station Eagle*, June 15, 2002, pp. 1-2)

The leadership role for the man is not a one-way street. Ephesians 5:25, 28, 31, and 33 says: "Husbands, love your wives, even as Christ also loved the Church, and gave himself for it (v. 25). So men ought to love their wives as their own bodies. He that loveth his wife loveth himself (v. 28). For this cause shall a man leave his father and mother, and shall be joined unto his wife, and they two shall be one flesh (v. 31). Nevertheless, let every one of you in particular so love his wife even as himself; and the wife, see that she reverence her husband" (v. 33).

Here's the way the submission/leadership concept needs to work in a marriage. Husbands and wives need to communicate with each other often about the goals that they want their marriage to achieve and how these will be accomplished. Hopefully—but not likely—there will be total agreement on these matters. When this does not occur, wives should reiterate their reasoning, then leave it to the husband to make the final decision and not whine and carp if the decision is not what they wanted. Believe me, the husband will remember the wife's position if his decision turns out to be the wrong one and he will probably be more responsive to her wishes in the future.

Of course, the radical feminists and the great number of women who have swallowed their insidious agenda don't want to even hear about what the Bible has to say, let alone embrace the fact that men are supposed to be the leaders and decision makers in a marriage and in society. These women do so, however, at their peril for many marriage counselors believe that the factor most likely to cause major fissures in a marriage is the inability of partners to resolve the issue of *control,* that is, who is the boss (the leader and decision maker). Perhaps the radical feminists and their legions of female followers don't really care if marriages fall apart. An advertisement for subscriptions to the *New Oxford Review,* a conservative,

Catholic publication which appeared in *Human Events*, claims that the "head of the flagship feminist organization, the National Organization for Women, says that 'maybe half' of NOW's members are lesbians."

A major controversy raging for some time is the role that women should play in the church; it is splitting many Protestant denominations asunder. The Bible takes a clear stand on this issue. God's word says in I Tim. 2: 11-12, in a section of the Bible dealing with *Instructions about Prayer and the Place of Women in the Church* (*Schofield Bible*): "Let the woman learn in silence with all subjection. But I permit not a woman to teach, nor to usurp authority over the man, but to be in silence."

Conservative Protestant churches allude to this scripture to justify their denying women the role of pastor, a position which appears to be in line with the above scripture (I Tim. 2: 11-12), as well as, in the passages dealing with the qualifications for two other important offices in the church, bishops and deacons. About bishops, I Timothy 3: 1-2 states: "There is a true saying, if a *man* desire the office of a bishop, *he* desireth a good work. A bishop must be blameless, the *husband* of one wife, temperate, sober-minded, of good behavior, given to hospitality, apt to teach" (emphases added). Clearly, the position of bishop (elder) is restricted to males, as is the *position of deacon*. I Timothy 3: 8-12 reads: "In like manner must the deacon be grave, not double-tongued, not given to much wine, not greedy of filthy lucre, holding the mystery of the faith in a pure conscience. And let these also be proved; then let them use the office of a deacon, being found blameless. Even so must *their wives* be grave, not slanderous, sober-minded, faithful in all things. Let the deacons be the *husband* of one wife, ruling their children and their own houses well" (emphases added).

The early disciples of Christ recognized this restriction when the first seven deacons were elected in order to take care of the widows of the Greek disciples. The 12 disciples (Peter, Andrew, John, etc.—all men) felt that it would not be prudent for them to have this responsibility because it would take them away from the "word of God," so Stephen, Philip, Procorus, Nicanor, Timon, Parmenas, and Nicolas—all Greek *men*—were chosen as the first deacons (see Acts 6:1-5).

What is the implication of God's limiting the offices of elders and deacons to men only? Obviously, if only men can be elders and deacons—which are church offices of lower stature than pastors—then women are not authorized to be pastors because of what I Tim. 2: 11-12 says about women's place in the church: "Let the woman learn in silence with all subjection. But I permit not a woman to teach, *nor to usurp authority over the man*, but to be in silence" (emphasis added).

Kenneth L. Woodward, *Newsweek's* religion editor, cogently presents the argument for women not serving as pastors: "Like it or not, congregations are also institutions that require the exercise of authority and demand that some distance be observed between those who stand in the pulpit and those who sit in the pews, traits that are more likely to be associated with men (Kenneth L. Woodward, "Gender and Religion—Who's Really Running the Show?," *Commonweal*, November 22, 1996, pp. 9-14.).

Are women "buying into" what God has to say concerning husband/wife and male/female relationships? Hardly! In 1995, the Virginia Slims opinion poll, conducted by Roper Starch Worldwide, found that 86% of women agreed with the statement, "It's no longer fair for men to be the sole decision maker in the household."

In 1994, the National Opinion Research Center of the University of Chicago conducted a major study of women's beliefs. One third of the respondents expressed some doubt about whether they believed in God; for women ages 18-29, the number was 42%. For sure, those women expressing some doubt about God's existence are not going to recognize God's laws regarding the mandated relationship between husband and wife and men and women. And even though a majority of women in this survey said they had no doubts about the existence of God, this is no guarantee that even these women will buy into God's expectations. In this regard, it is important to understand that, like it or not, any woman who is in rebellion against her husband—whether she believes in God or not—is, at the same time, in rebellion against God. For example it has been estimated that two out of every three *Christian* couples either separate or divorce.

In the fall of 2000, I received a newsletter from a local pastor, C. Russell Yates, who heads up the Family Foundation Ministry and has a Saturday morning radio program. Mr. Yates had grappled for 30 years with a wife who refused to yield to his Biblically-inspired authority and finally decided that he was justified in leaving her. Here is what he has to say about marriage with rebellious wives:

> Instead of complementing one another, they compete. But the woman often ends up dominating the man—she takes over. When that happens, the man is subjected to an emotional castration that makes it impossible for him to fulfill his God-given call. When a man is being castrated on a daily basis, he can also be pretty hard to live with. If a rebellious wife is allowed to continue, she will disrupt the home and contaminate the children. Researchers who have studied the home life of homosexuals and lesbians have discovered that almost always the pattern is a dominant mother and a passive father.[1]

No better (worse?) example of women breaking God's laws can be found with their reproduction "rights." Abortion (killing) contravenes God's laws and we have had over 41 million abortions since 1970 because women are not in harmony with God's mandates. Having children out of wedlock is another example of women breaking God's laws; it has been estimated that one third of children born in the United States will have an unwed mother *(The Economist World In 2001).*

Men Buy Into The Phoney Mystique Of Women

Women have been portrayed throughout history and currently, as well, as being super heroes, goddesses, as paragons of virtue, saviors, able to defend and protect due to the attributes of power and goodness. Societies that have been identified as matriarchal are often viewed as being benevolent and peaceful. Unfortunately, much of this is legend, wishful thinking, or downright misrepresentation.

Isis was the Egyptian goddess of fertility, usually represented as wearing a cow's horns and solar disk on her head. Ishtar was the chief goddess of Babyon and Assyria, the goddess of love and fertility, sometimes of war. Astarte was the goddess of fertility and love of the ancient Semites. She was known as Ashtoreth to the Hebrews.

But what is the truth about these females? The worship of Isis involved the annual drowning of a young virgin girl in the Nile in the hope for an abundant harvest. Ishtar's priestesses were temple slaves. Ashteroth supposedly had 70 children by the god, El—her brother. The worship of Ashteroth's son, Baal, involved the sacrifice of children in the worship services of the Canaanites who worshipped Baal.

But perhaps the most pronounced and widespread example of worship of females involves the Virgin Mary who is often, mistakenly, substituted for the Lord Jesus Christ as the way to obtain salvation.

Ascribing goddess-like qualities to women obscures the fact that, like men, women are sinners. For example, Barbara Ehrenreich, in reviewing Francis Fukuyama's article in *Foreign Affairs,* states that, historically, women have abused their children and committed infanticide (remember Andrea Yates), "mutilate the genitals of little girls, and cruelly tyrannize daughters, daughters-in-law, servants and slaves.... Historically, culture organized around war and displays of cruelty have had women's full cooperation."[2]

Don't make the mistake of assuming that women in present-day America don't buy into the goddess/saviour argument. Vice-president Al Gore reported that his wife, Tipper, when talking to one of their daughters, Karenna, about the cartoon character, Mighty Mouse, would become incensed because the girl mouse always had to be rescued by Mightly Mouse, the boy mouse. "Tipper would patiently explain to Karenna, no, no, no, that the girl mouse could take care of herself."[3]

Speaking of comic books, let's not forget Wonder Woman, the "first great comic book heroine, a displaced Amazon princess who helped the Allies defeat the Axis powers while seeking romance on the side." The creator of Wonder Woman was William Marston, a Harvard trained psychologist who also had a law degree; Marston was a strong early advocate of the lie detector and developed a prototype. He had four children, two by his wife and two by a mistress, Olive Richard, who lived with Marston and his wife. Marston viewed comic books as a way to get kids to read, but he had a sinister motive, as well, "to circulate radical feminine notions." He stated that the most "constructive comics were those that laid the groundwork for...... the coming age of 'American matriarchy in which women would *take over the rule of the country,* politically and economically'" (emphasis added).[4]

Some of the greatest figures in religion, philosophy and literature have been reluctant to buy into the deification of women. "In fact, the belief that women were less moral, less responsible than men has been an ancient and enduring theme in Western civilization." For example:

1. Virgil wrote that women are always fickle and unreliable (Varium et mutabile semper femina).

2. The apostle Paul wrote in the letter to Timothy: "But I permit not a woman to teach nor usurp authority over the man, but to be in silence" (I Timothy 2: 12).

3. St. Thomas Aquinas: "Woman is ... an imperfect being. Women are born to be eternally maintained under the yoke of their lords and masters, who are endowed by nature with superiority in every respect, and therefore destined to rule."

4. Philosopher Arthur Schopenhauer: "The fundamental defect of the female character is the lack of a sense of justice .... Fundamentally, women exist solely for the propagation of the race and find in this their complete fulfillment."

5. Alfred Lord Tennyson: "Man to command and women to obey; all else is confusion."[5]

Under Jewish law, around the time of Christ, the testimony of women was considered to be so unreliable that they were forbidden to testify in court (Lee Strobel, *The Case For Faith,* Zondervan Publishing House, Grand Rapids, Michigan, 2000, p. 82).

Women's Sins Are Excused or Covered Up

If we turn a blind eye to the sins committed by women in aborting their babies, it's an easy stretch to absolve them of other despicable crimes, such as, killing their young children. Between 1976 and 1999, mothers killed 4,118 children under five years of age; men murdered slightly more, 4,179. What happens to these women? Not much, according to Patricia Pearson, author of *When She Was Bad: Violent Women And The Myth Of Innocence:* "Of those who are convicted, about two-thirds avoid prison, and the rest receive an average sentence of seven years." Here are two high-profile examples, both of which made the national news because of their utter depravity:

1. Eighteen year-old Melissa Drexler murdered her new-born son by throwing him into a toilet bowl and strangling him with a conveniently available umbilical cord. She then pitched him into a garbage bin so she could dine and dance the night away. She was released from prison after serving only 37 months of a 15-year sentence for manslaughter.

2. Amy Grossberg and her high-school sweetheart, Brian Peterson, murdered their new-born son by stuffing him into a plastic bag and tossing him into a dumpster. Amy was out after serving all of 22 months.

Where do the feminists stand on the issue of "Mommy" child killers? Nancy Pfotenhauer, president of the Independent Women's Forum, says: 'The same liberals who purport to be advocates of everyone's children, in almost a collective approach, in individual cases embrace the mother regardless of what she has done.' Columnist Cathy Young decries the 'insidious brand of so-called feminism that absolves women of all responsibility for their actions.' Young's comments are right on in regard to Angela Yates, the Houston mother who murdered her five young children. (According to police, she chased two of them around the house before overpowering them and then drowning them in the bath tub). The National Organization for Women (NOW) held a candle-light vigil outside Yates' cell. NOW's president, Kim Gandy, suggests that the problem was that Yates' health insurance was insufficient to cure her of post-partum depression. "Today Show's Katie Couric urged viewers to contribute to Yates' legal fund." (Deroy Murdock, "Letting Baby Killers Off With A Slap On The Wrist And A Hug," *Washington Times,* December 17-23, 2001).

No better example of a cover up of women's sins occurs in the area of child abuse. The average person assumes that men are the gender most guilty of child abuse; it benefits women if men are viewed as the offender. But the truth about child abuse was cap-tured in an article by Stephen Baskerville, professor of political science at Howard University, that appeared in *Human Events,* April 29, 2002. Drawing upon a study conducted by the respected Heri-tage Foundation (authors Patrick Fagan and Dorothy Hanks), the 1996 book by Maggie Gallagher, *The Abolition of Marriage,* and comments by Kinaya Sokoya, director of the D.C. Children's Trust Fund, Baskerville states:

1. Child abuse is more likely to occur in a single-parent home.

2. "Research shows that the most likely physical abuser of a young child will be that child's mother, not a male in the house-hold" (emphasis added). 'Almost *two-thirds* of child abusers were *females*' (emphases added).

3. "Most child abusers first eliminate the father through uni-lateral divorce or separation, whereupon they can abuse *his* children with impunity" (emphasis added).

4. The safest venue for a child is a two-parent home that con-tains the biological father. "Biological fathers seldom abuse their children."

5. Courts routinely grant women's demands for separation or divorce. Child abuse goes up and government officials can then espouse the government as saviors; they, thus, have ammunition to get more tax payer funds and more workers, some of whom

have been known to abuse children themselves.

Radical Feminists Spew Out Their Anti-Male, Anti-God, Anti-Conservative Agenda

Most people associate the start of the feminist movement in the United States with the publication of Betty Friedan's book, *The Feminine Mystique.* Friedan and the other feminists who followed her pushed for female participation in the work force and equal pay as the means to escape the drudgery of housework. Ms. Friedan, however, may have been predated by Anne Lindbergh, Charles Lindbergh's wife, whose book, *Gift From The Sea,* reputedly foreshadowed the growth of the feminist movement; in it, she wrote that the routine of the home "destroys the soul."[6] In actuality, Ms. Friedan and Ms. Lindbergh were late on the scene; the true instigators of feminism were the suffragettes, whose efforts resulted in women securing the right to vote in 1920 through the ratification of the Constitution's 19th amendment.

Feminism has gone far beyond its initial objective of equality. Here are some examples, many of which, ironically, are provided by females involved with the feminist movement:

•In discussing Carol Gilligan's book, *In A Different Voice,* Barbara Eisenreich says "It stimulated efforts to restrict male behavior, stigmatizes males as generally brash and insensitive ...."[7]

•Jennifer Roback Morse, research fellow at the Hoover Institution, says that feminism "is the ideological veil for a political special interest group. This group is able to influence the outcomes of elections and legislative deliberations, and to generate patronage political appointments for its constituents." In discussing Norma Cantu's appointment to the Office of Civil Rights, Department of Education, she says that Cantu's "most expansive interpretation on definitions of discrimination and harassment create numerous opportunities for feminist attorneys to generate cases and earn legal fees. NOW, in essence, is in the business of ambulance chasing."[8]

•"On issues ranging from domestic violence to sexual harassment to divorce, the women's movement wants the law and society to view men as villains and women as their victims."[9]

•Rush Limbaugh: "Radical feminists are simply an *anti-male, pro-abortion attack team* masquerading as a legitimate advocacy group for all women." [10]

•Paul Craig Roberts, Senior Research Fellow with the Hoover Institution, says this about the feminist movement: "It is even more the case now that radical feminists have succeeded in making some women feel that they have a moral obligation to hate men with the same intensity that Nazis felt for Jews and Communists for the bourgeoisie." [11]

•Leonard Sax, PhD and M.D., asks about feminists: "What are they after? If you read what their leaders say, you get the impression that their paradise would be a world *without men*" (emphasis added).[12]

•Feminist Daphne Patai acknowledges that "it is plain and irrefutable that much contemporary feminism is indeed marred by hostility toward men. The virulence of it varies from group to group. But the antagonism is *pervasive*" (emphasis added).[13]

The radical feminist aims are pushed by a propaganda machine that is second to none and is bolstered by a supportive media which is controlled by women and biased toward their agenda.

The amount of information touting the causes of women in general and the radical feminists in particular is prodigious. A man can hardly go a day without being bombarded with their propaganda in some form or another—television, radio, magazines, newspapers, web sites, conferences, symposia, etc. And the number of women's organizations boggles the mind.

Here are some examples I noted as a member of the faculty at Texas A&M University. *Women in Discovery* was a symposium held on March 22, 2000. Touted as a "month-long celebration of Marie Curie's scientific and personal achievements," the symposium, as you might well imagine, was dominated by women. Except for a brief welcoming speech by the University's male executive vice president and provost, the participants were all female: Helene Langevin-Joliot, the grand daughter of Pierre and Marie Curie, and director of research emeritus, National Center for Scientific Research, Paris; Rosalyn Sussman-Yalow, 1977 Nobel prize winner in medicine for her work in the techniques of radioimmunoassay; Nancy W. Dickey, immediate past president, American Medical Association; and Shirley Jackson, president, Rennselaer Polytechnic Institute and former chair of the U.S. Nuclear Regulatory Commission. Panel members included Bonnie Dunbar, Carol Gross, Heidi Hammel, Mae Jemison (astronaut), and Carol Nacy. In March of 2000, the University celebrated Women's Week with a display, Rural Texas Women at Work, 1930-1960. "The award winning exhibit of photographs from the University archives portrays women engaged in all aspects of rural life from plowing to canning. Samples of equipment are part of the display." Here's another example:

Come and celebrate the diversity of women during March with Women's Spirit Month 2002. Many enlightening events geared toward women's interests support the 2002 theme, 'A Celebration of our Diversity' honoring National Women's History Month. A March 1st luncheon and awards ceremony will kickoff festivities with featured speaker Rebecca Walker. Named one of the 'future leaders of America' by *Time*, Ms. Walker has achieved recognition as an author and TV personality engaged in issues regarding young women's leadership and activism. Her talk, 'To Be Real: Changing the Face of Feminism,' is sure to inspire women of all ages. Other highlights include: a series of brown bag luncheons spotlighting 'Challenges of Female Athletes,' 'A 'History of Women's History at Texas A&M,' and 'American Women's Perspective: Living in Kuwait;' The Vagina Monologues, featuring local women performing the powerful, hilarious and provocative monologues from the theatre production by the same name;' the exhibit opening of 'Intended for All: 125 Years of Women at Texas A&M', and a 'Women's Celebration of Art,' to be held in the MSC Flag Room....

Since 1994, the Texas A&M community has been celebrating women's achievements with what was first a week-long event that expanded to a full month of festivities in 1999. This year, Women's Spirit Month continues to provide a stimulating schedule of events highlighting the many issues and interests that define women's lives.

Woman are taking advantage of computer technology. Here are some of their web sites: Abortion and Preproductive Rights, Gender and Sexuality, Institute for Women's Policy Research, The National Gay and Lesbian Task Force, Violence Against Women, Women's Bureau, Women's International Center, WW Women and, of course, the National Organization for Women.

How many women's organizations are there? Who knows? Pages 259-390 of the *Encyclopedia Of Women's Associations Worldwide* lists 1,027 different groups in the United States, including:

Alliance of Minority Women for Business and Political Development
Alliance for Women Bikers
American Library Association—Women's Studies Sections
American Mathematical Society—Joint Committee on Women in the Mathematical Sciences
American Medical Women's Association (AMWA)
American Musicological Society—Committee on the Status of Women
Clearinghouse on Femicide
Clearinghouse on Women's Issues
Equality Now
Equity Policy Center
Ex-Partners of Servicemen (Women) for Equality (EXPOSE)
Gay and Lesbian Parents Coalition International
Gay Nurses' Alliance
Institute of Electrical and Electronics Engineers—Task Force on Women and Minorities
Institute for Feminist Studies
Institute for Research on Women's Health
Hispanic Women's Council
Hollywood Women's Political Committee
National Network of Minority Women in Science
Women in Government Relations

Women Grocers of America

Women on Wine (WOW)

To be sure, many of the women's organizations in America are small and exist on contributions from members. Many are charitable in their orientations and have no axe to grind vis-á-vis men. Unfortunately, there are contrary organizations, many of which came to light when they manifested strong opposition to John Ashcroft (Christian, conservative, pro-life) as attorney general.

And here's the real zinger. These organizations receive money—big money-from the Federal Government—oops, from you, guys, the taxpayers. Planned Parenthood, the largest abortion mill in the U.S., got $10 million in 1996, $9 million in 1997, $16 million in 1998, and $27 million in 1999. The National Education Association (the teachers' union dominated by women with an anti-boy, anti-male bias) gets $1 million a year. Others that get your tax dollars include the Feminist Majority Foundation, National Black Women's Health Project, National Coalition Against Domestic Violence, National Council of Jewish Women and, of course, our old friend, the National Organization for Women (its Legal Defense and Education Fund).[14]

Pro-female propaganda is calculated to achieve females' desired ends. Recall two ads discussed earlier in this book. There is the long-running radio ad, sponsored by the Ad Council and the Women's College Coalition, that pushed for more girls in math and science. Using a female medical examiner, we are told "a girl can be any kind of scientist" and we are exhorted to "turn your daughter on to math and science." And there is the CNBC ad touting their program, "Powerful Business Women in Europe," which shows a winsome girl of eight or nine saying, "I want to be the boss of all things."

We noted in Chapter Four that at least half of the middle management employees at film studios and television networks are female, the same for editors, reporters and technical writers. Leonard Sax puts it much less charitably: "They are *infiltrating* the media" (emphasis added), suggesting that there may be hostile intent toward men. Indeed, Sax adds: "Now they can proceed to brainwash society as a whole."[15] The double whammy for men is that not only are the media controlled by women, but dominated by liberals. (Obviously, there is much overlap in these two categories, that is, most women are liberal). But, hold onto your hats, men, things will probably get a lot worse, In April of 2001, Barbra Streisand announced that she was seeking *Democratic* investors for a new cable TV news network.

Rush Limbaugh, in a promotional piece touting his newsletter, reports on a vote taken by the Society of Professional Journalists as to whether they should cover both sides of an issue. They voted against the resolution. Limbaugh also calls the radical feminists the "femi-nazis" and asserts that they are holding the mainstream media hostage. Larry Elder, a radio talk-show host on KABC, Los Angeles, speaking at a Cato Institute Book Forum, stated: "There is absolutely no question that there is a liberal bias in the media." He cites the results of a survey to prove his point. In 1996, 89% of Washington D.C. journalists said they had voted for Bill Clinton in 1992. This was more than double the figure of all voters (43%) who voted for Clinton. In that election, 38% of the U.S. voters opted for George Bush; only 7% of Washington D.C. journalists did.[16] According to Jennifer Roback Morse, the press always treats feminists with kid gloves, not asking them the tough questions leveled at other special interest groups like the tobacco industry or the National Rifle Association.[17] Dissident feminist reporter, Robyn Blumner, of the *St. Petersburg Times* and a syndicated columnist for Tribune Media Services, states that "so many of the shibboleths about men being bad and women being good, women being victims and men being oppressors, are inaccurate. Even so, popular culture is full of such images, as in the television show, *Men Behaving Badly*. The theme seems to have resonance." [18]

Women In The Military Have Weakened Our National Defense

In the previous chapter, we saw how unprepared our military became while the Clinton administration and the sycophantic women's groups pushed the social agenda of getting more females into the armed forces. Unfortunately, the achievement of this dubious objective wreaked havoc in our military and seriously jeopardized its ability to achieve its various missions.

A study of 12,000 servicemen and women found that two-thirds of junior enlisted men believed that women could not pull their load in combat; 56% of low-ranking *women* agreed. Forty percent of officers felt that women could not hack it in combat. Only seven percent of officers thought that sex integration improved military readiness. Women in active operational military units or in garrison were generally believed to have a negative effect on small-unit cohesion, or to put it another way, prevented male bonding in such units. Anna Simmons, in her book, *The Company They Keep: Life Inside The U.S. Army Special Forces*—a work developed from observing elite 12-man Marine A-teams over 18 months—claims that it is this bonding that "enables men to survive the stress of working closely under difficult conditions of cramped space, long hours, hardship, and extreme danger."

The failure of women to perform up to speed in military operations was clearly obvious in the Gulf War in *logistic and support units:* "Men in many units took over tearing down tents or loading boxes because most of the women simply couldn't or wouldn't do these chores fast enough."[19] If women could not do the job, or refused to do the job, in a support environment, what's to think they would perform at acceptable levels in a true combat situation?

Elaine Donnelly is president of the Center for Military Preparedness, an independent public policy organization that specializes in military personnel issues. Her father served on the submarine U.S.S. Menhadden. Ms. Donnelly wrote about the problems that would arise if women would be allowed to serve on submarines. These comments evolved from her membership on the 1992 Presidential Commission on the Assignment of Women in the Armed Forces; her visits to two SSN attack submarines; comments from enlisted personnel and officers, including the commander of the Atlantic fleet submarine force, Vice Admiral H. Chiles; and developments subsequent to 1992.

Submarine duty, the famed "silent service," is a primary target of feminists because it has been, according to the Secretary of the Navy, the "last male bastion" of the military services. He warned naval admirals in a speech to the Naval Submarine League on June 3, 1999 that they needed to get in touch with the rest of society, or be "left behind." This was a not-so-veiled threat that funding for the submarine service would be reduced if they didn't begin to accept female sailors. (Feminist senator Olympia Snowe, R-Maine, is a member of the Senate Armed Services Committee and chairs the Subcommittee on Seapower which decides ship procurement budgets. Mary Landrieu, D-La., another pro-feminist, is also a member of the Senate Armed Services Committee).

Close quarters in submarines intensify stress and friction. Body contact is unavoidable, especially during drills and emergencies. Admiral Chiles warned that the inherent loneliness of submarine duty could lead to sexual problems aboard ship and to marital problems at home.

The physical peculiarities of women would be an unmitigated disaster for submarine mission accomplishment. "Unplanned losses" among submarine crews are extremely harmful because replacements are not usually available. The Center for Naval Analysis found that the unplanned loss rate for female sailors of 23% to 25% was two-and-a half times that for males (8%-10%). "If proportionate losses and evacuation rates are extended to covert submarines, the negative effects on morale, safety and national security could be significant." During a 1999 deployment of the carrier, Theodore Roosevelt, 45 of 300 female sailors either could not begin the cruise or complete it due to impending childbirth. Eleven had to be flown off the ship while underway by helicopter, which obviously is not a viable option for submarines. (A 1998 study found that in 1996, 40% of all pregnancies among enlisted sailors on sea duty ended either in miscarriage or abortion).

Many tasks assigned to junior enlisted personnel aboard submarines are strenuous. Predictable physical strength deficiencies among female crew members—many tests have shown that even with extensive physical training, women are 50% to 60% less strong than males and have 25% to 30% less aerobic capacity for endurance than men—"would impose greater burdens on others, especially in emergencies."[20]

Tom Clancy is one of America's favorite authors *(The Hunt For Red October, Patriot Games, Red Storm Rising, Clear And Present Danger)* and one of the leading civilian authorities on our military *(Special Forces, Carrier, Airborne, Submarine, Armored Cav, Fighter Wing,* and *Marine)*. In his 2000 blockbuster novel, *The Bear And The Dragon,* Clancy's character, Admiral Bart Mancuso, commander of all U.S. forces in the Pacific (CINPAC), has the following thoughts as he ponders the implications of females in the Navy "…. a recent development in the navy which Mancuso would just have soon put off for another decade. They were even letting women on submarines now, and the admiral didn't regret having missed that one little bit. What the hell would Mush Morton and his crop of WWII submariners have made *of that?*"

National Review (December 8, 2003), in discussing the Jessica Lynch saga, has this to say: "Wars are about achieving objectives, not rescuing prisoners, important though that is to comradely morale. Not important at all is awarding brownie points on the basis of ethnicity and sex. The disproportionate coverage, so much of it grotesque, that Private Lynch has received is one more proof that women do not belong in the battlefield."

Women In The Work Force Open Up Pandora's Box

The feminist movement made women feel that their contributions in the home were meaningless—that they were nothing more than indentured servants who weren't even getting minimum wages. In order to be truly fulfilled, the argument went, they had to be employed outside the home; any efforts by the enemy (men) to keep them in home-bound bondage was simply designed to keep them from self-actualizing.

Unfortunately, the radical feminists have been successful. Record numbers of women are working outside the home. Most disturbingly, 59% of mothers with infant children are in the work force.[21] There is little likelihood that there is anything on the horizon to change women's attitudes toward outside-the-home work. Consider the results of a National Opinion Research Center survey of women concerning their attitudes toward work:

•Only 20.5% of women felt that it was more important for a wife to help her husband's career than to have one herself.

•Only 31.9% agreed with the statement, "It is much better for everyone involved if the man is the achiever outside the home and the woman takes care of the home and family."

•Only 36.2% felt that a preschool child is likely to suffer if his or her mother works.

•Only 33.5% agreed with the statement, "All in all, family life suffers when the woman has a full-time job."

•75% of working women ages 18 to 29 would continue to work even if they had enough money to live comfortably for the rest of their lives.

Here are the problems that arise when married women with children are in the work force. In many cases, the family may actually be worse off financially. By the time the cost of putting the wife into the work force is considered—new clothes, lunches, another automobile, gasoline—the additional income is less than the incremental costs. This situation is most likely to occur if the wife is working part-time or is employed full-time but is making a minimum wage.

Having married women work increases their interaction with males and the likelihood that adulterous relationships will develop. In turn, these liaisons can culminate in divorce with the calamitous implications for children of the marriage. And let's not forget the damage that can be done to husbands, which includes depression, shame, fear, and a reduced standard of living.

Recall from Chapter Four that in one-third of dual-income

families, women out-earn their husbands. Such a situation will lead to women gaining more power and the man's self esteem being eroded. The *Economist* states, "Certainly, there is a suspiciously close correlation between the rise in women's employment and their earning power relative to that of men, on the one hand, and the rise in marital breakdown on the other. Many women no longer need men to support them and their children financially; in addition, once out in the workplace, women whose marriages are not happy may find new and preferable partners. Going out to work may not increase conjugal unhappiness, but it certainly gives wives an easier way out." [22]

When women work, the family eats out more often because the wife complains that she is too tired to cook. Fully one-half of all meals in the United States are currently consumed outside the house. The result: more dollars spent on food than is necessary, less quality family time, and less nutritional, high-fat food consumed which contributes greatly to the significant obesity problem existing in America.

Children that come home to an empty house after school are prime candidates to get into trouble. T. Terry Brazelton, co-author of *The Irreducible Needs Of Children,* says, "Latchkey children shouldn't exist. The Academy of Pediatrics showed that latchkey kids were significantly more likely to get into drugs and sexual acting out and violent situations." [23] According to ABC radio, kids are most likely to experiment with drugs between 4 and 6 P.M. when parental supervision is frequently not available. "Latchkey children were more prone than non-latchkey children to have teenage sex, commit violent crimes and be involved as drivers in automobile wrecks." [24]

Putting infants in day school so women can work is not acceptable. Stanley Greenspan, the other author of *The Irreducible Needs Of Children,* feels that 85% of day care operations are not high quality. One of the reasons is that, on average, day-care workers switch jobs on average four times a year. "How could a child relate to four people a year? That's more than we can expect them to be able to respond to. Having too many people to identify with, too many choices, can be a deficit for a child."[25]

Women Buy Into Liberalism—And Everyone Suffers

Democratic politicians usually pursue liberal agendas. Women voters, as contrasted to male voters, generally favor democratic candidates. And, unfortunately, liberalism's legacy explains much of what is wrong in the United States today.

Data on the 2000 presidential election show that there were more women of voting age than men (105.5 million to 97.1 million), a greater percentage of them registered to vote (66.6% to 62.2%) and a greater percentage of female registered voters actually voted (56.2% to 53.1%). If these data are combined, it means that almost 39 million females cast ballots for president in 2000 as opposed to only about 32 million men (*Statistical Abstract of the United States,* 2001).

In 1976, 51.0% of both sexes voted for the Democratic candidate for President, but the 1996 and 2000 presidential elections showed much higher percentages of women voting for Clinton and Gore than did men: 56.0% and 46.0%, respectively, in 1996 and 2000 vs. 46.0% and 42.0%, respectively, for men.[26] Journalist Steven Stark, writing in the July 1996 *Atlantic Monthly,* states that "The gravitation of men and women to different political camps appears to be the *outstanding demographic development in American politics* over the last 20 years" (emphasis added).[27] An initiative by Patty Murray, Democratic Senatorial Campaign Committee Chairman, shows the lengths the democratic party will go to get women into senate seats. Her "Women On The Road To The Senate" effort raised $1.2 million for *female* senate candidates (*Human Events,* October 15, 2001).

While women are more likely to vote than men and make up a majority of the electorate, they "perform more poorly than men in most surveys measuring political knowledge." A study in 2000 by the Annenberg Public Policy Center at the University of Pennsylvania found that women were "considerably less likely" than men to be able to identify the candidates for president who were a former POW, a former professional basketball player or a current governor. In another survey, 46% of males knew that Republicans controlled both the House and Senate compared to 27% for females. In an extensive 1996 study by Michael Delli Carpini and Scott Keeter, *What Americans Know About Politics And Why It Matters,* it was found that "three fourths of females score well below the male average on tests measuring knowledge of national politics."[28]

Here is what liberalism, which apparently is the political/philosophical bent of women since a majority of them consistently votes for democratic candidates, stands for:

•There is no God. Or if there is a God, we don't have to know what He expects of us and, thus, we can ignore Him and do what we want.

•Man was not created by God. We simply evolved from a lower form of life to what we are today.

•Man is not inherently sinful but, rather, enters the world with a *tabula rosa,* a clean slate. Thus, man becomes "bad" through the environmental stimuli with which he comes in contact (parents, siblings, friends, television, schools, chance events, etc.).

•Because man is not inherently sinful, he can be manipulated to become good.

•The best and ultimate manipulator for good is government because it has a lock on knowledge and intelligence; it knows what to do, how to do it, and when to do it.

•Men and women are created equal.. That is, there are no significant physical, mental or psychological differences between them, nor should there be.

•Change for the sake of change is good. There is nothing sacrosanct about the past or the status quo.

Let's see how liberalism's basic tenets have poisoned our nation. If there is no God, we don't call on him individually and collectively as a nation for guidance. We don't follow His commandments and our society disintegrates—crime, abortion, broken homes, alcoholism, drug addiction, and so forth. Because we weren't created by God, we have no obligation to Him. Because man is inherently good, he is not responsible for his sins; these are simply "mistakes" which I made and the result of some external stimuli over which I have no control. When the right button is pushed, I will mend my ways (and yet the recidivism rate may be as high as 85%). We have a constantly expanding government which intrudes more and more into our lives and our privacy, spends ever-increasing amounts of dollars, and grabs more and more of our income in the form of taxes to whet its voracious appetite. Since it is obvious even to a moron that individuals are not all created the same, big government will inevitably institute policies which will artificially level the playing field. In other words, it will discriminate—through affirmative action, progressive income taxes that redistribute income, and so on. Because there should be no differences between men and women—but there are and everyone knows it—women are acting more like men and are trying to feminize men to be the same as women. Because liberals have no reverence for current institutions and historical precedents, they are fully free to engage in "social engineering." Thus, we end up with coed training in the military, coed barracks, and women in combat units—to the det-.riment of our armed forces' preparedness and effectiveness.

Education: Women Dominate, Learning Drops

Three-fourths of teachers in our schools are women. (A double whammy occurs because a disproportionate share of teachers in our public school have graduated in the bottom half of their college classes and in the bottom third of their high school classes). We have already seen how the educational system is stacked against boys in favor of girls or, as Leonard Sax puts it: "Our primary and secondary education systems, now dominated by female educators, are designed for *female success* and *male disengagement*" (emphasis added).[29] We also noticed that educational achievements of students have dropped such that the U.S. lags far behind other countries—some of the third-world variety—in educational achievement.

Three powerful, well-heeled, organizations have been in the forefront of educational development and reform in the United States and, thus, need to shoulder much of the blame for the anti-male bias and eroding levels of educational achievement, the latter despite tremendous increases in spending and lower classroom sizes. These are the two national teachers' unions—National Education Association (2.5 million members) and the American Federation of Teachers (1.0 million members)—and the U.S. Department of Education.

The National Education Association (NEA) is the higher profile of the two teachers' unions; 92% of its political contributions go to Democrats, as does 99% of AFT's. A majority of its members are women. Its annual income of $742 million is augmented by funds from its publishing, insurance and credit card operations. It is housed in an eight-story building in Washington D.C., worth $65 million. It has a 164-member board of directors; 54 state affiliates (two in Washington D.C., one in Puerto Rico and one overseas); a 9,044-member representative assembly—which is probably representative in name only—500 staff members, 50 of whom are involved with "government relations;" and 13,000 local affiliates. At least 2,000 NEA officials enjoy annual salaries of $100,000 or more.[30]

As indicated above, a distressingly high percentage of teachers in U.S. classrooms have graduated in the lower portions of their high school and college graduating classes. The powerful NEA can protect these individuals and make sure that more like them enter the teaching profession. It is also in a position to protect lazy, ineffective teachers and gave sanctuary to those female teachers that are discriminating against our sons in their classes. Political power is considered to be the NEA's *raison d'etre*. In the May 1984 issue of *Readers Digest*, NEA president Mary Futrell stated, "Instruction and professional development have been on the back burner for NEA, compared with political action."[31]

In November of 1999, the NEA issued a statement advocating the banning of school districts which hired teachers who, according to the NEA, lack "full credentials." NEA president, Robert Chase, said, "Let's have a fully prepared, qualified teacher in every classroom. No waivers. No exceptions. No excuses."[32] The result of such a self-serving agenda would be to perpetuate the mediocrity which the NEA has been so successful in doing for years. Also, you can bet that these "'fully prepared, qualified teachers" will only be those who belong to the National Education Association.

The teachers unions have aggressively resisted efforts to test students or teachers—to find out how well they are doing. Of course, they resist testing because such testing—as it has repeatedly shown in the past—would expose our public education system for the gigantic fraud that it is. Thomas Sowell, Senior Fellow with the Hoover Institution, hit the mark when he said:

> When teachers' union ads come on the TV screen, with some saccaharine-sweet spokesman promoting about how much they are 'concerned' about children and their education, ask yourself: Where were all these concerned people when our schools were being systematically dumbed down over the past generation?[33]

Sowell alluded to a *Time* magazine study which reported that American students spend about as much time in school each year as do English, French and German students. The problem is that U.S. schools devote only about half the time to such "serious" subjects as history, science and math as do these foreign schools.[34] Of course, girls do not do as well in these subjects as do boys, so women-dominated schools put more time on softer subjects. (Does this sound familiar? We mentioned earlier that the military was forced to put more emphasis on first aid and map reading—two areas in which females excelled over males—because males clearly outperformed females on the physical aspects of training).

Leonard Sax takes an especially dim view of the Department of Education. "The United States Department of Education—run almost entirely by women who toe the feminist-psychology line—continues to spend hundreds of millions of dollars a year on programs to make it easier for *women* to have 'equal access,' in the department's own words, to higher education, to ensure fairness."[35]

Title IX of the Education Amendments of 1972 "prohibits sex discrimination in any educational institution that receives public funds." The Women's Educational Equity Act (WEEA) Publishing Center is the "primary vehicle by which the U.S. Department of Education promotes gender equity." WEEA Publishing Corporation spews out 350 publications on gender equity and distributes them to over 200 conferences a year. Since 1980, this organization has gotten $75 million from the federal government! [36]

The Inspector General of the Department of Education indicated that the DOE has failed three consecutive audits. Over those three years, it has been guilty of $450 million in waste, fraud and abuse. Lorraine Lewis, the Inspector General, said in testimony before a House subcommittee, "No one can say with certainty if there are other problems. This is a big deal. Much work still remains" (*Human Events*, April 23, 2000).

You Are What You Believe: Women's Dubious Values Lead Us Down The Slippery Slope

Reverend C. Russell Yates, who we met earlier in this chapter, says, "The source of every human problem is the willingness to believe something that is not true." We have already seen earlier in this chapter some of females' false dogma regarding their relationship to God and whether they should be in the work force. Let's look at some additional fallacious thinking that harms their husbands, their children, themselves, and this nation. Margaret Thatcher, speaking at a Hillsdale College seminar in Fort Myers, Florida, February 19, 2001, eloquently expressed the importance of values to a society when she said:

> History has taught us that freedom cannot long survive unless it is based on moral foundations . . . The right to liberty is fundamental. But it is what a person or a people does with it that tells their caliber and their fiber, and that decides whether they will continue to be free, and whether their nation will be prosperous. I like very much what John Adams, your second president, wrote in 1798: 'Our Constitution was made only for a moral and religious people. It is wholly inadequate to the government of any other.'

The 1995 Virginia Slims Opinion Poll, conducted by Roper Starch Worldwide, found that large percentages of women agreed with the following statements:

1. "Men are just as competitive as ever." (84% agreed).

2. "People admire men who show a more sensitive side." (81% agreed).

3. "Men still find it difficult to think of women completely as equals." (79% agreed).

4. "Most men are confused about what women expect of them nowadays." (68% agreed).

5. "Men have become more able to express their feelings." (68% agreed).

6. "More and more men are questioning the 'macho' role." (54% agreed).

Let's look at these statements—all of which were agreed with by a majority (in some cases, a decided majority)—of the women interviewed. Statement #1 implies that there is something wrong with men being competitive, despite the fact that much of the culture in the United States today is competitively oriented and if men don't compete successfully, they and their families are less likely to enjoy a decent standard of living. Statements #2, #5 and #6 are especially pernicious in that they suggest a loss of masculinity for men, i.e., that they are becoming more feminine. Of course, this is a major objective of the feminist movement and their countless female minions. Statement #3 implies that men *should* think of women as equals, in other words, that men should not exercise their God-ordained mandate to be in positions of leadership and authority. Statement #4 chides us males for not knowing what females want—a likely occurrence if women don't tell us what they want (we're supposed to get this by osmosis)—or we are besieged with so many ludicrous demands that we become, initially, incredulous and eventually non-compliant.

Here is a particularly dangerous belief that apparently a majority of women have. In 1994, the National Opinion Research Center of the University of Chicago found that 52.3% of women believed that "astrology—the study of star signs—has some scientific truth." For anyone to believe that their destiny or fate is mandated by how stars line up is preposterous (despite what Nancy Reagan believes). In Biblical times, many of the unbelieving peoples, particularly the Chaldeans, who surrounded the Israelites, were heavily into astrology. This is wherein the problem lies: relying on astronomical bodies instead of God to direct our lives.

Women often don't bother to get the facts or choose to ignore or falsify them in order to further their dubious causes. In other words, they do not seek truth. (We saw plenty of examples of this in the first chapter). Here's another example. Ann Coulter, writing in *Human Events* (May 19, 2000), reports that women who favor gun control are greatly exaggerating their complicity in the death of children. "In the harsh light of facts, gun accidents do not even come close to being the leading cause of death for children. In fact, teddy bears and other toys actually do kill more children every year than gun accidents do." The U.S. Consumer Products Safety Commission reported in 1997 that toys cause at least 22 deaths annually, compared to 20 deaths for children under five from gun accidents in 1997.

Ms. Coulter *(Human Events,* February 18, 2000) exposes more fuzzy female logic. In chiding women for their failure to put economic issues (especially tax cuts) at the top of their political "wish list"—they, instead identified such issues as an insufficient effort to eradicate breast cancer, gun control, child care, equal pay, violence against women, medical benefits, pollution, the rising cost of a college education, and rescuing Social Security—Coulter points to their overwhelming emphasis on how to spend money rather than how it is earned. "The typical liberal woman's political calculus is based on budgeting, not earning. They have no idea how the money materializes, and are not particularly interested. But they have a lot of opinions on how to spend it."

Divorce In America: It Takes Two To Tango

As wives pursue their own dreams outside the home.....as they become more engrossed with themselves and less committed to their husbands and their children . . . as their incomes swell such that they can be self-supporting without their husbands' incomes... as their pride grows over what they have accomplished ....it is hardly surprising that the divorce rate in the United States would climb to the 50% level and that the blame for this sad commentary would be increasingly laid at the feet of women. Reverend C. Russell Yates says it succinctly: "When a couple splits, the culpability is usually on the feminine side." More specifically, Cathy Young, writing in *Reason* (June 2001) reveals that two-thirds of divorces *involving children are initiated by women.*

Female predilections toward divorce and their lack of knowledge about its consequences or cavalier attitude are reflected in the following survey results:

1. 42.6% of women believe that "one parent can bring up a child as well as two together." Horrifyingly, 61.1% of those 18-29 and 54.0% of those 30-39—ages when children are likely to be present in a marriage—concurred.

2. 25.3% of women believe that it should be easier to get a divorce. Only 47.8% felt it should be more difficult; 30.7% and 33.8% of women ages 18-29 and 30-39, respectively, agreed that it should be easier, while only 40.7% and 41.5%, respectively, believed that it should be more difficult.[37]

What is God's stance on divorce? In Mark 10: 11-12, Christ says: "Whosoever shall put away his wife, and marry another, committeth adultery against her. And if a woman shall put away her husband, and be married to another, she committeth adultery." In Mark 10:9, Jesus says: "What, therefore, God hath joined together, let not man put asunder." In other words, God takes a dim view of divorce; He did, however, allow for divorce in the case of fornication, that is, adultery (see Matthew 19:8-9).

As early as 1965, the dire consequences on boys not having fathers because of divorce was predicted by senator Patrick

Moynihan who said, "A community that allows a large number of young men to grow up in *broken families, dominated by women*, never acquiring any rational expectations about the future—that community asks for and gets chaos" (emphasis added).[38]

Women Like Men And Men Like Women

A major strategy of women and their spokespersons, radical feminists, is to homogenize the two genders (see Chapter Three), that is, to remake themselves or men so as to blur the physical, mental and psychological differences that exist between men and women.

These homogenization efforts are disastrous. They are an affront to God, the creator, who made men and women different for a number of reasons: to be attractive to each other, to complement each other in the striving to succeed economically, and to serve as appropriate role models for children. Role reversal, with the expected results, often occurs in families. Remember what Reverend Yates said: "Researchers who have studied the home life of homosexuals and lesbians have discovered that almost always the pattern is a dominant mother and a passive father."

Abortion and lesbianism logically occur when blurring between the sexes exists. An advertisement for *New Oxford Review*, a conservative Catholic publication, gets to the point:

> For the radical feminist, God committed the Original Sin by designing males and females differently, so that the female, not the male, would become pregnant. For today's militant feminist this is totally unfair: Bearing and nurturing children ties the woman down and handicaps her in her pursuit of career, money, and power. The only sure way to 'liberate' women from this natural order is, as the orthodox Catholic philosopher Germain Kipaczynski has noted, by means of abortion. While men are unpregnant by nature, abortion enables women to become unpregnant—by doing violence to nature. The 'unjust' order created by God is thereby undone, and women can in effect be men. This is why the litmus test of the feminist establishment is support for abortion-on-demand. Now if the link

between womanhood and motherhood is severed, and if women are identical to men, such that feminity is an antiquated and meaningless 'social construct,' then what's wrong with lesbianism? God knows—for He designed female bodies to bond with male bodies—but God's design is paid no heed. Not surprisingly, the head of the flagship feminist organization, the National Organization for Women, says that 'maybe half' of NOW's members are lesbians.

According to Christina Hoff Sommers, author of *The War Against Boys,* the effort to feminize boys "will render boys less competitive, more emotionally expressive, more nurturing—more, in short, like girls."[39]

Women In The Church = Stagnating Memberships And Marginalization Of Men

Membership in mainline Protestant denominations, like the Methodist, Lutheran, Presbyterian, Church of Christ, and Episcopalian, that have ceded power to women (they are serving as pastors, elders, deacons, committee heads, and are filling the ranks in seminaries) are experiencing stagnating or even declining memberships. On the other hand, membership is increasing among the Southern Baptists, Mormons and Pentecostals who, in accordance with Biblical mandates, limit women's roles.

Another outcome of women taking over churches: Men feel uncomfortable in such an environment and tend to withdraw from church activities to the extent of not even attending the Sunday morning worship services. There is danger when this happens. Kenneth L. Woodward, a senior religious writer and longtime reporter for *Newsweek,* states: "The best predictor of whether a child will remain religious as an adult is not the religiosity of the mother—for children tend to take that for granted—but of the father, because he is not expected to be religious. That is, if the father demonstrates that religion is not foreign to what a man is and does, the child—*especially the male child*—is much more likely to be religious upon reaching adulthood" (emphasis added). [40]

Let's quickly summarize what *The War Against Men* has to this point revealed. God has clearly defined male and female roles, but women, in general, and their attack dogs, the radical feminists, rebel against God and husbands' authority. Today, a number of factors—including a large number that can be laid at the feet of women—are making it increasingly difficult for men to operate effectively. Women, blatantly ignoring the obvious physical, mental and psychological distinctions between themselves and men, are trying to homogenize the sexes by either emulating men or trying to manipulate them in becoming more feminine. Over the last three decades in the United States, the power of women has increased greatly. Much of this "success" was achieved by outright discrimination against men and in favor of women, through the assistance provided by liberal politicians, favorable legislation and sympathetic courts.

Unfortunately, across a large number of fronts—medical, work, legal system, education, etc.—America has retrogressed over the last third of a century, with much of the blame attributable to the foilbles, fallacies and failures of women and the women's movement.

Men, do not despair, The war against us has not been lost, although we are currently losing a number of battles. We are still able to stem the tide and claim victory.

In order to win the war being waged against us we need to realize the danger that is confronting us, our families (especially our sons), and our country. Then, we need to mobilize ourselves and our resources (mainly our time) and take decisive action along two major fronts: the political and personal. The last two chapters of this book will provide sound, viable recommendations which, if implemented and implemented quickly (these is a sense of urgency), will bring about victory.

REFERENCES
1. Russell Yates, *Open Letter To Friends, Family, Church Family & Minsters*, 2000.
2. Barbara Ehrenreich, "Men Hate War Too," *Foreign Affairs*, January/

February 1999, pp. 118-127.

3. John Lofton, "Tipper Gore Meets Mighty Mouse," *Human Events*, September 15, 2000, p. 8.

4. Nick Gillespie, "William Marston's Secret Identity," *Reason*, May 2001, pp. 52-53.

5. Leonard Sax, "Guilty Until Proven Innocent," *Penthouse*, December 2000, pp. 123-148.

6. *The Economist*, February 17, 2001, p. 89.

7. Barara Ehrenreich.

8. Jennifer Roback Morse, "Is Feminism Finished?," *Forbes*, April 19, 1999.

9. *Penthouse*, January 2001, pp. 49, ff.

10. Promotional piece for Rush Limbaugh's newsletter, February 2001.

11. Paul Craig Roberts, "Columbia Targets Heterosexual Males," *Human Events*, November 17, 2002, p.11

12. Leonard Sax.

13. As quoted in Leonard Sax.

14. Joseph A. D'Agostino, "Ashcroft/Norton Opponents Receive Tax Funds," *Human Events*, January 22, 2001.

15. Leonard Sax.

16. Cato Policy Report, November/December 2000.

17. Jennifer Roback Morse.

18. *Penthouse.*

19. Stephanie Gutman, *The Kinder, Gentler Military,* as quoted in Matthew Robinson, "Playing Dolls With G.I. Joe," *Human Events,* September 1, 2000, p.13.

20. Elaine Donnelly, "Navy Bunks ROTC Coeds On Trident Submarines," *Human Events*, September 17, 1999, pp. 1, 8.

21. *U.S. News & World Report,* November 6, 2000, p. 10.

22. "I Do, I Can, I Will," *The Economist*, January 6, 2001, p. 77.

23. Katy Kelly, "Child Docs To Parents: Stay Home And Save Your Kids," *U.S. News & World Report,* October 30, 2000, p. 65.

24. News Report on KPGC Radio, Bryan/College Station, Texas, October 23, 1999.

25. Katy Kelly.

26. *Routledge Historical Atlas of Women in America* and the November 17, 2002 issue of *Human Events.*

27. As quoted in "Going Their Separate Ways," *American Demographics,* November 1996, pp. 10-12.

28. Kate O'Beirne, "Clueless—What Women Don't Know About Politics," *National Review*, October 9, 2000, pp. 20-21.

29. Leonard Sax.

30. "Treason Of The Educrats," *Human Events*, December 17, 1999.

31. As quoted in John Lofton.

32. John Lofton.

33. Thomas Sowell, "Teachers' Unions Get A-Plus For Self-Serving Propaganda," *Human Events*, November 10, 2000, pp. 15-16.

34. Thomas Sowell.

35. Leonard Sax.

36. Christina Hoff Sommers, *The War Against Boys*, Simon & Schuster, New York, 2002, pp. 47-51.

37. 1994 General Social Survey, National Opinion Research Center, University of Chicago.

38. As quoted in Christina Hoff Sommers, p. 129.

39. Christina Hoff Sommers.

40. Kenneth L. Woodward, "Who's Really Running The Show?," *Commonweal*, November 22, 1996, pp. 9-14.

EIGHT

Political Counter-Attack Strategies

"We will fight them in the halls of Congress, in the media, in places of work and worship, at the ballot box, in schools, colleges and universities and, yes, in the home."

"The only thing necessary for the triumph of evil is for good men to do nothing." Edmund Burke

This book was not written with the intent of discussing some social problem existing in the United States, but then not offering recommendations to cope with the problem. This chapter, accordingly, contains specific recommendations related to the political battlefield which, if men will implement, will measurably improve their lives. The good thing is that the lives of their wives and children (especially their sons) will also be enhanced. But the most important outcome may well be that the decline of the United States over the last 30 years—a decline that occurred as women were gaining more power as rank discrimination against men was surging— can be arrested.

What impact has this book had on you so far? Has it surprised you? Were you incredulous? Did it make you cry? Did you become despondent?

To be candid, I experienced all of the above as I gathered materials for the book, perused them, and tried to organize them into a meaningful format. I was surprised at how much the level of power has increased for women over the last three decades and how rampant anti-male discrimination was over the same period. I was incredulous at the distortions, outright lies and smear tactics used by the radical feminists and how gullible women and, yes, males were in buying into their nefarious anti-male, anti-conservative, anti-God agenda. I cried when I read how our young sons are degraded in school through the feminization efforts espoused by and, unfortunately, implemented by the female-dominated educational system. And I experienced despair when the data I analyzed clearly showed how the United States has lost ground over the last thirty years, in particular, how our values have eroded to such an extent that our families are torn apart through neglect and divorce, we condone the murder of over 41 million unborn children, and crime and drug use skyrocket in our society.

But, eventually, my despondency was offset by another more therapeutic, energizing feeling: anger. This is the reaction I hope many of this book's readers will have, for once this becomes your mind-set, you will see the wisdom of the recommendations offered in this chapter and Chapter Nine (counter attack strategies on the personal battlefield) and the need to be proactive in getting them implemented.

In Chapter One, you were exposed to the idea that men in the United States are at war, whether we know it or not—and many of us don't—and unfortunately, many of us will not buy into this notion even after reading this book. In war, you can either fight defensively or offensively. Let the men in the United States at least put up a defensive posture. However, it needs to be understood that an offensive posture will more likely achieve our aims and at a quicker pace than will a defensive one. (If you have trouble with being this aggressive, remember that much of the women's movement is spearheaded by women who have a deep and abiding hatred of men). Accordingly, the recommendations made in this chapter and the next one are of the proactive type.

To where should our anger be directed—an important question because the answer will indicate the targets of our proactive agenda? Each of us should direct some anger at ourselves and our fellow males for our overwhelming inertia and stupidity for not realizing what was happening to us, our families and our country over the last third of the preceding century. Of course, the radical feminists should be in our gun-sights, as well as those women who have bought into their agenda and worked vigorously to achieve it. And let's not forget the duplicitous politicians, judges, federal government departments and agencies, media, colleges and universities, churches, and corporations. In short, then, a parody of the famous speech Winston Churchill made when Great Britain was fighting Nazi aggression during World War II is in order: "We will fight them in the halls of Congress, in the media, in places of work and worship, at the ballot box, in schools, colleges and universities and, yes, in the home."

A major decision that men will have to make is, should we play the minority card in attempting to win on the political front? I am afraid we must, even though it smacks of weakness and desperation. The stakes are simply too high to do otherwise. As suggested in the Churchill parody, we need to use every weapon at our disposal. Keep in mind that we are not asking for unfair advantage but, in a society based on meritocracy, we only want a level playing field—the opportunity to succeed through our own abilities and productivity and not to be denied the chance to succeed because we are not wearing a skirt or a pants suit.

What does the minority card mean in actionable terms? Simply that whenever a job opening contains the affirmative action line, "We are sincerely interested in minorities and women," the employer will be made firmly aware of the fact that *males are a minority*. And we need to do the same whenever we see similar concessions being made to women in education, the military, and so on. When we see an organization that has a disproportionately small percentage of men, we should demand equal representation—as a minority—at least equal to our makeup in the general population (48.9%). And it would not hurt to refer to the Founding Fathers to give us more credibility as we play the minority card; they strongly feared that majorities would take unfair advantage of minorities. James Madison is a case in point. He worried that "moved by passion or greed, a majority would violate the rights of a minority." (Could Madison have been thinking of women when he referred to "passion or greed?"). A similar statement is made by Albert Jay Nock in his classic book, *Our Enemy, The State*; Nock maintains that governments exploit some people to enrich others with more political clout (remember that women have more political clout than men because there are greater numbers of voting age women than men).

As we move forward to regain what we have been losing over the last 30 years, two fundamental points should be remembered. First, we need to thank God that He has created us males, with all the rights, privileges and benefits—and yes, obligations—thereunto pertaining. In fact, we should go beyond merely thanking God; we should rejoice in our manhood. We should cherish the differences between men and women that God built into the two sexes. We should never forget that it has been primarily men who have made America the great country that it is. Men have designed and constructed our buildings, roads, bridges, and tunnels; men have developed the technology which has improved our standard of living and made it the envy of the rest of the world; men who have provided the successful political leadership in times of trouble; men who have started and run the great corporations that fuel our economic growth; and men who have fallen in defense of freedom: 117,000 in World War I (and 204,000 wounded), 407,000 in World War II (and 672,000 wounded), 37,000 in Korea (and 103,000 wounded), and 58,000 in Vietnam (and 153,000 wounded). On an individual basis, be proud, yet not boastful and complacent, about your achievements. You worked hard to get an education. You served in the military. You have provided for your family, got your children through college, and provided for your and your wife's retirement. Please don't let the radical feminists, women in general, or your wife denigrate—or even worse—take credit for your success. (Nothing is more repugnant to hear a man at his retirement party say he could not have done it without his wife, like the wife passed his college exams, ran his business, did his work at the office, dragged himself up before dawn for more than 30 years to go to work).

Second, you have got to keep yourself informed. You can not get so involved with work and family that you do not know what is going on in the U.S. and the rest of the world because these events will impact you. I believe that, like myself, many men over the last 30 years were not aware of the developments discussed in previous chapters and, thus, by our somnolence, allowed them to occur. Remember the statement attributed to Edmund Burke: "The only thing necessary for the triumph of evil is for good men to do nothing" and the words of Thomas Jefferson: "Eternal vigilance is the price of liberty." In addition, the words of James Madison are instructive, as well: "Knowledge will forever govern ignorance; and a people who mean to be their own governors, must arm themselves with the power which knowledge gives."

I strongly urge you not to rely on mainline media for your news. (Remember that they are controlled by women). They are simply too biased politically (liberal) and gender-wise and, worse, are not adverse to outright deception to further their anti-male agendas. Among major weekly magazines, *U.S. News & World Report* is probably the least biased; John Leo's editorials are usually right-on. Although George Will writes clear-thinking editorials for *Newsweek*, they may not be enough to overcome its liberal slant.

Don't bother with major metropolitan newspapers like the *New York Times*, *Washington Post*, and *Los Angeles Times*. You are much better informed by reading *Human Events* (an absolute must-read) the *Washington Times* and *The Weekly Standard*. *National Review* is great, also. G. Gordon Liddy, Rush Limbaugh, Neal Boortz, Michael Reagan, and Laura Ingraham give the straight scoop via their national radio talk shows and there are probably local ones around the country that are conservative, as well. News and talk shows on the major TV networks are an absolute waste— with the exception of Fox. There, you can get Bill O'Reilly ("The O'Reilly Factor") and "Hannity and Colmes" (Hannity is the conservative).

There are some excellent foundations and "think tanks" which have a conservative slant and publish excellent newsletters for their supporters. At the top of the list, I would put The Heritage Foundation and the Cato Institute. The Hoover Institution does a good job; so does the American Enterprise Institute.

Before specific counter attack strategies are enumerated for the political battle ground—in the areas of education, military, abortion, gun control, taxes, the war on drugs, and propaganda—some general recommendations concerning the political battle front are in order.

Men, you must take a more active role politically. This means knowing and deciding in your mind what the crucial issues are, knowing how candidates line up on them, *and voting*. (Remember the three basic political axioms about women articulated earlier in this book: There are more women voters than men, higher proportions of them vote, and they are more likely to vote for liberal candidates who embrace ideology often antithetical to what men believe). By voting, I do not mean punching a hole in a ballot every four years for president; I mean voting in all local, county and state elections, as well as national elections, and casting your ballot on propositions, amendments, referenda, etc. Don't underestimate the significance of local elections. Often, they will have a more direct effect on you than what is going on in Washington, D.C. Election results at the state level often serve as a barometer as to what eventually happens on the national scene, so you want to be involved there, as well.

We need to vet candidates for political office, especially those who are female, as to how they line up on issues affecting men. They need to be told point blank that men will no longer countenance having their rights eroded and being second class citizens. But don't focus only on female candidates. We certainly need to include liberal male candidates, too, who by their stupidity and lust for power to stay in office, will pander to female voters at the expense of male voters.

There is one female politician that men need to keep close tabs on. And that, of course, is Hillary Clinton. This is a woman who, I think, wants nothing else than to be president of the United States. (According to an advertisement for *NewsMax* magazine appearing in the June 17-23, 2002 *Washington Times*, Hillary and Bill engaged in a screaming match when she demanded Al Gore's office which is next to the Oval Office; Bill and Hillary often talked about their "12-year plan": Bill serving eight years, Hillary four). Believe me, Hillary could be elected president because of the majority of voters being women and their tendency to vote for liberals and the number of gullible men who think it would be only "fair" if a woman headed up the most powerful country in the world.

After Hillary was elected to the senate, *Human Events* decided to devote a column a week ("Hillary Watch") to track her actions, speeches and voting record. While recording old Hillary indiscretions, such as her pilfering White House property when Bill left office, *Human Events* accurately captures Hillary's political philosophy. "She is, always has been, and forever will be a revolutionary: a woman whose vision of America is completely and utterly contradictory to our founding, our history, our tradition and values" (*Human Events*, January 29, 2001). Another very disturbing view of Hillary's is her belief in pushing Ritalin into hyper-active young boys, a drug which many experts feels turns boys into walking zombies and increases the likelihood of their turning homosexual.

Personally, I feel that there could be nothing more dangerous to our country than for Hillary to be president for four years or, God forbid, for eight years and the Congress to be Democratic during her tenure. I say this in all seriousness: Under these conditions, a prudent man would be well-advised to think of every way possible to live with his family outside the United States until Hillary was out of office—that's how bad the situation would be.

As vacancies develop on the Supreme Court, a significant priority for men is to lobby aggressively for conservative replacements, particularly in those instances where the outgoing justice is liberal (the majority position on the Court in 2002, with only William Rehnquist, Antonin Scalia and Clarence Thomas consistently taking the conservative position). Eminent jurist, Robert Bork, writing in *First Things*, says that in recent sessions, the U.S. Supreme Court has made

> decisions redefining the family, altering the composition of the state and federal legislatures, striking down restrictions on contraception in the course of creating a right to privacy, protecting pornography, adopting rules rendering it virtually impossible to prosecute obscenity, refusing states the authority to support all-male military academies, creating special rights for homosexuals, limiting school disciplinary procedures, banishing religion from public life, protecting foul language in public as well as speech advocating violence and the overthrow of the government, and, of course, inventing the right to abort.

Human Events (December 29, 2001) describes the Court's decision in late 2000 on partial birth abortion—that there is a constitutional right for doctors to vacuum out a baby's brain the moment it is being born—as "madness."

There is strong support for "hate crime" legislation in America. Some states have already passed such laws, possibly providing a "bandwagon" effect for a federal statute. The danger in "hate crime" laws—and the reason why men should vigorously oppose a federal statute as well as lobby to have state laws repealed—is that there is only one group in America that will be targeted: white, heterosexual, able-bodied males because the assumption is that hate crimes are directed against women and minorities like Blacks, Hispanics, homosexuals, and the disabled. Hate crime laws are not needed because the requisite statutes are already on the books. Also, hate crime legislation violates the equal protection clause of the Constitution because it creates a hierarchy of victims. Minnesota governor, Jesse Ventura, addresses this point by asking how one explains to the family of a person murdered that it was not a hate crime and the person doesn't get sentenced as severely as someone else who does a hate crime?" [1]

A major effort in the political arena for men should be to gain elimination of the patently anti-male legislation, the Violence Against Women Act.

Repeal of VAWA is even more pressing because as pointed out by Howard University political scientists, Stephen Baskerville, domestic violence authorities, in an effort to ensnare more men, are expanding the definition of abuse to include whatever the alleged female "victim" *says it is*, such as, *depriving her of clothes or harassing her over bills*, in other words, "emotional abuse" has been added to physical abuse.

Did you know that there is a separate office in the Justice Department to oversee this legislation—the only office at Justice established to oversee a specific act? And, as you might well imagine, it is headed up by a woman, Catherine Pierce, Acting Director. Since women are increasingly committing acts of violence against men, there needs to be a corollary piece of legislation passed, Violence Against Males Act (VAMA).

Make no mistake about it, the female crazies and their unwitting dupes, a large proportion of American women, will aggressively push the notion that they are being victimized by males and, thus, the odious and discriminatory Violence Against Women Act will be the center piece of their efforts. Here's an example of what I mean. On February 14, 2000, "V-Day" celebrations were held at several hundred colleges and universities across America. Given the date, any rational person would figure that "V-Day" stands for Valentine's Day, right? Guess again; "V-Day" means "Vagina Day," the purpose of which is to "get people comfortable with talking about female genitalia as a key step in breaking the cycle of violence against women." At Texas A&M University, participants in the celebration could throw bean bags at paper vagina targets, flick condoms at a small container and could engage in an "interpretive activity" called 'dress the vagina' (whatever that is; I'm sure I don't want to know) (*Bryan-College Station Eagle*, February 14, 2002). I wonder what the response of college and university presidents would be if male students requested a similar day in their honor so that passersby could play ring toss?

The Albuquerque Tribune, in summarizing research findings from such institutions as the Centers for Disease Control and Prevention, National Institutes of Mental Health, the University of California, and the Annals of Emergency Medicine, provided strong ammunition to debunk the arguments women and their attack-dog groups use to accuse men of abuse with the hope of getting anti-male legislation passed. *The Tribune* found that:

1. "Hundreds of peer-reviewed studies show that *most domestic violence is mutual*, with women the first to hit as often as men, and nearly as likely to kill."

2. Women are much more likely to report domestic abuse than are men.

3. Because women are smaller in size and lack the strength of their male partners, they are much more likely to use weapons and surprise attacks.

4. Women and women's groups have brandished seemingly forever the statistic that a female is beaten every 18 seconds by her male partner. *The Albuquerque Tribune* says that there are an *equal or greater number of male victims* (see *Human Events*, June 10, 2002, p. 20 for a discussion of the *Albuquerque Tribune* article).

Letters by men to "Dear Annie," a feature that appears in newspapers across the country, provide graphic examples of the physical abuse they suffered at the hands of wives or girlfriends: "I tried to leave my girlfriend after she beat me. We have two children, so I foolishly begged her to take me back. I finally succeeded in getting out two months ago. Before I left, however, she beat me up and reported to the police that I had hit her...." "My ex-wife hit me so hard on one occasion that I was nearly knocked unconscious...." "After his last trip to the emergency room, I overheard his girlfriend laughing how she'd broken Joe's hand by repeatedly slamming it under the hood of her car..." "Although I had hot soup poured on me and was stabbed twice, I didn't leave my wife until she began abusing my son." Besides the abuse reported by these men, they were often charged by police as being the abuser, even when physical evidence supported their stories.

Is there a bias against men in the courts? That is, do juries made up of majorities of women or female judges discriminate against males? I do not have the answer to this question, but I believe that the potential for women to "get back" at men through our legal system is so great that I would want to make sure that, as far as possible, juries for trials involving men were composed of a majority of men and not women in cases involving sexual harassment, divorce, child custody, rape, and sexual assault—in other words, all trials which break down into a female vs. male thing, a "she said, he said" confrontation where there is often not a clear-cut idea of culpability. In such trials, I believe that men would probably be better off with male, not female, judges. In short, in the types of trials indicated above, guilt or innocence can swing on the prejudices of juries and judges and, thus, men would be better off with male juries and judges. Judges with track records of bias against males—decisions, sentences, restraining orders, etc.—should be voted out of office if they hold elected positions. Those appointed should not be reappointed; pressure should be applied to those officials who appoint judges.

The equal protection clause of the Constitution should be used as the basis for men to vigorously protest against all forms of anti-male discrimination. This means getting rid of affirmative action and quotas that give females an unfair advantage over men in a number of aspects of America, especially in the work force. America needs to return to being a nation based on merit, not giving preferential treatment to women simply because they are women.

In order to successfully implement their political agenda, males will need more political clout. This can be largely accomplished by having an "Office of Men's Affairs" (or some other, similar title) established in the governors' offices of each of the 50 states and at the White House. We also need to push for under-secretary slots in various federal departments (Education, Health and Human Resources, Defense, Justice, etc.) devoted solely to the protection of the rights of men in the United States—these already exist for women— and providing high-level forums for the promulgation of their interests.

On The Education Front

A two-pronged effort is required on the education front. First, the quality of education for boys at the primary and secondary levels needs to be raised. Second, a greater number of young men need to be getting post-secondary education at technical schools, junior colleges and four-year colleges and universities.

A critical starting point in achieving the first objective is to dismantle the U.S. Department of Education. This department has taken the leadership position on public education in the United States for nearly 20 years since it was designated a separate department (1979)—a period coinciding with much of the precipitous decline in educational achievements in our public school system— a decline which has made our public schools a laughing stock because they do not educate, are unable (or unwilling) to instill values and are incapable of providing a safe and secure environment for our children. Dominated by women, it has led to the anti-boy crusade which is rife in public school education today.

Republican members of Congress have called for the elimination of the U.S. Department of Education since 1994, but have been unsuccessful thus far. In fact, while the DOE had a budget of about $40 billion in fiscal year 2001, president George W. Bush has requested a $4.6 billion increase (+11.5%); the Democrats immediately began pushing for an $8.8 billion hike. Not surprisingly, DOE was cited by a congressional task force as being one of the most wasteful of federal departments when it was found to have paid $150 million in duplicate payments to vendors.[2]

On a broader scale, getting the federal government totally out of education would be another boon. Education decisions should be pushed as far down the government chain as possible—to the local level. Threats by federal bureaucrats that this would weaken education in the U.S. due to losses of funding should be dismissed since federal outlays for education amount to only 6% of the total bill, the rest ponied up at state, county and local levels. Influentials like James Dobson of Focus on the Family ("The new secretary of education must shift power away from wasteful Washington bureaucrats and into the hands of those at the local level"), Jared Young of People Advancing Christian Education ("Specifically, we'd like Congress to get the federal government out of education") and Ed Crane of the Cato Institute ("Another bad idea is expanding the federal government's role in local public education") have the same sentiment.

Let's go even further. The public school system in the U.S. has essentially failed. In a review of the book, *The 12-Year Sentence*, edited by William F. Rickenbacker, the following statement was noted: "People were reasonably well educated before 'public' schools gained a monopoly by serving the interests of ideologues and special interests." A review of Thomas Sowell's book, *Inside American Education—The Decline, The Deception, The Dogmas*, describes Mr. Sowell's work as a "scathing attack on the education establishment." Therefore, you, as the male parent need to be thinking about other education options for your children. These include private schools and home schooling and in order for parents to be able to better afford private schools for their children, they need to understand school vouchers and tax credits.

Sure, the cost of private schools is an added expense that perhaps you had not counted on when developing the family budget. You may think that the cost is prohibitive but remember that the level of education in the U.S. is a major variable in explaining the type of job our children will have and the level of income that they will achieve. Also, remember that 11.2% of all school children already are attending private schools.[3] In this light, private school expenditures should be viewed as an *investment* in your children's future and the cost does not go on *ad infitum*. Scholarships are available; loans can be taken out. More frivolous expenditures can be reduced, freeing up the necessary resources. And you can vote against school tax increases and hope that there will be enough like-minded people to prevent them so that the money saved can be used for your children's private schooling.

You will not regret the sacrifices you have made because your children will get a better education, they will have a better opportunity to acquire values (especially if they attend a private religious school), they will be less likely to be subjected to physical and psychological trauma from their classmates, and they will be better prepared for college.

As public schools have continued to tank, many parents have elected to home school their children. It has been estimated that there were one million children being home schooled in 2000.[4] This is a viable option when there is a parent who can be home to supervise the instruction. (Some home schooling is done by grand parents).

One fear that prevents many parents from home schooling is their own educational inadequacies or perceived deficiencies. In talking with many home schooling parents about this problem, I found a common solution: hire a tutor in those areas where you feel inadequate. Especially good ones are college juniors or seniors, resulting in a number of pluses. The tutor gets some invaluable teaching experience and extra income; the home schooler gets good instruction, a break from mom or dad doing the teaching, and gets to socially interact with a college-age role model.

Public school teachers—obviously with a vested interest—criticize home schooling on two counts: poor quality of education and social skills not being inculcated in the home schooler. These arguments are specious. Every report I have seen on the performance of homeschoolers has shown them with consistently higher scores on standardized tests, including the SAT. (Home schoolers in the inaugural class of Patrick Henry University had an average 1250 SAT). Julia Hunter, Harvard's admissions officer—Harvard arguably being the most selective of all U.S. colleges and universities—feels that home-schooled applicants are competitive with other students applying.[5] As far as the socialization reservation is concerned, home school parents are glad that their children don't have to be exposed to the "socialization" that goes on in public schools: the physical and psychological trauma meted out by public school bullies and quasi-bullies on a daily basis. And there are plenty of after-school opportunities for home schoolers to make friends, e.g., Boy Scouts, Girl Scouts, YMCAs, YWCAs, Boys & Girls Clubs, sports, music lessons, dance lessons.

Possibly the best arguments I have seen for home schooling were voiced by Mary Walsh, writing in *Human Events* (October 15, 2001):

> Primary reasons for homeschooling include better academics, religious or philosophical differences, alternative educational approaches, the ability to tailor the curriculum to suit the students, and safety concerns (physical, emotional, sexual or psychological) ....As a parent, what do I do with my freedom? I educate the children. I don't lay awake at night worrying about why a fifth-grader felt it necessary to expose my kindergartner to his private area. My kindergartner won't get off the bus after the first day of school spouting the 'f' word, nor will he fall asleep on that bus and be forgotten. None of my children will be molested in the lavatory by someone who is simply testing the new techniques taught in sex education class. And homeschoolers don't have to waste precious time to deal with bomb threats.

President George W. Bush has shown a partiality to home schooling. In his campaign for the presidency, he advocated eliminating federal legislation that impedes this educational option and has pushed for allowing home school parents to invest in Education Savings Accounts.[6]

School vouchers, which the Supreme Court said on June 27, 2002 could be used for religious schooling (*The Economist*, July 6, 2002, p. 34), would be a significant benefit to parents who want their children to get a better education. Advocated for 45 years by Nobel prize-winning economist, Milton Friedman, vouchers (payments) would be given to parents who, then, could use them to pay the cost of sending their children to any school of their choice—

private, public, church-related, near, far, specialized (music, science, art, math, etc.), general, whatever. Besides giving parents and/ or their children the right to select schools, there are other enormous benefits which would result:

1. School choice improves performance. According to *The Economist* (January 27, 2001), school choice in America results in an improvement of 1.4 grades in educational levels and an increase of 15% in the earnings of young adults. The Heritage Foundation released a most telling report on Washington D.C. schools. The District spends $8,055 per public school pupil annually (fifth highest in the U.S.); however, only 5% of its eighth graders can do math at the eighth grade level and only 12% can read at that grade level. On the other hand, private schools in the area, with the same *socio-economic profiles* as the D.C. public schools, have 72% higher scores.[7]

2. The cost of education will be dramatically reduced. The average annual cost-per-pupil in America's public schools is $6,549, compared to only $3,116 for private schools and $2,780 for Catholic private schools.[8] In Milwaukee, for fiscal year 2001, the American Enterprise Institute reported that the school district budgeted $9,500 per public school student, almost double ($4,894) the amount for the city's private schools. An explanation for this disparity is offered by Lois Maczuzak, administrator of the St. John Kanty school with the lowest cost-per-pupil in the city ($3,096): "We don't have to pay for a huge administration and a lot of red tape."[9]

3. According to *The Economist*, greater school choice will increase the demand for teachers who are better qualified, who went to better colleges and universities, are better prepared in math and science, and are willing to put in extra hours.[10] Do not underestimate the importance of getting better qualified teachers. I was shocked to learn, as indicated earlier, that a disproportionately large percentage of our public school teachers graduate in the bottom half of their college classes. I was more shocked to learn that, according to Martin Gross, author of *The Conspiracy Of Ignorance:*

The Failure Of American Public Schools, the typical public school teacher has graduated from the bottom third of their *high school class*, with no better than a C+ average (Martin Gross, "More Failed Federal Aid To Education," *Human Events*, January 21, 2002).

4. The Cato Institute maintains that school choice programs will increase the level of involvement by parents with their children's schools and the number of school-related activities in which they participate. Further, parents will have higher levels of satisfaction with schools' safety, discipline and instructional quality and are "likely to reenroll their children in the choice program." [11]

5. School choice vouchers will, hopefully, reduce the power of the national teachers unions—the bodies, dominated by women, which discriminate against boys in public schools, protect, through tenure, lazy and incompetent teachers, and have been a major factor in the decline of the quality of education in the United States over the last thirty years. But don't expect an easy fight; these unions are unalterably opposed to school choice because they clearly understand the threats vouchers and tax credits pose. Milton Friedman certainly recognizes the intransigence of these unions: "The teachers' unions are bitterly opposed to reform that lessens their own power, and they have acquired enormous political and financial strength that they are prepared to devote to defeating any attempt to adopt a voucher system." [12] In August, 2001 the National Education Association ran a series of radio ads requesting support of its "Make Public Schools Great" initiative. Guess how the NEA proposes to make our public schools great: by reducing the size of classrooms and increasing teachers's salaries, two so-called remedies that have proved fruitless but horribly expensive in the past. The only outcomes of these proposals will be to increase the number of inept teachers and ratchet up their salaries (according to Martin Gross, the typical teacher makes $42,000 annually and has "long vacations, enormous benefits and retirement"). Even more disgusting were TV ads running in August, 2001, cosponsored by the NEA and Home Depot. These ads reported that teachers con-

tribute $400 each annually to buy school supplies for their classes. The ad then requests donations to a fund so that this will not have to occur.

Tax credits provide tax relief to parents when they select a private school or alternative public school for their children. Thus, the credit would allow parents to deduct the amount spent for tuition, books, supplies, transportation, and so on, from their federal income taxes. (Some plans provide for an offset against property taxes). Most suggested options would cap the credit at 50% of what the government spends per pupil in public schools. This figure is believed to be adequate to cover the educational expenses at 90% or more of all private schools in the United States. Tax credits would have many of the same advantages as vouchers, as well as some additional upsides. According to Lawrence W. Reed, president of the Mackinac Center for Public Policy, Midland, Michigan: "The virtue of tax credits is that, unlike vouchers, they do not transfer money from the states, either to schools or taxpayers. Therefore, they carry less threat of government regulation of private schools and less risk of entanglement between church and state."[13] Another plus: Any taxpayer (parent, grand parent, friend, company, or church) could contribute to the education of a boy or girl and get the tax credit. The advantage of this is that it would enable low-income parents to participate. Without the possibility of these outside-the-family contributions, low-income families would be shut out because they usually do not pay any taxes so there would not be any tax payment to offset.

Certainly, the above recommendations will result in a great improvement in the quality of education for boys in America, thus increasing the possibility that they will be admitted to college and do well there. But much more needs to be done. The anti-male bias that exists in our public schools needs to be stopped dead in its tracks. This intolerable situation mitigates against boys fully developing the interest and intellectual skills they require to gain acceptance at colleges and universities; particularly odious are the efforts, often cryptic, of women teachers to emasculate our sons, essentially, to feminize them. As a dad who realizes the need for our sons to obtain a college degree, you should be on the lookout in your sons' schools for evidence of such treatment. This means you need to be involved—to know what is going on in your sons' schools by visiting them on a regular basis, talking to other parents, attending PTA meetings and other meetings, and so on, and complaining vigorously to teachers, school administrators and boards of education if you uncover even an iota of such anti-boy prejudice. Christina Hoff Sommers, author of *The War Against Boys* (a "must read" for any father interested in seeing that his son gets a good primary and secondary education), says: "If parents begin to stand up for their sons, if they refuse to allow schools to subject them to the tender mercies of the self-styled equity specialists, the prospects of America's boys will brighten immeasurably."[14]

One way to effectively blunt the anti-boy bias that permeates our public school systems and improve the educational climate for them would be to create public schools for boys only and staff them with male teachers. A move in that direction occurred in May of 2002 when the Department of Education announced that it was considering the establishment of all-boy and all-girl public schools; the education bill passed in 2001 contained $3 million for federal monies for these types of schools. However, you can bet that the radical, male-hating, radical feminists will claim discrimination because they do not want to lose the opportunity to feminize boys, humiliate them, prevent them from going to college, and unfairly catering to female students. Consider the following:

1. In 1989, Detroit wanted to open several all-male academies for at-risk, urban boys. The proposal was blocked due to the efforts of the National Organization for Women (is there any more odious group in America?) and the American Civil Liberties Union (not far behind NOW in obnoxiousness).

2. The female-dominated Department of Education's Office of Civil Rights—another boy-bashing organization—prevented Dade County, Florida from establishing two all-male *classes* (not schools) for under-achieving boys (let's not help those boys that

need help).

3. In 1994, senator John Danforth, offered an amendment to an education bill that would have allowed 10 school districts *to experiment* with all-boy classes. The Amendment was rejected in conference with the House after having passed the Senate. Danforth stated: 'I was stunned at the organized opposition to the amendment. Opponents argued vehemently that the provision would result in injustice to young girls, despite the amendment's requirement that same-sex classes be offered to both boys and girls. [15]

4. The president of the National Organization for Women's New York chapter, Anne Conners, says 'Public money should not be used to fund institutions segregated on the basis of sex.' [16]

5. Comments by Deborah Blake, senior counsel of the National Women's Law Center and Judith Shapiro, president of *all-female* Barnard College (New York City) show the true colors of the anti-male feminists vis-á-vis single-sex education: It's okay for women, but not for men. According to Ms. Blake, uni-sex schools for women are all right because of the "history of discrimination against women in education and the barriers that female students continue to face based on their gender ...."She also feels that the "considerable network" of public and private funds and programs for women are justified because of past inequities. Ms. Shapiro stated in the *Baltimore Sun*: "In a society that favors men over women, men's institutions operate to preserve privilege; women's institutions challenge privilege and attempt to expand access to the good things of life." [17]

About 15 years ago, Great Britain realized that its boys were significantly behind girls academically, particularly in reading and writing. They got a disproportionately high percentage of failing grades and tended to lose interest in school more than girls. Coming to grips with the problem, a council of British headmasters recommended single-sex schools as the major way to improve the academic performance of boys. Apparently, initial efforts have been successful; a 1997 article in *The Times* of London indicated that boys in all-male schools did 20% better than those attending mixed-sex schools. [18]

Proponents of all-boy schools for British boys point to the following as explaining their success:

1. Male teachers.
2. Teacher-dominated teaching.
3. Structured teaching environment.
4. High expectations of students.
5. Homework assignments that are thoroughly checked by teachers.
6. Penalties consistently applied if work is not done.
7. More emphasis on individual work instead of group work.
8. Frequent testing.
9. Less emphasis on "creative" assignments. (Notes one headmaster: "Boys do not always see the intrinsic worth of 'Imagine you're a sock in a dustbin'").
10. An emphasis on constructive competition. [19]

What the author finds significant about many of these rules-of-thumb is that these dominated classroom instruction in America until about the 1960s. Then, "progressive" educational ideology caught on, the old ways were summarily discarded (typical liberal strategy), and our nation's education began its precipitous decline.

Efforts by feminist groups to eliminate the SAT or ACT for getting into college need to be publicized, countered and stopped. Contrary to the shrill, cacophonous rhetoric of various anti-male groups, these tests were not developed with any gender bias but, rather, with the intent of measuring what the test developers perceived to be the skills and aptitudes needed for success in college. The fact that boys consistently do better on these tests than girls—especially in the math and science areas—is no justification whatsoever for their dismissal. In a similar vein, a perhaps more subtle and potentially more anti-boy connivance by female groups—the elimination of individual questions on these tests in which boys consistently outperform girls—needs to be exposed for the discrimination that it is (perhaps through application of the equal protection amendment of the U.S. Constitution), receive the highest level of outrage that we can muster, and be stopped. One way that should be considered to implement such an effort is to develop a similar organization for men, such as, the AAUM (American Association of University Men). One of the major goals of such an organization should also be the setting up of college scholarships for men—as the AAUW does for women—and to be in the vanguard of efforts to garner significant scholarship monies for young men from individuals, foundations and companies.

The decimation of men's athletic programs at college and universities due to Title IX needs to be halted. There may be little that can be done, however. Would it be possible for these men's teams to be resurrected and supported by private funds? This may not work due to colleges and universities dipping into the federal coffers, but it is an option worth investigating.

We read in Chapter Three about Heather Sue Mercer, the place kicker wannabe for Duke University. During the fall of 2001 another female place kicker actually began playing for a Division I team, Jacksonville University. (I wonder how she will react when some 300-pound defensive lineman nails her after she has to run with the ball following a botched field goal attempt or tries to tackle a 230-pound linebacker who picks up a blocked kick and runs with it?)

What probably needs to be done is for men to demand to play on female college and university teams, in particular, those women's teams which are a sport normally played by men but for which a team no longer exists for them due to Title IX. For example, at my university, Texas A&M, there are women's volleyball and soccer teams (but not men's teams). Using the equal protection clause of the 14th amendment, why could not a man try out for these teams? What a great experience this would be: playing a sport you love at the college-level, using the same locker room and showers, and having attractive (hopefully) ladies for team mates!

Prepare your sons for the anti-male bias they will face in college. Perhaps the most loathsome is their having to take "women's studies" courses. One thing that we men need to push is for colleges and universities to offer and require "men's studies," once again using the leverage of the equal protection amendment of the Constitution to call attention to the discrimination occurring against males.

On The Military Front

Even before the treacherous attacks on the United States on September 11, president Bush was making an effort to deal with some of the problems our military was facing. Increasing defense budgets, military pay raises and better housing will be helpful. But it will be interesting to see if he and his administration will come to grips with the problems caused by the previous administration's effort to "socially engineer" the military by caving in to the radical feminists and other women who pushed for more women in the military, more of them in combat units, coed training, and relaxed standards for female recruits but, of course, wanting to hold men to the same rigorous standards—the result of which is a military ill-prepared to accomplish its missions and defend our country.

What can those of us do who want our military to become strong again and remain strong? We should vociferously recommend to our congressmen, senators and the president that the following agenda be adopted:

1. No preferential treatment for women in the military. They will have to meet the same set of standards that men have to meet and these standards will not be relaxed to accommodate the physical or mental deficiencies of female recruits.

2. No coed training in the military. And no females being housed in the same barracks as men.

3. No women in combat units, especially the marines, army (infantry, airborne, armor, artillery, etc.), navy surface ships and submarines, helicopters and fixed-wing aircraft, and front-line logistics operations. Women in our armed forces have a contribution to make in clerical, intelligence, legal, medical specialties, and rear echelon logistics operations, but not in front-line units where their inherent physical inadequacies and temperaments will compro-

mise their safety, the safety of their comrades, and the completion
of the mission.

4. Under no circumstances should women ever be subjected to
a military draft.

Don't expect it to be easy to get this agenda passed. Military
personnel will not admit in any public forum the problems caused
by women in the armed forces for fear of being reprimanded or
worse. (Even the Marines appear to be caving in. I was horrified to
hear radio ads put out by the Marine Corps during the summer of
2001 designed to attract female recruits. I know I will sleep a lot
better at night after hearing the soprano voices in the ads cooing
about how proud they are to be marines, how much they over-
came, and saying: "I never thought I could do it.").

One way that the above agenda can be achieved and achieved
more quickly would be the election of men to the House and Senate who have had previous military experience. A start in this
direction may be found in the formation of the National Defense
Political Action Committee which actively supports candidates with
a military background. Getting organizations like the American
Legion and Veterans of Foreign Wars involved would be immensely
helpful, as well.

On The Abortion Front

In the centuries ahead, how will the United States be remembered; what will our posterity be? Nations tend to be recalled mainly
for their transgressions and no nation has greater culpability than
the United States through the 41 million innocent children slaugh-
tered by the abortion mills since 1970. And, unfortunately, the
count is still growing as we refuse to stop the carnage.

Here is what we need to do to rid our nation of this horror.
First, we should play the minority card and the equal protection
amendment in the forefront of an aggressive, *unrelenting* effort to
make abortions illegal. In other words, we push our minority status and the discriminatory outcome of abortions since they murder
more males than females (close to one million more since 1970, as

noted previously).

Second, support Supreme Court nominees who are anti-abortion. Make their stance on abortion—there can be no more important issue than this—your litmus test as to whether they should be appointed. Some of the more liberal members of the Court may soon be retiring—like pro-abortion Sandra Day O'Connor—giving us the opportunity to replace them with God-fearing jurists who have anti-abortion views.

Hopefully, Justice Ruth Bader Ginsburg will soon be retiring. Phyllis Schlafly (*Human Events*, August 18, 2003) calls Ginsburg a "feminist extremist" who favors abortion at tax payer's expense and "hates everything masculine." In Ginsburg's radical feminist manifesto, *Sex Bias in the U.S. Code*, written before she was appointed to the Supreme Court, she espouses women in military combat units, affirmative action for women in the military, federal funds for comprehensive day care, and the integration of the Boy and Girl Scouts.

Third, publicize adoption as a viable alternative to abortion. In support of this recommendation, it is important to understand that James Dobson, head of Focus on the Family, stated on his organization's radio program (July 25, 2000) that there are as many people wanting to adopt babies as there are abortions each year in the United States.

Fourth, stop federal funding for the organization that is the leading proponent of abortion and the largest provider of them (197,000 in 2001 and 3 million since Roe v. Wade), Planned Parenthood. (I continue to be amazed that this organization has "parenthood" in its name, when the logical outcome of its lies and operations eliminates the need for parents). This organization was given $27 million of your tax dollars in 1999. In other words, taxes paid by you and me are being used to destroy our posterity. If you want an idea as to why Planned Parenthood is in favor of abortions, you need to know something about its founder, Margaret Sanger. Ms. Sanger was a staunch supporter and early advocate of "eugenics," the "science concerned with improving a breed or species, especially the *human* species, by such means as influencing or encouraging reproduction by persons presumed to have desirable genetic traits" (*Webster's Universal College Dictionary*) (emphasis added). Eugenics, as one might logically assume, became the basic tenet for the Nazis who touted the supremacy of the Aryan, or master race. Consider the chilling words of Dr. Leo Alexander, who worked with the chief U.S. counsel at the Nuremberg tribunal:

> It started with the acceptance of the attitude, basic in the euthanasia movement, that there is such a thing as life not worthy to be lived. This attitude in its early stages concerned itself with the severely and chronically sick. Gradually, the sphere of those to be included in this category was enlarged to encompass the socially unproductive, the ideologically unwanted, the racially unwanted, and finally all non-Germans. But it is important to realize that the infinitely small, wedged-in lever from which the entire trend of mind received its impetus was the attitude towards the non-rehabilitable sick. [20]

Cal Thomas, nationally syndicated columnist, echoes the same sentiment: "A nation that will not protect babies at the moment of their birth is not likely to acquire a latent morality on the way to exterminating them at ever-earlier stages" (*Washington Times*, Vol. 8, No. 34, 2001). In the same oped piece, Mr. Thomas addressed the peril that *elderly men* face (remember they usually die five to six years earlier than their wives): "If we can steal the essential elements of life from others not yet born, why not exterminate those at the other end of life? Why not kill the elderly and the infirm when they have become a 'burden' on Social Security and Medicare, on society, or even on relatives eager to access an estate before much of it goes for lone-term care?" (Remember Will and his loving, caring wife, Joan, in the first chapter). A possible analogy: Could the stance on abortion taken by radical feminists be because they want to be the "master race" (remember Wonder Woman in Chapter Seven) achieved, in part, by eliminating more men than women through abortion? God forbid, but have they been willing to sacrifice 20 million female fetuses, as well as 21 million male fetuses, in order to eliminate one million more males than females?

Fifth, keep a close eye on Hillary Clinton and be poised to thwart her legislative efforts in support of abortion. Hillary has unequivocally come down on the pro-choice side: "I'll be on your side in the fight against Republican efforts to undermine family planning and take away a woman's right to choose." [21] (Notice that she doesn't say a woman's right to murder her unborn child). How far will Hillary go to push her pro-abortion agenda? Pretty far. She has co-sponsored with Teddy Kennedy an Equal Rights Amendment to the Constitution that, if passed, would lead to a vast expansion of abortion rights because it would end the prohibition on taxpayer funds for abortion, would eliminate all federal or state restrictions on partial birth abortion (where the baby's brains are sucked out after its head emerges from its mother) and tri-semester abortions, and would go after government supported medical facilities and personnel who refuse to perform abortions. [22]

Sixth, work to prevent our tax dollars from going overseas to support abortion outside the U.S. Unfortunately, during the Fall of 2000, the House and Senate appropriated $425 million to foreign nations for "population control" but without the usual restriction that these dollars could not be used for abortion except in cases of rape, incest, or to save the life of the mother (the so-called President Reagan "Mexico City Policy").

And, seventh, do not assume that president George W. Bush is a slam dunk to aggressively fight abortion even though this was a promise he made on the campaign trail in 2000. In August of 2001, he approved limited stem-cell research which involves the removal of an inner cell mass from a five-to-seven day old embryo, resulting in its death. While Mr. Bush's speech advocated this research only on already-destroyed cells, anti-abortion foes feel that it sends mixed signals on the abortion issue. And the pressure on Mr. Bush not to work for repeal of Roe vs. Wade will be unrelenting. For example, although Kate Michelman, head of the National Abortion and Reproductive Action League (NARAL), feels that 'Bush does not appear to be zealously in pursuit of the overturn of

Roe', nevertheless, NARAL pledged $40 million to pressure the Senate not to confirm Supreme Court nominees who are anti-abortion. ('Bush is a wolf in sheep's clothing,' she says). [23] And what about the pressure Mr. Bush will face from his own family—three women? During a series of television interviews, Laura Bush said that she doesn't think Roe vs. Wade should be overturned. [24] Mr. Bush's true sentiments concerning abortion may have been revealed in a speech to participants in the annual March for Life. Mr.Bush decried partial birth abortions (a ban on which was passed by the Senate on October 21, 2003 and was signed by Mr. Bush) and public funding for abortions but, most significantly, did not denounce abortions in general. (*Human Events*, January 28, 2002).

Eighth, if you know a woman who is contemplating an abortion, consider what can be done to dissuade her. Are you aware of a couple who would want to adopt the child? Can you help with medical expenses? Can you refer her to a right-to-life clinic where she can get help? Can you help with day-care expenses if the woman has to work after the baby is born? In other words, be helpful, not condemnatory; be part of the solution, not part of the problem.

On The Gun Control Front

The second amendment to the Constitution gives government military units ("militia") the right to bear arms but many scholars, including famed *liberal* constitutional scholar, Lawrence Tribe, believe that it also gives *individuals* the right to bear arms. This can be the only conclusion one can draw upon reading the actual language: "A well regulated militia, being necessary to the security of a free State, the *right of the people* to keep and bear arms, shall not be infringed" (emphasis added). Why would our Founding Fathers have included this amendment and make it the second amendment, behind the first, which guarantees freedom of religion, speech and press? Many of colonial Americans, and not a few of the Founding Fathers, were of Scottish descent. England forced the Act of Union (1707) on Scotland, thereby ending Scotland's sovereignty. This act was followed by a period of "reconstruction" that had no aim other than the total destruction of Scottish civilization. This despicable effort was made possible by the Disarming Act of 1756, which took away the right of Scots to bear arms. [25] Listen to the words of Thomas Jefferson: "No man shall ever be debarred the use of arms. The strongest reason for the people to retain the right to keep and bear arms is, as a last resort, to protect themselves against tyranny." And those of Alexander Hamilton: "If the representatives of the people betray their constituents, there is then no recourse left but in the exertion of that original right of self-defense which is paramount to all forms of positive government:"[26] Little wonder that our second amendment was passed. And let's not forget that one of Adolph Hitler's first acts as Chancellor of Germany was the abrogation of that country's right to bear arms.

So what we have seen from history is that the citizens of a country, without this right, are in grave danger of being controlled and, worse, are in extreme danger of being annihilated by a despotic government (the Jews in Nazi Germany, the Kulaks in the USSR, etc.). Men, we need to blunt the efforts of the powerful, anti-gun lobby to strip us of this important prerogative. Here is the ammunition we can use:

1. According to Florida State University criminologist, Gary Kleck, guns are *primarily* used by victims or *potential victims* to *thwart* criminals.

2. Mr. Kleck believes that seizing guns from criminals—probably an impossible task—would be fruitless. 'A year's worth of theft would easily rearm them within a single year.' [27]

3. John Lott, author of *More Guns, Less Crime*, analyzed 18 years of crime data from every county in the United States. His conclusion: "Widespread gun ownership has proven to save lives, reduce crime rates, and help citizens protect themselves. Fees, training requirements, waiting periods, and other gun laws have the negative effect of limiting gun ownership, often when citizens most need guns to protect themselves." [28]

4. In a most insightful book, *The Seven Myths Of Gun Control*,

Richard Poe, an award-winning journalist, points out that terrifying crime waves are now sweeping England and Australia—after both nations passed laws making it virtually impossible for their people to own guns. The vast majority of rank-and-file police in the U.S. favor an armed citizenry. Switzerland, which has more guns per capita than any other developed country, is the world's most peaceful nation. [29] (Switzerland requires all males to be a soldier until age 50 or 55, depending on rank. Each man keeps an automatic weapon, ammunition, helmet, and uniform at home. Subject to periodic call-ups, the Swiss claim that they can mobolize 625,000 men in less than two days, a level of preparedness that helped deter the Nazis from attacking them during World War II). (See Andrew Borowiec, "Swiss Army Strife? Move To End 'Citizens Army' Shot Down," *The Washington Times*, December 31-January 6, 2002).

5. Point out to your wife and daughters that gun control laws will put them in harm's way. Use the comments by Janalee Tobias, President of Women Against Gun Control (tell them about the existence of this organization as well), to substantiate your argument: "Women have the primary responsibility for protecting our children. And it's just a physiological fact that women are not as strong as men. The criminals will always have guns. The rapist and the murderer do not obey the law anyway. The housewife, the church-going woman won't have one....A woman needs to know how to responsibly and safely handle a firearm so she can deter crime."[30]

6. Join the NRA (National Rifle Association). It provides firearms education and safety training to such groups as the Boy Scouts, American Legion, 4-H, and Future Farmers of America (FFA) that reach one million youngsters annually. But an even more important reason to join is to help them in their effort to thwart the nefarious aims of the gun-control lobby.

7. Abigail Kohn is a practicing anthropologist whose research interest is gun use in the United States, although she had not "grown up" with guns. After visiting shooting ranges and gun shows, tak-

ing lessons from NRA-certified instructors, and eventually firing hand guns, rifles, shot guns, and pistols on ranges and in competition, she concluded:

> There was a time when I would not have wanted to touch a gun of any kind, much less spend part of an afternoon riding the back of a rocking mechanical pony and blazing away at a series of targets with revolvers, rifles and shotguns. But that improbable picture is the culmination of a journey that took me from the ivory towers of academia to the shooting ranges of Northern California. Bluntly, I was surprised by what I found there. As a practicing anthropologist, I had set out in search of gun crazies, but what I found were regular folks—enthusiasts who relate to their guns in generally positive ways. These people are usually ignored by most media accounts of America's 'gun culture'...Contrary to my initial expectations of the 'gun nuts' who presumably constitute what critics disparagingly refer to as 'the cult of the gun in America,' most members of the 'gun culture' I've talked with are typical citizens. They live normal American lives, insofar as any of us is 'normal.' They have complex and sophisticated ideas about what guns do, what guns are for, and why guns are an important part of American history, society, and culture.[31]

Ms. Kohn ran across some very informative data during her odyssey, while studying Gallup polls of adults in 1999 and 2000. There are between 77 million and 90 million gun owners in the U.S.; 39% have guns in their homes, including 47% of men and 27% of women. Two-thirds of Americans have fired guns (86% of men and 51% of women). Almost two-thirds of gun owners (65%) own guns to protect themselves against crimes; 64% of gun owners own a handgun.[32]

8. Where will the "crazies" stop in their zeal to control our lives and strip away our freedoms? They brutalized the tobacco industry, have mounted attacks against the gun industry, and now seem poised to go after the automobile, fast-food and alcohol beverage industries because they are "killers." If they are not stopped, we will be defenseless, have to walk everywhere, drink nothing but lemonade, and eat only tofu.

On The Taxes Front

President Bush's tax plan, passed in 2001, may have lowered the tax bite, but, in the long-run, will do little to change what we pay in taxes and how we pay them. The reason: The Bush tax plan did not address the fundamental flaws in our tax system.

In a nutshell, we pay too much in taxes. The wealthiest are particularly hard hit, being taxed at a marginal rate of 36%. Because we are penalized for being more productive (making more money), there is a disincentive for working harder. The high tax rates mitigate against savings and investment which create jobs. Each year, we spend countless hours and incur astronomical expenses in preparing our tax returns or having them prepared for us. And we have to deal with a tyrannical Internal Revenue Service which has been guilty of all kinds of gross injustices against U.S. citizens: taking money out of our bank accounts (often without our even knowing it), seizing our property and selling it off, sending people to prison, even shooting innocent victims. (Many of these horror stories came to light in Congressional hearings held several years ago).

If we really want to improve our tax system, make our nation more productive, get rid of inequities and, perhaps, even more important, eliminate the IRS, our nation should adopt a national retail sales tax, which is essentially a tax on consumption (purchases), not on income. (Please do not try to sell me on a flat tax. The problem with a flat tax is that it will—unlike a national retail sales tax—still require the existence of the IRS because the tax will be based on income, deductions and exemptions).

Here's the way a national retail sales tax would work. When you buy an item covered by the tax, you would pay an extra percentage—15% and 17% are two figures suggested—that would be remitted to Washington D.C. Look at the benefits that would result from the institution of this kind of tax:

1. There would be no need for the IRS. Taxes would be collected by the various state agencies that now collect state sales taxes.

2. The federal government would no longer withhold income taxes from your paycheck. You, not the federal government, would collect the interest on these monies should you choose to invest them.

3. There will be more incentives for people to work harder. Extra income would *not be taxed at all* (only if you spent some of the incremental funds). Investment and savings would be increased, spurring economic growth and employment.

4. Taxpayers would not spend hours preparing tax forms—and worrying that they might be audited. They would not have to keep receipts and maintain detailed and voluminous financial records.

5. The possibility of random acts occurring that can hurt tax-payers would be eliminated. For example, ABC radio (September 5, 2001) reported that employees of Mellon Bank, hired to screen federal income tax returns, threw away 40,000 of them—they, of course, never reached the IRS—because they were falling behind in their work and wanted to "get caught up."

Liberals (including women) will attack this plan by saying that it discriminates against the poor. There is a simple remedy: not make the tax applicable to basic items that account for large percentages of the expenditures of the poor.

Support for a national retail sales tax can be found in the history books. Most people do not know that for the first 137 years (1776-1913), the United States did not have a tax on personal incomes, except briefly during the Civil War; the tax on incomes was initiated by the Sixteenth Amendment to our Constitution. Prior to that time, we got by with essentially a set of consumption taxes—like excise taxes—and we did just fine. In 1815, England was broke. It had just fought an expensive war to defeat Napoleon on the continent of Europe. What to do? Parliament decided to eliminate the country's tax on personal incomes and replace it with a national consumption tax. (As part of the agreement, all tax records were to be burned, eliciting the loudest cheer ever heard in Parliament). Unfortunately, England made the foolish mistake of reinstating the income tax in 1894. But in the eight decades without it, England became the greatest economic power in the world. Why did this happen? Because the Brits could take risks and enjoy the results of their success without the government taking away huge chunks of their income. What has happened to Britain since 1894? Its status as an economic power has waned after it reinstituted the income tax, which at one time reached a rate of 90% on "high income" citizens.

Another tax that needs eliminated now is our nation's inheritance taxes, the so-called "death tax." This tax is especially onerous on the heirs of small business owners and ranchers and farmers. What happens is that the heirs can't pay the taxes on the ranch, farm or business, so they have to sell them often at a bargain basement price in order to pay the taxes, thus passing the asset—which may have been in the family for several generations—on to someone outside the family. People without businesses or ranches or farms as an inheritance can be hard hit, too, and don't think you have to be rich to be at risk. Our rapacious federal government provides currently only a $1 million exclusion for surviving spouses and then the tax bite begins, reaching 55%. Guys, this is a paltry amount in today's economy when one considers that the feds will consider the value of pensions and insurance proceeds in determining the size of an estate. This death tax is considered so onerous that many wealthy individuals are renouncing their U.S. citizenship in order to escape them, such as, the Dorrance family, which owns Campbell Soup. (Can you believe that the IRS, in cahoots with the Treasury department, is trying to make this ploy to eliminate these horrific taxes illegal?) Of course, the most telling argument for getting rid of this tax is that it accounts for less than one percent of federal income.

Reducing corporate capital gains taxes to 15% has been suggested by such people as Stephen Moore, president of Growth and Economic Affairs, and should be implemented. Doing so would increase corporate revenues, individual savings and the value of assets—all benefits which occurred during the last cut in capital gains. [33] Another tax which rightly has come under fire are corporate income taxes. Currently, this tax is at a rate of 35% but it is actually more than that because the 65% of profits not grabbed by the Feds can be paid to corporations' shareholders in the form of dividends and, you guessed it, individuals have to pay taxes on dividends—a classic double taxation example. Cutting the corporate rate would increase dividends and allow companies to expand their operations, thereby creating more jobs. It is important to note that many leading economists—such as Joseph Bankman of Stanford and William Vickery, a Nobel prize winner from Columbia—are advocating the abolition of this tax, which annually represents only about 10% of federal tax receipts.[34]

I am by no means a financial planner but I do know the one type of financial product to avoid at all costs: One that has a low return and high risk. There is one such product in the United States and, unfortunately, it is institutionalized by law. Its name: Social Security.

Earlier in this book you saw how meager the returns are on Social Security. And, if you listen to the critics of privatizing even a part of social security, it is very high risk ("It will be broke by such and such a date;" "the baby boomers, when they reach retirement age, will bankrupt the system," and so on).

The percentage of your pay check taken out for Social Security continues to increase, as does the upper limit; as of January 1, 2003 these were, respectively, 6.2% on $85,000. In other words, the federal government takes $5,270 a year from many wage earners to fund this low return/high-risk program. And don't forget, it takes an *equivalent amount from your employer.*

Mr. Bush wants to privatize a portion of your contributions. In other words, you would have the power to invest some of the money taken from your pay check. I recommend something even more radical: Give people the choice of leaving all of that deduction in the Social Security system or investing all of it themselves. Frankly, I would be surprised that anyone would take the first option; it doesn't take a rocket scientist to find an investment product that would guarantee a no risk, 6% return—a return four times what I have seen experts estimate the returns of Social Security to be, that is, 1.5%.

Some of the above tax recommendations, however, will not be possible unless we stop the OECD dead in its tracks. I know what you are thinking: What in the world is the OECD and what does it have to do with internal tax matters of the United States of America? Located in Paris, the Organization for Economic Cooperation and Development is an international organization of 30 developed countries, including the U.S., most European nations and Japan, Australia and New Zealand. It makes economic and political policy recommendations for its member nations. Recently, it has come down hard on countries, many of which are not members of the OECD, which it says have unfair tax policies—policies which entice people and corporations to locate there to enjoy the benefits of low (or no) taxes, claiming that such policies are unfair (to the high-tax countries). The consequences would be catastrophic if the OECD is successful; by "criminalizing territorial tax systems," the United States would be precluded from ever implementing a flat tax or national retail sales tax and would significantly reduce the level of foreign investment in the United States. A number of prominent political leaders and private citizens are leading the fight against this assault on our financial privacy and fiscal sovereignty, including Rep. Dick Armey (Texas), House majority leader; Senate minority whip Don Nickles (Oklahoma); Sen. Jesse Helms (North Carolina), Sen. Judd Gregg (New Hampshire); Rep. Sam Johnson (Texas); Rep. Tom Reynolds (New York); Grover Norquist (Americans for Tax Reform) and Walter Williams (John M. Olin Distinguished Professor of Economics, George Mason University). [35] (I have visited the OECD in Paris and have perused much of their literature. Their personnel are typical "one worlders" and United Nations lovers, in other words, threats to the success and sovereignty currently enjoyed by Americans.

On The War-on-Drugs Front

The Economist reports that nearly 25% of America's prison inmates are serving time for drug-related offenses, cost tax payers $10 billion, and result in a host of other undesirable outcomes, including children of incarcerated women being sent to foster homes, a disproportionate share of Blacks being locked up, loss of voting rights for individuals committing minor crimes (possessing and using), and the great increase in crime likely to occur when these drug offenders are released from prison because the prison experience has made them hardened criminals. Little wonder that *The Economist* refers to our war-on-drugs as "failed."[36] *Reason,* in one of its promotional circulars, terms it a "complete failure" because of its cost (($100 million *every day),* number of arrests (4,246 *every day),* tearing families apart, destroying fundamental Constitutional protections, and undermining our foreign policy. Like the misguided thinking that more money would solve our country's education woes, pumping billions more into the War-on-Drugs has not eradicated—has not even reduced—the drug problem.

America would be better off reducing the intensity of the War-on-Drugs—targeting large-scale dealers instead of "recreational users"— and using the freed-up funds for treatment instead of prison. (There are an estimated five million hardcore drug users in the U.S. and only 40% are in treatment). With the change in priority, we could then eliminate many of the Draconian laws passed to supposedly "fight drugs" but often used to intrude on the rights and privacy of law-abiding citizens. (Remember the Bank Secrecy Act, the Comprehensive Crime Bill of 1984, the Money Laundering Act of 1986, and others discussed in Chapter Two.)

On The Health-Care Front

Under no circumstances, support Hillary Clinton's national health care agenda which the respected Heritage Foundation says will destroy the high-quality health care we have and our relationships with our doctors and will become the "biggest bureaucratic nightmare our country has ever seen." Vowing to get her ideas accepted, piecemeal (remember the boiling frog analogy), she has introduced 10 health-care bills directed toward achieving her "single-payer health care" idea, which is simply an euphemism for putting our health care system in the hands of our federal government. (The Heritage Foundation says that this would be "health care with the efficiency of the postal service and the compassion of the IRS."). Don't buy into the argument that this is the norm in other countries. It is, but here's the result. In Britain, people are having to raise large sums of money to get *private* surgery done because the National Health Service is jammed up. Seventy-eight percent of Canadians recently polled said that their health care system is in crisis. Why? Because people have died waiting for help in emergency rooms; waiting times for MRIs are usually at least a year and newer, life-saving drugs are not available.[37]

Push aggressively for equitable federal funding for men's health concerns, particularly for research on prostate cancer which, as we saw in Chapter Five, receives much less funding than is allocated for women's cancers. A step in the right direction may be on the horizon. In February 2001, Rep. Randy Cunningham (R-Cal.) introduced a bill in the House to establish an Office of Men's Health within the Department of Health and Human Services.[38]

Expand on Mr. Cunningham's embryonic effort by aggressively pushing for a men's health office or department in *every* major health agency. The leverage that we can use is that there is *already* a women's office or department in all major federal health agencies.

In order to counter the pro-female, anti-male bias that exists in federally funded health-care research, demand that males be part of all appropriate subject pools. After all, this is only going to level the playing field since the National Institutes of Health now require funded scientists to include women in their medical research studies.

On The Propaganda Front

The female propaganda machine is relentless. We are bombarded daily with anti-male, pro-female material, whether it's radio, television, newspapers, what have you. Little wonder, since a majority of people working in the media are women. A double whammy: Not only are women in media likely to be biased against men, they tend to vote for liberal politicians who are the architects of many of the anti-male laws and regulations that spew out of Washington D.C. and our various state capitals. (The December 23, 2000 issue of *The Economist* indicated that 90% of journalists in 1996 voted for Bill Clinton and, currently, do not approve of President Bush's positions on abortion and the death penalty).

Don't expect to see a diminution in the female drum beat. In 1999, *Electronic Media* (November 8, 1999) announced the establishment of a fund to increase the ownership of television and radio stations by women and minorities. (Note how women have craftily tied into minorities to gain their ends). The fund was established by the National Association of Broadcasters and 15 major TV and radio companies.

Men, we need a national organization, similar to the National Organization for Women, that will aggressively advance men's positions, interests and needs. It needs to have a catchy name that captures the imagination of men and what it means to be a man in the United States in the 21st century. Here's one to consider: "No Ma'am" (National Organization for Men Against Anti-Maleness). And whatever the name, this organization needs to be involved in all facets of American life to counter the anti-male propaganda that is poured out—in education, religion, politics, etc. One example: We need a countervailing organization to thwart the aims of those women's groups which advocate the elimination of all math questions on the SAT on which men do better than women.

I hope this book might be the catalyst for national syndicated columnists to take up the cudgels for men. Radio and television shows dealing with topics of interest to men and their concerns would be appropriate. (With over 3,500 radio talk shows in the

United States, surely at least a handful would be interested in men's issues).

There are some pro-male organizations that have sprung up that appear to be helpful in advancing the cause of men in the United States. These include American Coalition for Fathers and Children, The Fatherhood Coalition, The Men's Center, Men's Health Center, The Men's Issues Pages, Men's Rights, Inc. and The National Organization on Male Sexual Victimization.

✗ Finally, be very skeptical about "information" coming from women's organizations; remember the examples of deliberate lies put out by various women's groups to further their ends that are contained in previous chapters. Be suspicious; check out all of their "facts and figures."

REFERENCES

1. C. Russell Yates, Newsletter, Fall, 2002.

2. The Heritage Foundation Newsletter, April 16, 2001.

3. Peter Brimelow, "Private School Surge," *Forbes,* November 27, 2000, p. 104.

4. Peter Brimelow.

5. Susan B. Garland, "The ABCs Of Home Schooling," *Business Week,* March 5, 2001, pp. 110-111.

6. *Human Events,* November 17, 2000, p. 3.

7. Matthew Robinson, "GOP Retreats On Bush Education Plan," *Human Events,* May 7, 2001, p. 5.

8. Matthew Robinson.

9. *Human Events,* September 29, 2000, p. 28.

10. *The Economist,* January 27, 2001, p. 78.

11. Philip Vassallo, "More Than Grades—How Choice Boosts Parental Involvement And Benefits Children," *Cato Institute Policy Analysis* #383, October 26, 2000.

12. Excerpt from communication from Milton and Rose D.Friedman Educational Choice Foundation.

13. *Imprimis,* July 2001.

14. Christina Hoff Sommers, *The War Against Boys,* Simon &

Schuster, New York, 2000, p. 71.

15. Christina Hoff Sommers, p. 171.

16. Christina Hoff Sommers, p. 171.

17. Christina Hoff Sommers, pp. 171-172.

18. Christina Hoff Sommers, pp. 171-172.

19. Christina Hoff Sommers, p. 161.

20. Michelle Malkin, "Award-Winning Letter Harkens Back To Days Of Nazi Holocaust," *Human Events,* May 18, 2001.

21. Terence P. Jeffrey, "Here's A Job For Hillary," *Human Events,* February 18, 2000, p. 7.

22, *Human Events,* April 9, 2001, p. 10.

23. Mimi Hall, "For Bush, Abortion Not Policy Priority," *USA Today,* April 29-22, 2001.

24. *The Bryan-College Station Eagle,* January 25, 2001.

25. Flyer from the Conservative Book Club.

26. Conservative Book Club Announcement #901.

27. *Human Events,* December 29, 2000.

28. *Cato Institute Publications,* May/June 2000, p. 6.

29. Conservative Book Club Flyer #901.

30. Joseph A. D'Agostino, "Women Against Gun Control," *Human Events,* March 31, 2000.

31. Abigail Kohn, "Their Aim Is True—Taking Stock Of America's Gun Culture," *Reason,* May 2001, pp. 27-32.

32. Abigail Kohn.

33. Stephen Moore, "Tax-Cutting Advice For President-Elect Bush," *Human Events,* December 29, 2000.

34. Bruce Bartlett, "Cut Corporate Taxes To Raise Standard Of Living," *Human Events,* November 10, 2000, p. 15.

35. Daniel J. Mitchell, "International Bureaucrats Seek Control Of U.S. Tax Law, *Human Events,* March 12, 2001, p. 3.

36. Sebastian Mallaby, "Two Million Behind Bars," *The World In 2001, The Economist,* 2001, p. 28.

37. The Heritage Foundation Newsletter, July 11, 2001.

38. Cathy Young, "False Diagnosis," *Reason,* May 2001, pp. 22-24.

NINE

Personal Counter-Attack Strategies

"If you have conscientiously tried to be responsive to your wife's needs, don't let her blame you for her lack of happiness."

"It is not at all inappropriate for you to indicate to your wife the expectations you have of her and the extent to which they are being met."

The final chapter of *The War Against Men* will offer additional counter-attack strategies that men should aggressively move to implement as soon as possible. These deal with the personal aspects of their lives and, as such, are more emotional, more immediate and more people-oriented than those offered in Chapter Eight, where our concern was what men must do to win the political battles we face. Included in this chapter are indications as to what needs to be accomplished on the following fronts: men/women, father/son, work force, religion, and health care.

On The Men/Women Front

In discussing this front, I will address male/female relations before and after marriage.

Before Marriage

There is only one decision a young man will make that is more important than his relationship he has with God through Jesus Christ: that is deciding which woman to marry. This decision will affect all facets of your future life—work, children, your faith, your relationship with your parents—so you better make the right choice.

You are urged not to trivialize this decision with the notion that if it does not work out, you can always get a divorce. God hates divorce—perhaps mainly because of what it does to the children involved—he wants you to make a life-long commitment to your spouse, not a two-,three- or five-year one.

What qualities should you look for in a potential mate? At the top of the list should be your prospective mate's set of values, not her looks or her sex appeal. If these come with the appropriate values, great; if not, choose values over looks. Believe me, inappropriate values will cause more problems in a marriage than will the lack of looks or sex appeal.

What values should you desire? A young women who is a committed Christian is the chief priority. With this set of values, you will be marrying someone who will likely seek God's help in your lives—a tremendous plus in your marriage. If you, yourself, are a committed Christian and your potential partner is not, do not make the mistake of thinking you can get married and then change her. It does not work this way. In fact, the normal strains of marriage may have the opposite effect: watering down your Christian commitment.

It is totally wrong in God's eyes and potentially harmful to you on a personal basis for you to be engaging in pre-marital sex. Here are the downsides. Pregnancy could result, forcing you to marry someone you really do not care for. This is a sure-fire formula for an early divorce. Or, the unwanted pregnancy may result in the

woman getting an abortion and the extent to which you are involved with this decision may haunt you for the rest of your life.
You may eventually decide during the relationship that the woman
is someone you do not want to marry but because of your guilt
from having "violated" her or taken away her virginity, you capitu-
late into a marriage doomed to fail. For all of these and additional
factors, as well, abstinence is the way to go. (Do not let your buddies' tales of sexual conquests deter you from your commitment to
abstinence. In many cases, they are probably making these up and,
even if they aren't, let them suffer the consequences described
above—but not you).

Many young men will ignore this abstinence recommendation
because they will rely on condoms to keep them out of trouble.
Big mistake; Pat Buchanan (*Human Events*, March 11, 2002) sum-
marizes the results of a 2001 study conducted by the Department
of Health and Human Services, *Scientific Evidence on Condom Effectiveness for Sexually Transmitted Disease Prevention*, thusly: "The
study then coldly concluded there is no 'clinical proof' of the effectiveness of condoms in preventing genital herpes, syphilis,
chancroid, trichomoniasis or chlamydia ...."

Do not be in a hurry to get married. The old adage, "Marry in
haste, repent at leisure," is certainly applicable here. Take time to
really get to know the woman you think you want to marry. Let
her be exposed to a variety of situations and see how she responds.
And pray about this decision, seeking God's guidance.

It is always a good idea for you and your future spouse to go
through marriage counseling before you tie the knot. From the
perspective of a Christian counselor, you will gain an understanding of the importance of faith in your marriage and the
responsibilities each of you will have toward each other and your
children. A good counselor will also address an area that frequently
causes significant levels of dissension in a marriage—finances.

In regard to the financial issue, I think it is mandatory that you
and your future wife hammer out and sign a pre-nuptial agreement. While such an agreement includes mainly economic

dimensions of a marriage, it can also touch on such non-economic issues as what faith children will be raised in and which spouse will get custody of them should there be divorce.

The advantages to men of a pre-nuptial agreement are many:

1. Your financial interests will be protected. These can be divided into two categories: the assets you had before you got married and the income and assets you acquire after you are married, including pension plans and stock options which many courts, in the absence of a pre-nup, are now more inclined to award a hefty share to wives.

2. Your future wife will have to declare what her debts are, such as, college loans, credit cards, etc. This way, you will not be ambushed after you are married. It is a foolish move on your part to co-sign any of your future wife's debts which she incurred before marriage.

3. You can decide who, in your marriage, will be responsible for paying bills and long-run financial planning.

4. Both you and your spouse will better appreciate the importance of the financial aspects of marriage.

5. Your prospective partner will be forced to declare what assets she is bringing into the marriage.

6. The time taken to develop a pre-nuptial agreement will lengthen the courtship process, allowing you to be more certain that you are marrying the right woman.

7. You can sequester for yourself those assets you had acquired before you were married.

In developing a pre-nuptial agreement, several points are worth remembering. First, you and your future wife will each need to have your own lawyer. This eliminates the possibility of your wife saying later on that she was coerced or "didn't understand." Second, don't hide assets, although it is certainly all right for you to keep for yourself those that you bring to the marriage. You need to be honest, in this regard, and disclose any future assets you reasonably expect to get, such as, an inheritance. Third, decide how any appreciation in value of assets is to be allocated between you and your wife. [1]

Don't be stampeded into getting married because you are getting older and all of your friends are already married and your mother is pushing hard. Wait for the right woman and the right timing. Couples are getting married later in life so, if you want to get married, but are already in your late 20s or early 30s, don't panic—there will be enough time to marry, raise children and retire at a relatively early age.

While we are on the subject of time, let's consider the implications of any age differential that might exist between you and your future wife. While, obviously, this should not be the major factor in deciding whom you marry, there are some important ramifications if you are older than your wife—as apparently are most of the husbands in the U.S. As the number of years for which the husband's age exceeds that of the wife's increases, the greater the number of years the wife will have remaining after the husband dies. For example, if it is assumed that the expected life span is 79 for women and 74 for men, a wife has on average 11 more years to live if she is six years younger than her husband. This has important implications for decisions about pensions, insurance, social security, retirement, long-term care, etc, Also, a wife who is likely to live a great number of years beyond her husband is more likely to be "concerned" about her financial security (remember Will's situation in Chapter One?). As the ages of the wife and husband become closer, of if the wife is older than the husband, there is less concern on the part of the woman and the temptation to do something she should not do should decrease.

After Marriage

Don't berate yourself if you did not hammer out a pre-nuptial agreement. Simply develop, along the lines suggested above, a *post-nuptial* agreement. A major benefit of such an agreement is that it will force you and your wife to think carefully about how your marriage is currently progressing, particularly in the financial and economic arena. If, in general, you have a good marriage, you are fortunate. If not, a post-nuptial agreement is a good way for you to get on track because it will provide you with an opportunity to articulate your concerns in a less heated environment.

It is vitally important that you indicate to your wife how much you appreciate her contributions to your marriage. I urge you, in particular, to thank her for taking care of the house and your children. To be perfectly honest about it, much of what wives do is unadulterated drudgery, but it is so important— almost as important as the job you have and the income that is derived from it. A couple's house may be its highest-valued asset and it is important that it be maintained, straightened up and cleaned on a timely basis. And the yard needs to be well-maintained, but this should probably be your responsibility. How important is your wife's contribution to child care? Absolutely critical. Psychologists estimate that virtually all of a child's personality is determined by the age of seven and it is moms who are mainly with children from birth until that age.

You need to thank your wife for these contributions because they are well deserved but, also, because you need to blunt the onslaught of radical feminist rhetoric that demeans the stay-at-home mom. Consider what Ann Crittenden says in her book, *The Price of Motherhood: Why Motherhood Is The Most Important—And Least Valued—Job In America*: 'Motherhood is now the single greatest obstacle left in the path to economic equality for women." [2]

If you have conscientiously tried to be responsive to your wife's needs, don't let her blame you for her lack of happiness. After all, the Constitution says the *pursuit* of happiness, not the *guarantee* of happiness. Wives, themselves, are largely responsible for their happiness, or lack thereof. A woman's happiness should first be a function of her relationship with God, then largely from how she relates to her children. Next in importance are the female friends she has. So, it can be argued, that her relationship with her husband is, in the overall scheme of things, not that important in determining her level of happiness.

It is not at all inappropriate for you to indicate to your wife the expectations you have of her and the extent to which they are being met. After all, if you are like most husbands in the U.S., you are probably on the receiving end of a litany of expectations and criticisms from your wife—on an ad infinitum, ad nauseum basis. Thus, turn about is fair play.

If at all possible, keep your wife out of the work force. Even if you don't have children, I don't advise her working for all of the downsides indicated previously. I can think of no instance in which the benefits would override the downsides which, as we have seen, are horrific. Be particularly wary of part-time employment. It is most unlikely that the incremental income will cover the additional outlays required for clothes, transportation, lunches, day-care, and so on.

Finances are a significant part of marriage and you need a solid plan to ensure your success in this area. Larry Burkett, the premier Christian financial counselor, has two major pieces of advice: Avoid going into debt and develop a budget. Burkett bases his debt verboten recommendation on the notion that debt is bondage, according to such Bible verses as "Owe no one anything except to love one another" (Rom. 13:8) and "The rich rule over the poor and the borrower is servant to the lender" (Prov. 22:7). He maintains that taking on a mortgage is the one asset for which it is okay to go into debt. He does not recommend the incurring of debt for automobiles, preferring instead that cash be paid for a used vehicle. Credit card debt is viewed as being totally unacceptable and dangerous. [3]

Many wives are, unfortunately, going to be resistant to the notion of a budget. However, it is critical that couples develop an idea as to what categories of expenses income will need to cover and the amounts required, and you need to stick to it. Account for all categories of expenditures, being sure to allocate funds for charity and Church-giving—Christian financial counselor, Paul Swaes, maintains that couples that tithe don't experience financial problems—[4] and fun times (vacations, eating out, etc,). I think it is also a good idea that each partner—if at all possible—have at least a small amount of money each month to spend as they see fit on themselves, without having to be accountable to the spouse.

A 1996 survey conducted by DDB Needham Worldwide, Inc. found that a large percentage of women "took care of the checkbook and paid the bills." The proportion with this responsibility increased with age: 82% under 32 years-of-age, 83% ages 32-50 and 87% for the 50-and-over group. Unfortunately, many wives will take advantage of the situation to not stay within the budget, indulge themselves, and sequester funds in advance of a separation or divorce. While men may feel that they don't want to "mess around with the finances," I urge you to take on this responsibility in order to protect yourself and to ensure that your financial game plan is progressing as expected. If you do not want this responsibility for yourself, at least consider two other options: "Audit the books" periodically to make sure nothing untoward is occurring or manage the checkbook and pay bills jointly with your wife.

I don't know how you can accomplish this, but wives need to have an understanding of basic economics. At the top of the list should be the concept of finite resources, that is, that a family has only so much money, so much time. Coupled with the notion of finite resources is the idea of trade offs. This is particularly applicable to the family budget. For example, the more money spent on entertainment, the less funds available for other wants or needs. Supply and demand analysis is important, also, as it affects the prices that have to be paid and product availabilities. Of a more financial nature, the time value of money and compound interest are quite important, especially for retirement planning.

It is of utmost importance that you plan successfully for retirement. There is nothing more demoralizing to a man than to work a lifetime and find that he has less than $250 in the bank and will have to rely solely on social security to survive—circumstances which apparently are being faced by a majority of individuals who retire today.

Many jobs have attractive retirement programs whereby an employee contribution is matched or exceeded by the employer.

These are the lucky employees as compared to others who need to provide for their retirement solely on their own. However, even the lucky ones may find that they need to supplement their company retirement program with an investment scheme of their own.

However you are going to do it, understand that a person can be comfortable at retirement even though monthly contributions are not excessive and only "reasonable" rates of return are achieved. (I feel that, for the foreseeable future, you can forget about the 15%, 20% and 25% annual returns that investors enjoyed during much of the 1990s; they were an aberration). For example, a monthly contribution of $400 for 30 years with a rate of return of 6% will provide a retirement nest egg of $402,000; an 8% return on a monthly contribution of $800 over 30 years will grow to about $1.2 million. Keep in mind that if you are willing to accept lower rates of return, you are incurring less risk, that is, the likelihood that you will lose money decreases. Another point: You need to start early so that you can let compound interest work for you; starting early also allows you to accept lower rates of return and the accompanying lower levels of risk.

A 30-year time frame means that a man could begin contributing to a retirement program in his middle 20s and quit work in his middle fifties. For many men, their children would be out of the house, they would not need as much money to live on, and they and their wives could enjoy themselves early enough in life so that their retirement would not be beset by health problems. Another advantage: By starting early for retirement, men would provide themselves with additional time to reach their financial goals by their early 60s if their retirement funds did not achieve the rates of return hoped for and/or the level of contributions had to be reduced.

Don't let your wife jeopardize your and her retirement by having you buy various extravagances which will reduce the amount of funds you and she will have at retirement. She doesn't need expensive jewelry, a fur coat, a more ostentatious house, and so on. I saw an excellent ad campaign on television in the Spring of 2001 stressing this same theme. The ad showed how devastating to retirement an expensive diamond necklace bought today would be; another made the same point with a luxury car. To show how damaging to your retirement such frivolous purchases can be, consider what $20,000 would be worth 20 years later at retirement instead of being used to purchase some unnecessary item now. Even assuming a relatively low annual rate of return of 6%, it would be worth $65,000; at 10%, $135,000.

How much life insurance should you carry? A good rule-of-thumb is enough to provide for your family should you die, but not such an excessive amount that it would be a temptation for anything to happen to you. You also need a tightly crafted will so that your post-mortem wishes can be carried out as you would like them to be.

What should you do if your marriage has disintegrated to the extent that carrying on appears to be utterly futile and most of the blame lays with your wife? Certainly, the decision as to what you will do is made infinitely more difficult if you have children still at home. What must be done is for you to sit down with your wife and, as dispassionately as possible, tell her of your concerns. At this point, do not let yourself be flummoxed into listening to her complaints against you. You have probably been hearing these for years and, besides, it is her turn to hear what your concerns are. Give her a certain time period in which she has the opportunity to make a change for the better. If she flat out refuses during the confrontation to make a change, or has not made satisfactory progress toward same at the end of the stipulated time period, follow through with what you have articulated will be the consequences—separation, divorce, whatever.

You should have kept enough money aside for a situation like this—an apartment, food, transportation, utilities, etc.— so that you do not have to stay in an intolerable situation because you can't afford to leave. And don't keep hanging around because you think you can't handle the cooking, washing and cleaning responsibilities—I've known some men who felt this way and, thus, continued to live in most disagreeable circumstances—they aren't that big a deal.

With children at home, you will have a gut-wrenching decision. Here's what I suggest you do. Try and stick it out, but get out if your wife is submitting you to a constant barrage of humiliation and degradation that your children are aware of. Why? Because your children will be worse off in that kind of a situation than if you leave. But remember that, if you do leave, you *absolutely must* take care of the financial needs (legally and morally) and emotional needs of your children by spending as much time with them as you can. Of course, one way to assure this is to get custody of your children, especially if you believe that your wife is an unfit mother. One of the most heart-rending examples of neglecting children I have ever encountered is that engaged in by Larry Bird, the basketball great, but a real dud as a father. Bird fathered a daughter out of wedlock with his ex-wife while attempting a reconciliation with her—which failed. Bird subsequently remarried and had several additional children by his second wife but, except for an occasional card and a monthly support check (which I am sure he could easily afford), had little or no contact with her. She was not even invited to his induction into the Basketball Hall of Fame; but the half-siblings and the new wife attended. The neglected daughter, an attractive young lady in her middle 20s, appeared in one of the documentaries made about Bird, and made excuses for him, but you could see and feel the hurt on her face and in her voice.

If you have decided to divorce your wife, you will want to be fair to her and to yourself, as well. Don't give the store away because you have a guilt feeling; you need to be able to survive also. Don't be embarrassed to ask the court for alimony payments from your ex-wife—especially if she makes more money than you do—and don't be reticent to nail her for child-support funds if you have custody of your children. As you press the court for financial equity, be sure to have your lawyer indicate three economic factors prejudicial to men that dissident feminists Cathy Young (*Boston*

Globe) and Robyn Blumner (*St. Petersburg Times*) admit exist: the extra money men need when visiting their children, funds required for them to move out, and discriminating tax laws to which men are subjected. [5]

On The Father/Son Front

I consider this a battlefield because in many families, wives and even daughters will either unwittingly or knowingly attempt to encroach on the bond that exists between fathers and sons or prevent them from forming such a bond in the first place. Of course, you will want to be loving and helpful to your wife and daughters, also, but you need to forge a special relationship with your sons. You are essentially derelict in your obligations to them if you don't.

Four recommendations are offered that should form the bedrock for a successful relationship with sons. First, tell them that you love them. I don't care if they are teenagers or even young adults; they need to hear this. Oh, sure, they may make light of it, but deep down they will be grateful—perhaps not today, but down the road. Second, you must live a life that they will respect. Your sons will watch you like a hawk to see if your actions square with the credo you verbally provide them. They will only get confused or deem you a hypocrite if your actions are at variance with what you say. If fact, I think you do your sons more harm if they see a gulf between what you do and what you profess than if you had not verbalized any "code of conduct" and your modus vivendi were less than desirable. In other words, your credibility will be destroyed if the former situation exists. Third, spend time with your sons. I am sure that you are as appalled as I am to learn that the average dad spends 10 minutes a week with his children. Do not buy into the cop out that you spend "quality time" with your boys; there needs to be quantity, as well. Fourth, spending time should include a set of activities *over time* in which both of you are interested and that will, hopefully, be continued when your sons reach young adulthood, Examples include all kinds of sports, tinkering with cars, collectibles (coins, stamps, baseball cards, etc.), fishing and/

or hunting, working out, playing musical instruments—the possibilities are virtually endless.

It is important that you stress to your sons how important it is to further their education at the college or university level. This objective should permeate their learning throughout their elementary, junior-high and high-school days.

Dads, you need to put together a financial plan to help pay for your sons' college bills. Some states have developed education savings plans (Section 529 College Savings Plans which in 2002 became tax exempt) which might prove helpful but there are other non-governmental strategies which can be implemented, as well. For example, regular savings plans and insurance policies which will ensure that your son will have at least some financial assistance when starting college. These do not have to "break the bank." Putting $100 a month aside for 18 years with a nominal rate of return of 6% will accumulate a nest egg of $40,000. And do not forget loans, scholarships and sons' contributions from working.

If your son is having trouble getting accepted by a four-year school and/or money is tight, consider his enrolling at a junior or community college. The tuition at these two-year schools is usually a fraction of that charged by the public four-year institutions, even less that what would have to be paid to top-tier, private colleges and universities. Four-year schools which turned away your son earlier may accept him two years later if his grades are good. In fact, some four-year, state-supported universities have agreements in place with two-year institutions which obligate them to accept those two-year students that have performed at certain designated levels.

Another benefit of two-year schools worth noting: It is possible to get professional training somewhat comparable to what is available at four-year schools—in half the time. For example, many junior or community colleges offer an Associate Degree in Business which can be obtained in two years. How is this possible? The Associate Degree, unlike the four-year baccalaureate degree in business, does not require history, English, sciences, political science, psychology, etc., but only courses in accounting, management, marketing, sales, retailing, information systems, etc.

Another way to save on the cost of educating your sons is to have them live at home rather than on campus or in an apartment. I know that many college-bound young men will balk at this idea—they want to "get out of the house," to be on their own—but if finances are strained or if they lack the maturity to be on their own and the college they want to attend is close by, they can "suck up" a few more years of living at home. After all, they will still have 40+ years to be on their own and live in a style *they* can afford. Another point: Whether they live at home, on campus or in their own apartment, they do not need a brand new, $30,000 vehicle. A decent, affordable used vehicle is perfectly acceptable; after all, we're talking about only four or five years. When they graduate, they can acquire a new, expensive mode of transportation. In fact, many car dealerships offer great deals to the new college graduate.

Another option for young men to finance college is for them to, first, join the armed forces, then take advantage of educational funds that will be available. Besides the dollars they will be getting, they will acquire discipline, self-reliance and pride—all attributes that will help them succeed in college—and in life.

On The Work Force Front

Remember Gary Bauer, candidate for the Republican nomination for president in the 2000 election? His detractors all but accused him of sexual misconduct because he had several meetings with a female subordinate behind a closed door. No matter how far fetched the allegation, it illustrates a valid point: Unless men protect themselves on the job from instances like this, we may be sued by women with a vendetta against men who claim our talk is inappropriate, they were groped, we leered, and so on, and our weak-kneed employers, believe me, will side with the female because they are afraid of being sued.

What can you do? Keep your door open when conversing with a female co-worker, especially if she is a subordinate, and even if she is your superior. If the conversation is to be sensitive, or turns out that way, have another male colleague sit in, or even tape it. Be very careful not to tell female workers that they look nice, or that you like their new dress or hairdo because even such innocuous comments as these can be construed by women, your employer or the courts as sexual harassment. Under no circumstances would I ever tell a joke with sexual innuendoes to a woman. And you need to be even more careful than this: Don't tell a joke or make a comment with sexual overtones to another male for fear a woman might be listening (eavesdropping?). They might take offense and accuse you of sexual harassment.

Don't allow yourself to be in close quarters where women are for fear of being accused of groping, making sexual suggestions, etc. If you are moving through an area where women are and the space is tight, it is probably a good idea to put your hands in your pockets so you accidentally don't touch them.

Be prepared to fight for your rights if you are being sexually harassed by a female. It does happen. It happened to a married male correctional officer in New Jersey who rejected the sexual advances of a female co-worker. The man reported the situation to his supervisors who did nothing to stop the unwarranted advances, telling him to "handle it yourself." The man sued and was awarded $10 million. [6]

The effect of these precautionary measures on your part will be to reduce the probability that you will be falsely accused of wrong doing. The downside is that the work environment will be less open and accommodating to women. So be it. Much of this can be blamed on females who have manipulated sexual harassment and equal opportunity laws to unfairly advance their careers.

The essence of what I am saying was substantially corroborated in an exchange between the two dissident feminists mentioned earlier, Cathy Young and Robyn Blumner:

Blumner: "You have written extensively about the growth of sexual harassment law, saying it 'has grown like the Blob, swallowing up trivial or ambiguous acts, sexual jokes, compliments, leers, requests for dates, and spreading over an ever-wider range of inter-actions between men and women who work and study together.' Why do you think women are willing to let this Blob grow?"

Young: "I mean, it codifies women as the weaker sex in need of legal protections against the indelicacies of men. It undermines, as opposed to advances, an equal-work environment where women are included in the dirty jokes and made to feel like part of the group. Instead, victim feminists want to erect a Victorian-era wall between women and their male colleagues."[7]

Women have chosen to invade the work force and, as described earlier, they are often getting ahead not through merit but because of rank discrimination in favor of them and against men. I have several suggestions for combatting this situation:

1. Push hard for repeal of all legislation that gives preferential treatment to women over men in the work place, the so-called "affirmative action" laws.

2. Compete aggressively with women for jobs, pay increases and promotions. You should view women in the work force as an even greater threat to your career and economic well-being be-cause they are being given preferential treatment. In other words, do not hold back because they are the so-called "weaker sex."

3. Any time you feel you are discriminated against on the job because you are not a female—and the discrimination is gross, not at the margin—complain to your superior and, if you feel that you have a strong case, consider taking legal action. This is what the male faculty did at Virginia Commonwealth University (and won) when the administration excluded merit factors in the pay raise process and gave an across-the-board raise to *all women* faculty, but not men.[8]

On The Religion Front

Remember that we said previously that the best predictor of whether a child remains religious throughout adulthood is not the religiosity of the mother, but the religiosity of the father. This is especially true for boys as they see that religion is not something alien to the father but, rather, an integral part of his life. [9]

In practical terms, what does this mean? The religious father regularly attends church and Sunday school and sees to it that his wife and children do also. The father, at home, reads and helps his children read and understand the Bible. The religious dad teaches his children the value of prayer; he regularly prays himself and leads his family in prayer. He explains to his children the need to accept Christ and the dire consequences if this is not done. The religious dad scrupulously tithes to his church and supports other Christian ministries with gifts. But, most important, his daily living reflects his commitment to Christ: slow to anger, nice balance between work and family, gentleness toward his wife, providing a climate in which children can fail and still continue to encourage them, yet has reasonable expectations regarding the behavior and performance of his children and, yes, meting out appropriate punishment when warranted.

Because of the feminization of churches occurring today in America—most predominantly in the Catholic and mainline Protestant churches—dads need to take leadership positions in their local churches. Examples include serving as an elder or deacon, singing in the choir, teaching Sunday school, coaching an after-school church athletic team, etc.

There are very tangible and meaningful benefits that result when dads and their families are active participants in their churches. David G. Myers, in an excerpt from his book, *The American Paradox: Spiritual Hunger In Age Of Plenty (Yale University Press, 2000)*, which appeared in *Christianity Today* (April 4, 2000), says "We now have massive evidence that people active in faith communities are happier and healthier than their unchurched peers." Studies of thousands of lives conclude that religiously-involved individuals outlive their unchurched peers by several years. Stanford psychologist, William Damon, says 'faith has clear benefits for children . . . enabling some children to adapt to stressful and burdensome life events.' The bipartisan National Committee on Children concluded that, for many children, 'religion is a major force in their development; for some, it is the chief determinant of moral behavior.' Vanderbilt University criminologist, Byron Johnson, drawing on the findings of several national studies, concluded that a disproportionately high number of delinquent acts are caused by juveniles who have low levels of religious commitment. Sociologists Shalom Schwartz and Sipke Huismans studied a variety of religious groups, including Jews in Israel, Calvinists in the Netherlands, Orthodox in Greece, and Lutherans and Catholics in West Germany. They found that "people of faith tended to be less hedonistic and self-oriented." Noted sociologist, Seymour Martin Lipset, concludes that charitable donations and voluntarism are higher in America than they are in less religious countries.

On The Health Care Front

The main point to be made—and the overall basic philosophy that should guide your health care efforts—is that you are primarily responsible for the health you enjoy (or suffer from). By not smoking, following sound rules of nutrition, and exercising, you can dramatically increase the likelihood of your living a longer life with fewer health complications.

Dimitrious Trichopoulous, Frederick P. Li and David S. Hunter, writing in the prestigious *Scientific American* (September 1996), concluded that smoking causes about one-third of all cancer deaths. Smoking, essentially of cigarettes, causes the following types of cancers: lung, upper respiratory track, esophagous, bladder, and pancreas. It probably has an effect on stomach, liver and kidney cancers and may be related to colon and rectal cancers.

These authors, all associated with either Harvard University's Center for Cancer Prevention (Trichopoulos is director, Hunter the executive director) or its Medical School (Li is professor of medicine), blame diet for causing as many deaths from cancer annually in the United States as does smoking. Particularly suspect are colon and rectal cancer and, to some extent, prostate cancer.

Of course, obesity is a significant health risk, leading to diabetes, stroke, heart disease, and contributing to some cancers. In an exhaustive discussion of obesity in his book, *The Fat Of The Land: The Obesity Epidemic And How Overweight Americans Can Help Themselves* (Viking, New York, 1998), Michael Fumento, resident fellow at the American Enterprise Institute, consistently states that people are overweight because they eat too much and do not exercise enough. Cutting down on the amount you eat and exercising regularly will have positive effects on your health; you will lose weight and reduce the potential for severe medical problems. In the Finnish Diabetes Prevention Study, several hundred men and women with increased risk for diabetes—they had impaired glucose intolerance—were put on a modest weight loss program featuring exercise and sensible eating. After three years, they showed half the rate of diabetes as did a similar group not following the same regimen. [10] A massive study involving German and British civilians during World War II showed the health benefits resulting from not overeating. Forced to live on 800 calories a day and increase the level of their physical activity, both groups showed a 50% reduction in the incidence of diabetes and heart problems.

If you are currently overweight or want to avoid becoming so, what kind of nutritional game plan should you be following? (Notice I did not say "diet." This word suggests a crash, often bizarre, effort to reach some predetermined weight, which you will probably put back on—and then some—faster than you took it off). The best strategy is to develop a nutritional program of sensible eating—both portions and types of foods—that becomes a part of your daily modus operandi for the rest of your life.

Daily caloric intake of no more than 2,000-2,500 should help you take off unneeded weight and keep it off. As to what should make up these calories, Jean Carper, author of *Your Miracle Brain*, recommends the following:

1. Lots of olive oil, especially extra virgin. It has beneficial effects on blood pressure, cholesterol and longevity and helps prevent heart disease, cancer, arthritis, and wrinkles.

2. Whole grains, such as, oatmeal, shredded wheat, whole-grain bread, brown rice, popcorn, and bulgur wheat. They reduce the

incidence of heart disease, cancer, diabetes, obesity, and premature death.

3. Fatty fish, like fresh or canned salmon, tuna, sardines, and mackerel. Because they contain high levels of Omega-3 oils, they keep arteries clear, hearts in rhythm and help the brain and joints to function well. Recent research indicates that fatty fish reduced the rate of fatal heart attacks by 44%.

4. Nuts, such as, pecans, walnuts, almonds, and peanuts help to reduce the possibility of heart disease (up to 50%), lower bad LDL cholesterol (up to 30% in a week), and increase longevity. This regimen has worked as well as such drugs as Lipitor and Mevacor.

5. Tea, especially the black and green varieties, helps prevent strokes, heart attacks, cancer, and neurological damage. The most benefit comes when it is brewed for five minutes. Bottled and herbal teas are ineffective.

6. Fruits and vegetables, especially berries, citrus fruits, and deeply colored greens. Eating five or more servings a day will reduce the incidence of high blood pressure, heart disease, diabetes, cancer, arthritis, stroke, obesity, age-related mental declines, and wrinkles.

7. Good carbohydrates. Dried beans, lentils, peanuts, yogurt, oatmeal, cherries, and prunes help prevent colon cancer, heart disease, diabetes, weight gain, and poor memory.

8. Lower intakes of meat, animal fat, trans fat, and sodium. Especially suspect are red meat (made worse when fried) and the saturated fat contained in whole milk, butter, cheese, sausage, steak, and poultry. Many margarines, processed snacks, and baked goods clog arteries. Excessive salt intake can induce heart disease.

9. Eating less. This is a priority because more calories accelerate aging, cancer, heart disease, diabetes, and Alzheimer's.

10. Supplementing with vitamins and minerals, such as, B_{12}, B_6, C, E, folic acids, niacin, and zinc. Without these, DNA is damaged, bringing on cancer. Even eliminating minor deficiencies will improve immunity, prevent chronic diseases and perhaps prolong

life. Supplements have recently been reported as being important in the fight against prostate cancer. It was found as a by-product of a study in the 1980s that analyzed the effect of selenium on the incidence of skin cancer that males who were taking selenium supplements had a much lower chance of getting prostate cancer. In a similar, serendipitous situation, vitamin E was found to significantly reduce the incidence of men getting prostate cancer when the link between vitamin E and lung cancer was being investigated. These findings have prompted a 10-year trial of 32,000 men to fully examine the linkages between selenium and vitamin E and prostate cancer. [11]

Such a nutritional regimen as this is going to only work if you avoid eating fast foods. Once in a while—as a treat—is okay, but don't get in the habit of eating one-third or more of your meals at McDonald's, Long John Silver's, Wendy's, Burger King, etc. because your wife doesn't "feel like cooking."

As far as exercise is concerned, moderation and consistency are the keys. Don't set out to break any speed, endurance or strength records. A half-hour of aerobic exercise, such as a rapid walk, three or four times a week and several 15-minute weekly sessions of strength and flexibility exercise should do the trick. I would be quite reluctant to getting your wife or girl friend involved in your work-out routine as such a concession usually results in either a watered down program or its eventual (usually quick) demise. (Example: I noticed two women walking for exercise in our local mall. They appeared to be moving at a brisk clip but talking quite a bit—no problem. Later on, however, their "workouts" were marred by window shopping and respites for examining and purchasing sidewalk sale items).

Here's a good example of how a sensible nutrition/exercise program can pay off. My twin brother, Ted, was due to go into the Army for six months active duty in 1961. About three months before his reporting date, he experienced soreness in his shoulder. His doctor recommended that he begin lifting weights to ease the pain. He did so, the soreness disappeared, but the weight loss he hoped would also occur did not materialize; on a 5'8" frame, he believed that at 160 pounds, he was 15 pounds too heavy. After eight weeks of basic training, he was down to 145 pounds. Upon being discharged, he vowed never to get overweight again. On Mondays, Wednesdays and Fridays, he lifted weights for a half-hour. Several years later, he began a half-hour jog on Tuesdays, Thursdays and Saturdays. As he got older, these were turned into a half-hour brisk walk. Eating regular-sized meals and eschewing snacks and desserts, he has maintained to this day a weight in the 145-pound range, a tribute to his dedication and will power and a sensible regimen. On his 25th wedding anniversary, he took his wife to Bermuda. Prior to boarding the ship, with its culinary temptations of six, six-course meals a day, he weighed himself—146 pounds. A week later, upon his return to New York, he weighed himself on the same scales—145 pounds!

I can't overstate the importance of what I'm about to say next. If, as a concerned and loving dad, you notice that you son is overweight, I urge you to immediately put into play a plan (nutritional and exercise) similar to what I have described above in order to correct the problem. Now don't take offense if your son is overweight—you probably also are so a viable way to deal with his and your problem is for the two of you to work together (one of the "projects" discussed earlier). Make no mistake, obesity for your son is a one-way ticket to eventual health problems and derision, scorn and rejection from teachers, siblings (yes), and school mates, especially girls. Obesity for boys and young men is analogous to being a left-handed batter facing Randy Johnson who already has you down 0 and 2 and is getting ready to send you back to the dugout without your having gotten a foul ball off of him.

If you don't want to expose yourself to getting herpes, syphilis, gonorrhea, AIDS, and other sexually transmitted diseases (STDs), I have a one-word recommendation for you: ABSTAIN! The more sexual partners you have, the greater the likelihood that you will contract "one of the above." Although I am no epidemiologist, I assume that increasing the number of sexual partners you have does not enhance linearly the potential for your being exposed to such diseases, but, rather, exponentially. And don't buy into the fallacy of assuming that you will protect yourself with condoms. Condoms do have holes (15% are estimated to be defective), they may come off, passion may preclude you from even getting them on, etc. An even bigger problem: Andre Nahmias, of Emory University's School of Medicine, believes that condoms provide only partial protection from herpes; it can be contracted from other parts of the body not covered with a condom. [12] And, disturbingly, getting herpes may increase the possibility of getting HIV *nine-fold*, according to Sharilyn Stanley with the National Institute of Allergy and Infectious Diseases. [13]

You need to have a program to ensure that you can be adequately cared for should your health deteriorate. Proper insurance is a big help here. Strongly recommended is long-term disability insurance. This will pay you a certain percentage of your monthly salary—usually two-thirds—should you become disabled to the extent you can't work. Such coverage will give you peace of mind at an astonishingly affordable cost. I checked my most recent pay stub and found the monthly cost to be only $31.89. If your wife works full-time, she should have this coverage, also.

You also need to have long-term care insurance which pays so much per day to a nursing facility should you require such care. These costs can be catastrophic as the average cost of a yearly stay in a nursing home in the United States is $55,000.[14] These plans pay so much a day—$80, $100, $120—and, like long-term disability insurance, are surprisingly affordable. Another glance as my most recent pay stub showed a monthly cost of $40.72 for a daily payout of $100. And, while you are getting this coverage for yourself, get it for your wife. In fact, for your protection, it's probably more important to get spousal coverage; you do not want her stay in a nursing home to bankrupt you. Like the cost of your coverage, long-term care insurance for your wife is quite reasonable ($31.89 a month under the plan I have).

As I went through the process of proofing *The War Against*

Men galleries, I grappled with how to craft a concluding statement. Frequently during the writing of the rest of this book, I would run across an article or quote at just the right time that would provide the inspiration needed for a particular passage. Such was the case when I read items in the March 10, 2003 issue of *Human Events* and the U.K.'s *Daily Mail.*

Melanie Phillips' article in the *Daily Mail* revealed that many of the injustices American men are suffering, as described in this book, are also happening in the United Kingdom. They are falsely being accused of abusing wives and children, subjected to restraining orders and evictions based solely on women's uncorroborated testimony, being deprived of contact with their children, and being denied protection under that country's Human Rights Act. Even more sobering is the following from *Human Events*:

"The French magazine *Elle* will release a Centre for Advanced Communication study this week demonstrating that women's liberation in France has led to the emasculation of French men. Thirty years of feminism, says a report on the study by the Bloomberg newswire, has 'left French masculinity in tatters in an increasingly feminized society.' According to a report on Agence France Presse, *Elle* says, 'Masculinity is in crisis...there is no longer a model for building a masculine identity. Man no longer exists.'"

Will American men be next? God forbid. However, *The War Against Men* clearly shows that it is already happening. Unless we recognize and face the danger, I am afraid our fate will be the same. Chapters Eight and Nine provide a template to win the war that has been waged against us for 30 years—the same time frame referred to in the *Human Events* piece for the demise of French masculinity. Let's get going before it is too late, for I fear we may be at the eleventh hour.

REFERENCES
1. Chandra Schoenberger, "Til Lawyers Do Us Part," *Forbes*, December 27, 1999, p. 248.

2. Crittenden's book is discussed in Cathy Young, "The Mommy Tax," *Reason*, June 2001, p. 27.

3. Larry Eskridge, "When Burkett Speaks, Evangelicals Listen," *Christianity Today*, June 12, 2000.

4. Larry Eskridge.

5. "Feminism's Wrong Turn," *Penthouse*, January 2001, pp. 49, ff.

6. "Feminism's Wrong Turn."

7. "Feminism's Wrong Turn."

8. Ann Coulter, "Keep Your Laws Off My Judiciary," *Human Events*, May 21, 2001, p. 5.

9. Kenneth L. Woodward, "Order And Religion—Who's Really Running The Show,?" *Commonweal*, November 22, 1996, pp. 9-14.

10. *U.S. News & World Report*, June 25, 2001.

11. Linda Kapusniak, "Diet Counts In Prostate Cancer War," *Bryan-College Station Eagle*, November 14, 2000.

12. Betsy Carpenter, "Her Turn," *U.S. News & World Report*, November 10, 1997, pp. 77-82.

13. Betsy Carpenter.

14. Ellen Hoffman, "Nursing Homes Don't Have To Break You," *Business Week*, November 20, 2000, pp. 169-170.

INDEX

Printed in the United States
16862LVS00003B/133-174